Alexander Pushkin

Revised Edition

Twayne's World Authors Series
Russian Literature

Charles A. Moser

George Washington University

TWAS 82

А. С. Пушкин.

Портрет работы В. А. Тропинина. 1827.

ALEXANDER PUSHKIN

Alexander Pushkin

Revised Edition

Walter N. Vickery

Twayne Publishers • New York
Maxwell Macmillan Canada • Toronto
Maxwell Macmillan International • New York   Oxford   Singapore   Sydney

Alexander Pushkin, Revised Edition
Walter N. Vickery

Twayne Publishers
Macmillan Publishing Company
866 Third Avenue
New York, New York 10022

Maxwell Macmillan Canada, Inc.
1200 Eglinton Avenue East
Suite 200
Don Mills, Ontario M3C 3N1

Macmillan Publishing Company is part of the Maxwell Communication Group of Companies.

Library of Congress Cataloging-in-Publication Data

Vickery, Walter N., 1921–
    Alexander Pushkin / Walter N. Vickery.—Rev. ed.
        p.   cm.—(Twayne's world authors series : TWAS 82. Russian
    literature)
    Includes bibliographical references and index.
    ISBN 0-8057-8268-0 (alk. paper) :
        1. Pushkin, Aleksandr Sergeevich, 1799–1837—Criticism and
    interpretation. I. Title. II. Series: Twayne's world authors
    series ; TWAS 828. III. Series: Twayne's world authors series.
    Russian literature.
    PG3356.V53   1992
    891.71'3—dc20   91-34029
                                                                     CIP

The paper used in this publication meets the minimum requirements of American National Standard for Information Sciences—Permanence of Paper for Printed Library Materials. ANSI Z3948-1984. ∞™

10 9 8 7 6 5 4 3 2 1

Printed in the United States of America

For Tina, Helen, Carl, and Eileen

Contents

Preface

While most Russians and students of Russian literature unhesitatingly rate Pushkin as Russia's greatest poet, his merits have been insufficiently recognized outside his own country. The reasons for this are several, and they have a direct bearing on the peculiar difficulties confronting the writer who would attempt to present Pushkin to the non-Russian reader. The main obstacle to Pushkin's reputation abroad has been the language barrier; until recently the Russian language, compared with French, German, English, Italian, or Spanish, has been studied and known by relatively few people. This barrier has not prevented the rise to fame of Tolstoy, Dostoevski, Turgenev, or Chekhov; ill-served at times by their translators, these writers have nevertheless secured for themselves positions of preeminence—thanks to the fact that they wrote in prose. Pushkin, who also wrote in prose but whose principal claim to fame is as a poet, has been—in this limited respect only—less fortunate than a Tolstoy or a Dostoevski; for the loss incurred in translation must, with a few possible doubtful exceptions, inevitably be more damaging in poetry than in prose. And in Pushkin's case this unavoidable problem has been aggravated by the manner of his writing. His style is characterized by an unobtrusiveness and self-restraint that in the original are among his chief assets. Such virtues are not, however, easy to convey in translation. If, in spite of the difficulties, this introductory essay on Pushkin's life and work proves instrumental in giving something of the flavor of the original and some idea of Pushkin's greatness, it will have accomplished something worthwhile.

While Pushkin has suffered abroad from neglect, he has not gone unscathed at the hands of his fellow countrymen. Full tribute must be paid to Russian and, in particular, Soviet scholars for their invaluable achievements in collecting and documenting materials on Pushkin's life and works. However, their critical judgments (often echoed in Western scholarly works) have been all too often faulty. Adulation combined with a one-sided theoretical approach has caused emphasis to be placed on qualities that are either nonexistent or irrelevant to a critical appreciation of Pushkin as a poet, at the same time obscuring some of the essential qualities of his work.

The avowed intent of this essay—to provide an introduction to Pushkin—argues against an overly polemical tone. On the other hand, it would obviously be purposeless to compose a synthesis of viewpoints I do not share. It is my hope that the present volume may serve a purpose not only in introducing the new reader to Pushkin, but also in stimulating fresh inquiry and discussion among those already acquainted with Pushkin and Pushkin criticism.

I have approached Pushkin in two ways. First, I have attempted to provide as much background information as space permitted relating to Pushkin's development, his literary environment, the influences he experienced, his writing of individual works, and the findings of previous literary scholarship. Second—and this has been my principal aim—I have attempted to arrive at a critical appreciation of Pushkin's work: to define what Croce would have called its fundamental theme or themes, to interpret as far as possible Pushkin's poetic personality.

I would like to express my gratitude to the Baring Trustees for permission to reproduce two translations by the late Maurice Baring, "The Prophet" and "Remembrance." The remaining translations are my own. In some cases I have been tempted to rhyme. More often I have sought only to reproduce roughly the English equivalent of Pushkin's Russian meters. In all cases I am conscious of my inability to approach the original.

Considerations of space have obliged me to be selective, and Pushkin connoisseurs will readily spot the omissions. I have, in general, omitted Pushkin's unfinished works and his historical and critical writings and have paid only perfunctory tribute to his literary prose. The decision to be selective was prompted by the fear that all-inclusiveness would turn a monograph of this type into something approaching a catalog, and by the hope that, in devoting more space (often required by the need to translate or recapitulate) to Pushkin's most famous works, I could better give the non-Russian reader some feeling for his magnitude as a writer.

Every chapter of this revised edition has undergone some modification since the first edition of 1970. The most important changes are a new first chapter, "Biographical Introduction," that brings together biographical facts that were earlier spread over a number of chapters, and a commentary on some of the circumstances leading to Pushkin's duel and death. In addition, there are substantial changes—reflecting changes in my own preferences—in the choice of lyrics in chapter 8, "Lyric Poetry." Of course this solution is still far from ideal. With

Pushkin lyrics we always cry for more. But anthologies are by their very function unlikely to please—perhaps least of all the anthologist.

The debts of gratitude incurred in the writing of this book are too numerous to mention. Discussions with colleagues, both at home and abroad, and with students have been immeasurably helpful. For her assistance in making ready the manuscript, I wish to express my sincere thanks to Ms. Stephanie Bigley. And finally, I acknowledge with pleasure a special debt of gratitude to Liz T. Fowler, to Charles A. Moser, and to Cornelia Wilde for their painstaking work, and no less for their sensitivity and understanding in editing and very significantly improving the present manuscript.

Chronology

1799   Alexander Pushkin born 26 May (old style) in Moscow.

1811   Enters lycée in Tsarskoe Selo, near Saint Petersburg.

1813   Writes earliest surviving verses.

1815   Reads his "Memories in Tsarskoe Selo" at a lycée examination in the presence of the poet Gavriil Derzhavin.

1817   Finishes lycée and is appointed to the Ministry of Foreign Affairs.

1817–1820   Lives mainly in Saint Petersburg. Becomes famous for liberal verses.

1820   Completes *Ruslan and Lyudmila.* Transferred compulsorily away from Saint Petersburg. From May to September, travels with the Raevsky family in the Caucasus and the Crimea.

1820–1823   Lives mainly in Kishinev. Writes *The Prisoner of the Caucasus* (1820), *Gavriiliada* (1821), *The Fountain of Bakhchisaray* (1821–23); starts work on *Eugene Onegin* (1823).

1823   Transferred to Odessa.

1824–1826   Exiled to Mikhaylovskoe. Completes *The Gypsies* (1824), *Boris Godunov* (1825), *Count Nulin* (1825). Decembrist revolt takes place 14 December 1825. In May 1826 requests reprieve from exile and is pardoned by Nicholas I on 8 September 1826; he takes up life mainly in Moscow and Saint Petersburg.

1828   Pushkin's authorship of *Gavriiliada* is investigated, August–October. Writes *Poltava.*

1829   Reprimanded for traveling without authorization to the Army of the Caucasus.

1830   Becomes engaged to Natalya Nikolaevna Goncharova on 6 May. Obliged by cholera epidemic to spend September to December at Boldino, near Nizhny Novgorod, where he writes *Tales of Belkin, Little House in Kolomna,* the little tragedies, a number of lyric poems, and almost completes *Eugene Onegin.*

1831 Marries Natalya Goncharova on 18 February; moves from Moscow to Tsarskoe Selo and then to Saint Petersburg. Their married life is spent mainly in Saint Petersburg, and they have four children. Writes *The Tale of the Czar Saltan.* Appointed to the civil service as historiographer.

1831 Completes *Eugene Onegin.*

1833 Elected to the Russian Academy. Visits Orenburg and Kazan to collect material for a history of Pugachev. Spends October and November at Boldino, where he completes *The Bronze Horseman, The History of Pugachev,* and *Angelo.* On 30 December appointed *Kammerjunker,* which he deeply resents.

1834 Writes *The Queen of Spades.* His request to be allowed to retire is refused. Writes *The Tale of the Golden Cockerel.*

1835 Request for temporary retirement refused.

1836 Completes *The Captain's Daughter.* On 4 November receives anonymous "diploma" certifying he is a member of the "Order of Cuckolds." Challenges d'Anthès, but a duel is averted.

1837 D'Anthès marries Pushkin's sister-in-law on 10 January, but continues to court Pushkin's wife. On 25 January Pushkin writes an insulting letter to d'Anthès's adoptive father, and on 26 January receives a challenge to duel. On 27 January he is mortally wounded in a duel with d'Anthès, and dies on 29 January. On 6 February Pushkin is buried at the Svyatogorsky Monastery near Pskov.

Chapter One
Biographical Introduction

Alexander Sergeyevich Pushkin was born in Moscow on 26 May 1799 (old style), the second of three children. As a boy he lacked a close relationship with his parents, particularly his mother, who did not attempt to conceal her preference for his younger brother. What adult affection he did receive seems to have come from his maternal grandmother and the family nurse. An important stimulus for Pushkin's literary development was the fact that both his father Sergey and his uncle Vasily were writers; the latter in particular enjoyed quite a reputation among his contemporaries. From a very early age the young Pushkin was exposed to a literary atmosphere. Distinguished men of letters used to gather at his father's house, and Pushkin had free access to his father's library, which contained, among other things, a good collection of French literature. By the time he was twelve the future poet had read widely for his age, though without systematic guidance; had tried his hand at writing poetry (his earliest verses, which do not survive, were apparently in French); and had almost certainly conceived the ambition of making his name as a poet.[1]

Pushkin was descended from the old Russian aristocracy—he proudly traced his family tree back six hundred years—but the family had by Pushkin's time lost almost all of its earlier wealth. These two factors, consciousness of aristocratic lineage and lack of money, were to have a decisive influence on the poet's life.

In 1811, at the age of twelve, Pushkin entered the newly founded lycée at Tsarskoe Selo, near Saint Petersburg. The lycée was designed to provide what was then considered a broad liberal education to young boys, "especially," in the words of its charter, "those destined for high administrative posts in the state service."[2] The education was free. Pushkin was one of the first class of thirty pupils.

Pushkin spent six formative years at Tsarskoe Selo. Although not one of the more popular members of his class, he did make some lifelong friends there and, like many of his classmates, always looked back on his lycée days with tenderness and a certain nostalgia. He had strong personal likes and dislikes, and other people tended to react strongly toward him, both positively and negatively. He had a lively disposition, but could be moody. His teachers varied in their assessments of his scholarship, but most considered that Pushkin was more gifted than diligent and that he was unwilling to make an effort in subjects that did not appeal to him, such as ethics, political philosophy, or history. On the other hand, they acknowledged his proficiency in the French language and literature and his brilliance in all things relative to his native language. In particular, he established himself as the outstanding poet in a class that numbered no fewer than six aspiring poets among its members.

Before he left Tsarskoe Selo Pushkin's talent and promise received recognition from such distinguished writers as Konstantin Batyushkov, Vasily Zhukovsky, Nikolay Karamzin, and the aged Gavriil Derzhavin, the dean of Russian poets at the time. During their last years at the lycée Pushkin and his classmates were invited to the homes of some of the residents of Tsarskoe Selo; in this way Pushkin became an intimate of the Karamzin household. They also became friendly with some hussar officers stationed there, through whom they not only learned about drinking and womanizing, but also were exposed to the philosophical and political ideas beginning to stir the youth of those years. Petr Chaadaev, the philosopher, was a hussar officer at the time; it was at Tsarskoe Selo that Pushkin struck up a lifelong friendship with him.

Early Career

On leaving the lycée in 1817, with little or no interest in a conventional career but eager for poetic fame, Pushkin obtained a civil service appointment in the Ministry of Foreign Affairs. After spending two summer months at his mother's estate, he went in September 1817 to live in Saint Petersburg. Freed of the restraints of Tsarskoe Selo, he now set himself to lead the dissipated life of a young blood.

He was short, about five feet, three inches tall, solidly built, with a dark complexion and with dark curly hair inherited from an Abyssinian forebear. He could not be described as handsome, but he had considerable charm. At this youthful stage he practiced the art of love in the Ovidian sense, but emotional by nature, he could seldom restrict himself cold-bloodedly to the techniques of seduction, and his heart was constantly vulnerable to falling in love. He also indulged, like many of the younger set, in late-night partying, actresses, and brothels. All this was natural enough. Meanwhile, Pushkin was writing.

While he continued in Saint Petersburg to compose comic lightweight and at times elegiac verses, a new influence soon appeared in his poetry—that of political liberalism. Pushkin's awareness of the intellectual and political ferment agitating the younger generation of the aristocracy dates back to the end of his stay in the lycée. Chaadaev at Tsarskoe Selo had been the original mentor of Pushkin's intellectual awakening. But it was the brothers Alexander and Nikolay Turgenev in Saint Petersburg who were primarily responsible for the strongly liberal antiauthoritarian streak that now developed in Pushkin's political attitude.

It should be borne in mind that, in the years following Napoleon's defeat, political discontent was rapidly taking definite shape throughout much of Europe. In Russia young people were forming secret societies. Members of the generation that had fought the Paris campaign, in particular junior army officers, were heavily involved in these societies. In the next few years their ranks were augmented by contemporaries of Pushkin's, and at least two of his classmates were to be found guilty for the part they played in the abortive Decembrist Revolt of 1825. The members of the secret societies varied in their degree of political radicalism. The institution of serfdom came under criticism, but the more widely felt opposition was to the principle of unlimited autocratic rule. Some would have been satisfied with a constitutional monarchy, while others were belligerently antimonarchical, in some cases to the point of advocating regicide. Although he wished to become a member of the secret societies, Pushkin was never asked to join one. This has been attributed to their members' hesitancy to involve a poet who was rapidly winning national acclaim. The more substantial reasons given by I. I. Pushchin, Pushkin's classmate and very close friend who was later exiled to Siberia for his part in the Decembrist plot, were, however, different: Pushkin's impulsive nature made him a poor security risk, and in any case Pushkin's Saint Petersburg activities—in particular his willingness to court the favor of the conservative aristocracy—raised the question of whether his liberalism was sufficiently consistent. He was not, in the Decembrist sense, "dedicated."[3]

Reliable or not, Pushkin's emotions during these years in Saint Petersburg (1817–20) were with the liberals. The verses he wrote to support the liberal cause could not be published, but were circulated in manuscript form from hand to hand until they were known to many by heart. These verses, especially "Ode to Freedom" and "Christmas Fairy Tales," were brought to the attention of Alexander I in 1820 and motivated the czar to take disciplinary action against Pushkin. Neither of these poems was, strictly speaking, revolutionary. The former used the title that was used by the radical A. N. Radishchev in a well-known eighteenth-century ode; but ideologically it fell within acceptable bounds of exhorting a reigning monarch to eliminate abuses and implement reforms. The latter, though also not revolutionary, was probably more offensive; it lampooned Alexander I personally. Pushkin was interrogated and transferred out of Petersburg.

Exile

For a time it seemed Pushkin might be exiled to Siberia. But various people (among others, Karamzin, Zhukovsky, Pushkin's former lycée principal, V. V. Engelhardt, and even Count M. A. Miloradovich, military governor of St. Petersburg, whose official duty it had been to interrogate Pushkin concerning his subversive poetry) interceded on his behalf with the czar, and a more moderate form of punishment was agreed upon. On graduating from the lycée Pushkin had, we recall, received an appointment with the Ministry of Foreign Affairs, and during his Saint Petersburg years he had remained officially, though not very actively, it seems, attached to that ministry. It was now decided, rather than exile Pushkin, to use his official position with the Ministry of Foreign Affairs to *transfer* him away. Russia had, after all, invested six years of free education in Pushkin and looked for dividends from both him and his classmates. The official attitude toward Pushkin's liberal writing and rebellious conduct was thus one of chagrin and disappointment tempered by the hope that the misguided youth would mend his ways and employ his obvious talents more appropriately. This is precisely the tone Pushkin's superiors in St. Petersburg took in a letter to his new superior in the south, General I. N. Inzov:

After an extremely unhappy childhood, young Pushkin left his paternal home without feeling any regrets. His heart, devoid of all filial affection, could feel only a passionate desire of independence. As a student, he quickly showed signs of possessing an extraordinary genius. . . . He entered the world endowed with a fiery imagination but lacking completely those inner feelings which serve as a substitute for principle until such time as experience has completed our education. There are no excesses to which this unfortunate young man has not given himself over, just as there is no perfection he could not attain through the great excellence of his talents. . . . Certain poems, especially an ode to freedom, have brought Monsieur Pushkin to the attention of the government. Beautiful in conception and style, this poem reveals dangerous principles stemming from the modern school of thought, or, rather, from that anarchical system which people deliberately misrepresent as the system of the rights of man, liberty and the independence of peoples. . . . Monsieur Pushkin seems to have mended his ways, at least if we can believe his tears and promises. At least his protectors [Karamzin and Zhukovsky] believe that his repentance is sincere and that by sending him out of Saint Petersburg for a while, giving him work and surrounding him with good examples, it will be possible to make of him an excellent servant of the state or at least a first-class writer. . . .[4]

The czar approved the letter. The decision to send Pushkin away from the capital was not entirely unwelcome to the poet. He was not well suited to dissipation, and the life he had been leading did not satisfy his more serious spiritual needs. As he confided in a letter of March 1820 to his fellow poet and lifelong friend Petr Vyazemsky, "Saint Petersburg is suffocating for a poet. I crave new horizons." In fact, Pushkin seems to have more or less consciously courted official displeasure, prompted either by some inner need to see himself chastised or by the desire to provoke a mandatory removal.

Pushkin was given a thousand rubles for travel expenses. He left Saint Petersburg on 6 May 1820 and traveled south to join General Inzov in Ekaterinoslav (now Dnepropetrovsk). A little more than a month before he left Saint Petersburg, Pushkin had completed his first major long poem, *Ruslan and Lyudmila.*

When Pushkin arrived in Ekaterinoslav, he appeared to be ill. General Inzov—who throughout his relationship with Pushkin would prove himself an understanding, tolerant, indulgent, almost paternal superior—lost no time in showing his kindness. One of his first acts was to grant Pushkin leave. It happened that at the time of Pushkin's illness a certain General N. N. Raevsky, a hero of the 1812 war, was passing through Ekaterinoslav with his family on his way to the Caucasus and the Crimea. Since the Raevskys were accompanied by a doctor, Pushkin was entrusted to their care. Thanks to Inzov's generosity, Pushkin experienced three of the most memorable and significant months of his life. From the end of May into September he traveled and lived as a member of the Raevsky family. The superb scenery of the Caucasus made a deep impression on him and was reflected in his poetry. At the same time, members of the Raevsky family introduced Pushkin to the works of Byron, who came to exert an important influence on the Russian poet.

Reluctantly leaving the shores of the Black Sea, Pushkin returned to place himself once more under the supervision of Inzov, who had in the meantime been transferred to Kishinev, near what is now the Romanian border. For the next three years Kishinev was Pushkin's home; although the city was in many ways unappealing to him, he had every reason to be grateful for the patience and good will of his superior. This became doubly clear to him when in July 1823 he was transferred to the more entertaining city of Odessa, only to discover that it was quite impossible to get along with his new superior, Count M. S. Vorontsov, governor-general of Novorossiya. Their mutual antipathy was instinctive, wholehearted, and, for a variety of reasons, unavoidable, although it was undoubtedly aggravated by the attentions Pushkin paid to Vorontsov's wife. It was probably more than anything else Pushkin's persistent and indiscreet courtship that caused Vorontsov to decide to get rid of him. Such an adroit bureaucrat had little difficulty in finding a pretext, but Pushkin provided him with a very convenient one: in a letter of May 1824 addressed to his friend Vyazemsky he had spoken in praise of atheism, a serious matter at the time. The governor-general used this information not only to have Pushkin removed from Odessa, but dismissed from the Ministry of Foreign Affairs. On 30 July 1824, now officially an exile, Pushkin set out by a prescribed route for his mother's estate in the Pskov area, where he was to live under his father's direct supervision.

The four years since Pushkin left Saint Petersburg, the years of his so-called southern exile, had been productive. They saw him well launched into what would become his best-known poem, *Eugene Onegin.* During this same period he had surreptitiously composed his brilliantly blasphemous *Gavriiliada,* written a number of excellent shorter lyrics, and—what most sets the tone for the period—nearly completed his three "Byronic" or "southern" poems: *The Prisoner of the Caucasus, The Fountain of Bakhchisaray,* and *The Gypsies.*

Pushkin's dismissal from the civil service ended the fiction, maintained until that time, that he was being transferred from one post to another. He was now officially an exile. Upon his arrival at his mother's estate at Mikhaylovskoe, he was met by his mother, father, older sister, and younger brother. But his family reunion was not a happy one. His relations with his father had never been good; the latter's stinginess was a constant source of irritation. Worse, however, was the fact that his father had agreed to act as a semiofficial supervisor of his son's activities. The father regarded the son as a disgrace to the family and something of a threat to its security; for the son, the father appeared in the role of spy and jailer. Relations between them deteriorated rapidly, and they would quarrel violently. On one occasion the father accused Pushkin of having struck him or having gestured as if to strike him—a very serious offense in the Russia of those days. Pushkin was sufficiently alarmed by this accusation to write to Zhukovsky asserting his innocence and asking for the latter's protection if that should become necessary. This intolerable situation came to an end when his father relinquished his supervisory duties and moved away from the estate, taking the rest of the family with him.

For the next two years Pushkin lived in virtual isolation at Mikhaylovskoe. He suffered greatly from loneliness. The presence in the house of the family nurse, Arina Rodionovna, for whom Pushkin felt genuine affection, helped to alleviate his unhappiness; she told him many of the folk and fairy tales that he came to love and that would find a place in his work. He was also fortunate in having as neighbors on the nearby estate of Trigorskoe a large family, with whose female members Pushkin enjoyed varying degrees of intimacy and where he was always a welcome guest. There were also visitors to Mikhaylovskoe, but they were few and far between. Pushkin attempted to escape from his isolation by requesting permission to go abroad for treatment for his alleged varicose veins, but did not receive permission. Meanwhile he rode, read, and wrote. He also fathered a child by a serf girl on the estate, but he missed the social life and activities of the city.

However, the two years at Mikhaylovskoe were among the most fruitful of his life. His enforced isolation gave him more time for reading—thus expanding his intellectual horizons—and for writing. His productivity as a lyric poet continued, and he made considerable progress in his work on *Eugene Onegin*. He also completed two major works during this period: the drama *Boris Godunov* and the less serious but brilliantly witty short poem *Count Nulin*.

A change in Pushkin's life came from an unexpected event, the death of Alexander I at Taganrog in November 1825. The czar's death produced a temporary state of confusion regarding the succession to the throne. Konstantin, the next oldest brother and therefore presumably next in line to succeed, had previously renounced his claim to the throne, and his younger brother Nicholas was in fact the legitimate heir. However, the fact of Konstantin's renunciation was not generally known, and some time elapsed while attempts were made to have Konstantin, who was in Warsaw, make a statement clearly establishing Nicholas's right of succession.

Meanwhile the secret societies that had begun to emerge in 1816 were growing increasingly impatient with the government's reactionary policies; by this time their activities assumed a definitely conspiratorial character. At the time of Alexander's death there were two main groups of conspirators, both composed largely of army officers—a northern group and a southern group. The decision was made to take advantage of the confusion over the succession by staging an uprising.

The uprising occurred on 14 December 1825 in Saint Petersburg, and was speedily suppressed. Pushkin, aware of the troubled atmosphere then prevailing, had contemplated leaving his place of exile and traveling surreptitiously to Saint Petersburg. The story has it that the poet actually started out but encountered bad omens—Pushkin was extremely superstitious—and decided to return to Mikhaylovskoe. If this is true, it was very fortunate, for the poet would apparently have arrived in Saint Petersburg on the eve of the uprising and would inevitably have been involved in the catastrophe, which led to the hanging of five conspirators and the exiling of more than one hundred others to Siberia. Pushkin's own exile and his decision to remain at Mikhaylovskoe undoubtedly saved him from sharing the fate of the conspirators, a number of whom were his friends.

Return

With the Decembrist uprising crushed and Nicholas I clearly in control, Pushkin again decided to use the state of his health as a pretext to petition for clemency. At some point between 11 May and mid-June 1826 he sent the following letter to Nicholas I:

MOST GRACIOUS SOVEREIGN!
In 1824 I had the misfortune to incur the wrath of the late Emperor by an ill-considered judgment regarding atheism set down in a letter, and I was expelled from the service, and exiled to the village where I still am under the surveillance of the provincial authorities.

Now, with reliance upon Your Majesty's magnanimity, with sincere remorse, and with the firm intention for my opinions not to be at variance with the generally accepted order (in which matter I am ready to obligate myself by my signature and by my word of honor), I have decided to have recourse to Your Imperial Majesty with my most humble request.

My health, which was shattered in my early youth, and a kind of aneurism, have now for a long time been needing constant treatment in support of which I present the testimony of physicians: I make bold to request most humbly the permission to go for this purpose to Moscow, to St. Petersburg, or to foreign lands.

Most gracious Sovereign,
Your Imperial Majesty's
Loyal subject,
ALEXANDER PUSHKIN

And, on a separate sheet:

I, the undersigned, obligate myself henceforth not to belong to any secret societies, under whatever name they may exist; I hereby certify that I have not belonged and do not belong to any secret society, and that I never had knowledge of them.

Civil servant of the Tenth Class Alexander Pushkin
11 May
1826[5]

Nicholas I's reign can scarcely be said to have begun auspiciously, so it was natural that the czar now felt the need to balance his stern treatment of the Decembrists with measures of mercy and compassion. An example of this desire was the granting of a pension to the widow of the poet Kondraty Ryleev, one of the five conspirators hanged. Pushkin's case also offered the czar the opportunity to demonstrate to the Russian people his capacity for generosity and humane feeling. Pushkin had, as was pointed out earlier, never been a member of any of the secret societies. In the eyes of the authorities his main sins were the liberal verses that in 1820 had led to his removal from Saint Petersburg, and Count Vorontsov's charge in Odessa that he was an atheist. It was true that Pushkin's liberal verses had exerted a powerful influence on many of those involved in the Decembrist uprising. Nevertheless, Pushkin's letter to the czar was, in effect, a pledge that he not only would not become a member of any secret society, but that his writings would not be in opposition to the established regime. Nicholas I undoubtedly also calculated that Pushkin could be induced to lend his influential writings to the support of the regime, and that in any case he would be less dangerous if shown mercy than if left in the bitterness of exile. This time, then, Pushkin's plea for clemency met with a positive response. The decision was taken to summon Pushkin to Moscow.

"Not as a prisoner and under the escort of the courier only"—as the order stipulated—Pushkin set out for Moscow and arrived, travel-weary and rather unwell, on 8 September 1826. He was ordered to present himself to the czar that same afternoon, and at four o'clock was received in private audience by Nicholas.

The exact details of this man-to-man conversation will probably never be known. However, accounts of the meeting emanating from both sides differ very little on the essentials. Apparently, Nicholas I sought to persuade Pushkin that he was not merely a tyrannical despot and that his love of Russia was no less than that of the poet. The czar insisted, however, that any reform must come from above—a by no means ridiculous stipulation when we reflect that in czarist Russia progress normally had come from above. The crucial question between the two was clearly that of the recent Decembrist uprising. Pushkin was asked what role he would have played if he had been in Saint Petersburg on 14 December, to which the poet replied: "I should have been in the ranks of the rebels." Pushkin also acknowledged his friendship with many of the conspirators and his sympathy for their plight. However, he agreed, as indeed his letter had pledged, that he would no longer be part of any opposition to the regime. Another question, from the poet's point of view, was that of his suffering under bureaucratic censorship. Nicholas I appears to have expressed sympathy with the poet's predicament and to have reassured him, "You will send me everything you write; from now on I will be your censor." Pushkin was told that he was now free. The meeting appears to have lasted between one and two hours.[6]

The meeting itself was an unqualified success from the viewpoint of each man. Nicholas was pleased with Pushkin's showing and the fact that he had apparently persuaded the poet to abandon his past attitudes. The czar allegedly remarked that evening that he had talked earlier in the day to "the most intelligent man in Russia." Pushkin was no less pleased. He found himself powerfully drawn to Nicholas I, whose personality for some years afterward seems to have exerted an almost magnetic charm on the poet. There *were* limitations on his freedom: for example, he could not visit Saint Petersburg without permission. Meanwhile the returned poet was the most popular hero in Moscow. The social pleasures deprived him for so long were his once again, and he had the satisfaction of knowing that he had held his head high in conversation with his czar, had spoken frankly to him, and had kept his honor intact. Before long, though, the poet realized that his problems with the regime, and with himself, were far from solved.

It was not long before he once more began to run into trouble. He found himself under police supervision. It was not enough that he, a member of the Russian aristocracy, had given his word of honor to his czar; he was constantly obliged to account for his actions to Count Benkendorf, chief of the Third Section of the czar's private chancery and in effect head of the security police. Upon requesting permission to visit Saint Petersburg, Pushkin had to endure the latter's admonitions that he be on his best behavior while in the capital. Furthermore, the czar did not keep his promise that he would become Pushkin's personal censor. Either through indifference or lack of time, Nicholas delegated these duties to Benkendorf and his staff. One pinprick after another made Pushkin feel he was being constantly surveyed and harassed. A genuine crisis arose when in 1828 a copy of the blasphemous *Gavriiliada* came to light, and Pushkin was accused of having written it. Nicholas I set up a special investigating commission; Pushkin, required to appear before it, denied authorship. His denial was not accepted, for in all probability the authorities had in their possession reliable evidence showing that Pushkin was indeed the author. The czar ordered the commission to summon Pushkin once more and to "tell him in my name that, knowing Pushkin personally, I believe his word. But I desire that he help the government in discovering who could have composed such an abomination, and who could offend Pushkin by placing it under his name." Driven to the wall, Pushkin asked permission to send a sealed letter to the czar. Permission was granted and the letter written. Pushkin confessed that he had written *Gavriiliada* and begged forgiveness. The czar ordered that the investigation be dropped.[7]

Partly as a result of the government's harassments, Pushkin developed a growing sense of restlessness. He requested permission to take part in missions to Paris and even to China, but his participation was not required. In 1829 his restlessness, aggravated by lack of success in the courtship of his future wife, drove Pushkin to make an unauthorized journey south to the Army of the Caucasus, where his brother was serving and where he found many of his friends. The journey was not made in secret; Pushkin's moves were closely followed by the authorities, who warned the commanding officer of Pushkin's impending arrival and told him to allow him to visit. However, on Pushkin's return he was greeted by a letter from Benkendorf demanding an explanation for his unauthorized journey.

The trouble did not lie entirely with Nicholas I or with Benkendorf, but also with Pushkin himself. The social round of Saint Petersburg did not entirely suit the poet and tended to produce in him a sense of

aimlessness. While on the one hand he professed to despise social life, on the other hand he found it difficult to abstain from it when it was available. He was also a near-compulsive gambler and frequent loser. As a result of these varied activities, his productivity diminished. He was also becoming convinced that his youth was past and that so far he had failed to achieve a satisfying way of life. All in all, Pushkin was becoming increasingly subject to moods of despair, and in 1828 and 1829 his poetry displays a sense of life's futility and a preoccupation with the thought of death.[8]

Marriage

The most feasible way out of this impasse, to Pushkin, was marriage. It was not, perhaps, that marriage would lead to ecstatic happiness, but rather that marriage seemed to be the conventional thing at Pushkin's age, and Pushkin felt that the conventional paths—which he had hith-erto neglected—might offer the possibility of a more peaceful and more stable existence. The woman he finally chose to court was Natalya Nik-olaevna Goncharova, a young and beautiful girl just coming out in Moscow society. His choice could scarcely be considered felicitous if stability was his goal. Natalya Nikolaevna had little understanding of literature, considerable social aspirations, and no money. For Pushkin, who himself had no money, to take upon himself the burden of pro-moting Natalya Nikolaevna's social career was in itself an act of pure folly. Aspirations to a stable life aside, Pushkin was strongly attracted to Natalya Nikolaevna and his ego was flattered by the thought of winning this great beauty.

From the Goncharov family's standpoint Pushkin was hardly a desir-able match. He lacked money, had a record of dissipated bachelor liv-ing, and had been in trouble with the authorities. Here again, ironically enough, Benkendorf played a role in Pushkin's life. In order to satisfy the Goncharov family that he was *persona grata* with the authorities, Pushkin was compelled to request a letter of recommendation from Benkendorf. Natalya herself was not in love with Pushkin, but was simply following her mother's orders.

After Pushkin eventually obtained the mother's consent, the engage-ment was constantly marred by quarrels over money. The impoverished Pushkin was obliged to provide his bride's trousseau and help finan-cially in other ways. More than once the engagement seemed on the verge of being broken. When the marriage finally took place, on 18

February 1831, almost no one—friend of bride or groom—was predicting a happy future for the couple.

Pushkin hoped desperately that marriage would bring him new happiness and give new meaning to his life. But he too was prey to misgivings. It is remarkable that the writings of the period of his engagement are marked by a constant nostalgic looking backward to the past—past loves, past experiences, past freedoms. Not surprisingly, this was one of the most productive periods of his life. During the autumn of 1830 in particular, when he was confined to his father's estate of Boldino because of a cholera epidemic, Pushkin wrote more than he had before or after. The anticipation of marriage caused Pushkin to weigh very deeply some of life's most basic problems. This found expression in many of his lyrics and in the so-called little tragedies of 1830.

Pushkin's choice of a marriage partner was an unwise one, but this does not mean that the marriage was catastrophically unhappy. Natalya Nikolaevna bore him four children and was in many respects a dutiful wife. There was a great physical disparity between the two; in fact they were compared, not very kindly, to Vulcan and Venus. More important was the difference in interests. Natalya Nikolaevna had little or no love for literature and little or no understanding of her husband's work; she was nevertheless jealous whenever Pushkin showed his work to other intelligent and attractive women. Another strain on the relationship was Natalya Nikolaevna's almost frenzied interest in social activities. As early as 1831, when the Pushkins moved from Moscow to Tsarskoe Selo for the summer, Pushkin's wife made an impression in court circles. She was fond of flirtation, which for her cast a sort of romantic aura over her life. Pushkin, although himself not averse to flirtation when he was the one involved, could not but feel somewhat jealous as he saw himself forced to the sidelines. Moreover, he disliked the exaggerated importance his wife attached to her successes.

Nevertheless, the summer of 1831 in Tsarskoe Selo was not unhappy. Pushkin was pleased, at least at first, with his wife's social successes and the improvement of relations between himself and Nicholas I. The Polish uprising took place in 1831, and Pushkin's pen was wielded in patriotic defense of Russia's position—which, although it brought Pushkin criticism from his more liberal pro-Polish friends and acquaintances, certainly met with Nicholas's approval. That same year Pushkin was restored to the civil service with a small but helpful salary and the title of historiographer. His position, in effect, imposed no obligations on him but did give him access to the state archives, which was for Pushkin highly desirable in view of his growing interest in Russian history, particularly the figures of Peter the Great and Pugachev. The only possible disadvantage to Pushkin's reappointment was that it indebted him to Nicholas. This growing dependence on the czar's favor marred the remaining years of Pushkin's life. His wife's social aspirations were far too lofty for Pushkin's limited means, and he found that he was obliged to ask the government—Nicholas I, that is—to subsidize first his history of the Pugachev uprising, and then his family life. By 1837 his indebtedness—both private and to the government—had reached disastrous proportions.

For a while after 1826 Pushkin was favorably disposed toward his new czar. At one time, as noted above, Nicholas's personality seems to have exerted an almost spellbinding hold on the poet. The czar's handling of the *Gavriiliada* episode in 1828 may well have given cause for gratitude and surely cannot have diminished Nicholas in Pushkin's esteem. The poet also appears to have attributed the irksome tribulations he suffered from time to time to the overly zealous supervision of Benkendorf's Third Section and felt little or no rancor toward the czar. The summer of 1831 was marked by good relations between monarch and poet, but by 1834 Pushkin's attitude had altered. One of the unkindest blows for him was his appointment as *Kammerjunker* (gentleman-in-waiting) on 30 December 1833, which he keenly resented. This court position corresponded to Pushkin's service rank (he had lost several years' seniority), but this did not change the fact that it was usually reserved for far younger men, aristocrats of about twenty years of age. Pushkin was also aware that this court appointment was a device to bring his lovely wife closer into court circles. Pushkin poured much of his bitterness about the appointment into a diary he kept in 1834.[9] His letters to his wife during the summer of 1834—she was resting in the country after a miscarriage following a ball—also reveal Pushkin's unhappiness.

Another cause for bitterness was the opening of a letter to his wife that was then passed on to Nicholas I, who not only read it but discussed its contents with others. Increasingly bitter, making use of his wife's being away in the country, Pushkin requested permission to retire. Permission, he was told, would be granted, but at the czar's displeasure, and the state archives would be closed to the poet. Pushkin was also accused of "ingratitude."[10] Pushkin hastily withdrew his request for retirement, assuring all concerned that his motives had been misunderstood: it was only his wish to repair his financial situation that had led him to request retirement. In the summer of 1835 Pushkin once more requested permission to retire—this time for only three or four years, and again to repair his finances. Permission was again refused.

End of a Career

Natalya's zest for society life would have been somewhat more tolerable for Pushkin had he not had the feeling that his own role in society was insignificant. The fact that he was Russia's greatest poet counted for very little with many of the philistine aristocrats surrounding the throne in Saint Petersburg. Not many of them would give Pushkin what he felt was his due by treating him as an equal. He considered himself in many cases their superior by virtue of his aristocratic lineage, which reached back six hundred years. But Pushkin was poor, and many of them were rich. That in many cases their riches and titles had been acquired as recently as the preceding century made no difference in their attitude to the poet, whom they treated with condescension. He for his part thought of them as upstarts, *nouveaux riches.* Their condescension wounded his pride deeply and offended his honor, about which Pushkin had always been sensitive and was now becoming increasingly, sometimes paranoically, so. Added to his many discomforts, he felt that his later works were greeted with far less acclaim than had been accorded his earlier efforts, he frequently found himself the target of unfriendly criticism from hostile and mediocre writers, and he was becoming embroiled in often trivial journalistic polemics. All in all, the general circumstances of his social life and literary career offered Pushkin little satisfaction. Marriage had held out the hope of a more stable and meaningful life, but the situation in which he found himself as a result of his marriage was turning out to be a straitjacket. Meanwhile, Natalya Nikolaevna's star continued to rise.

His wife's flirtations had undoubtedly vexed Pushkin, but he had not felt his marriage seriously threatened before the arrival in Saint Petersburg of a young Alsatian, Georges d'Anthès. D'Anthès was a royalist who had resigned from St. Cyr, the foremost French military academy, as a result of the 1830 Revolution. He was now seeking his fortune in Russia, where through highly placed connections he secured a commission in the cavalry guard. Georges d'Anthès was handsome, good company, and there was no doubt that he was successful with women. He first met Natalya Nikolaevna sometime in 1834, either after her return from the country or possibly that spring, before her miscarriage. A strong attraction developed between d'Anthès and Pushkin's wife. At first, his courtship remained within the bounds of propriety, but by 1836 d'Anthès attentions had become so blatant that they aroused gossip and scandal in Saint Petersburg society. In at least one household d'Anthès was told to desist from his courtship of Natalya Nikolaevna or carry it on elsewhere. The situation came to a head on 4 November 1836, when Pushkin received the follow- ing anonymous letter, or "diploma," circulated in about eight copies among his friends:

The Grand-Cross Commanders and Chevaliers of the Most Serene Order of Cuckolds, convened in plenary assembly under the presidency of the venerable Grand Master of the Order, His Excellency D. L. Naryshkin, have unanimously elected M. Alexander Pushkin coadjutor of the Grand Master of the Order of Cuckolds and historiographer of the Order.

Permanent Secretary
Count I. Borch (XVI, 180)

The personalities in the letter were well known. Naryshkin's wife had been for years the mistress of Alexander I, and the wife of Count Borch was notoriously promiscuous. The mention of Naryshkin's wife, mistress of Alexander I, has led commentators to argue that the anonymous letter was in reality aimed at Nicholas I, who had not hesitated to pay court to Pushkin's wife either. However, this theory seems very improbable. Pushkin's contemporaries, and Pushkin himself, linked the anonymous letter to d'Anthès's courtship. Pushkin immediately challenged d'Anthès to a duel. After lengthy negotiations on the part of several mediators, all equally interested in avoiding a duel, Pushkin was induced to withdraw his challenge. The stated pretext was that d'Anthès had actually been courting not Pushkin's wife, but his sister-in-law, Ekaterina Nikolaevna, who was living with the Pushkins. D'Anthès intended to propose marriage, but *only* would do so provided the challenge were withdrawn without any reference to his intended proposal, so that d'Anthès could not be suspected of having been forced into an unwanted engagement through cowardice. Pushkin withdrew his challenge but was never far from believing that d'Anthès had in fact acted out of cowardice—although few of his contemporaries thought so. Another suspicion that poisoned Pushkin's life was the unfounded belief that the anonymous letter had been the work of d'Anthès's adoptive father, Baron Heeckeren, the ambassador of the Netherlands. (In 1927 a Soviet handwriting expert determined that the letters were the work of a young aristocrat, Prince P. Dolgoruky.) Somewhat contrary to Pushkin's expectations, d'Anthès did marry Ekaterina Nikolaevna, on 10 January 1837. His motives for marrying her will probably never be clear, and were perhaps not fully understood by d'Anthès himself. But his supporters maintained—to Pushkin's mortification—that this was a noble act of self-sacrifice to protect the honor of Pushkin's wife, the woman d'Anthès truly loved. The marriage in no way affected d'Anthès's conduct toward Natalya Nikolaevna. While showing every tenderness to his bride, he continued his pursuit of Pushkin's wife, now his sister-in-law. The uneasy truce could not last. Pushkin continued to snub d'Anthès in public, and d'Anthès's courtship of Pushkin's wife appeared at times an almost deliberate provocation, meant presumably to disprove any suspicion of cowardice, and motivated also, it would seem, by d'Anthès's growing dislike of Pushkin.

Pushkin's troubled domestic life had by late 1836 become an object of public amusement in Saint Petersburg society. His unhappy situation was further aggravated by rumors—probably true—that the poet was carrying on an affair with his other sister-in-law, Alexandra Nikolaevna Goncharova. From 1834, Alexandra Nikolaevna, the second of the Goncharov sisters, and Ekaterina Nikolaevna, the oldest, had been living in the Pushkin household. Alexandra Nikolaevna, the only Goncharov sister to display an interest in poetry, appears to have been infatuated with her brother-in-law from the beginning of their acquaintance. The rumor of a relationship between the two only rendered the spectacle of the Pushkin ménage more ridiculous. Nor was Pushkin's own public conduct calculated to gain him sympathy. Undoubtedly under severe stress as a result of his growing feeling of imprisonment in society life and the attention focused on his personal life owing to the d'Anthès affair, Pushkin's behavior in 1836 was extremely erratic. While at times he appeared controlled, relaxed, and in good humor, there were frequent occasions when he showed himself caustic, sardonic, melodramatic, and rude. Those who had never greatly cared for him disliked him even more than before, and people genuinely well disposed toward him began to regard him as an object of ridicule. In his own mind he felt pursued, harassed, and resentful. His sense of honor was deeply wounded. And the score was still to be settled with d'Anthès and Heeckeren.

The final showdown was apparently sparked by a secret rendezvous

demanded by d'Anthès of Natalya Nikolaevna (under the false pretense
of discussing family matters), of which Pushkin was informed by an
anonymous letter. Pushkin could no longer afford not to take action,
and indeed he was eager enough to do so. On 25 January 1837 Pushkin
wrote the following insulting letter to Heeckeren, whom he had now
come to hate almost more than d'Anthès:

Baron! Permit me to set down briefly everything that has happened. The
behavior of your son has been known to me for a long time past, and I could
not remain indifferent. I contented myself with the role of observer, ready to
intervene when I should consider it necessary. An incident, which at any other
time would have been extremely unpleasant to me, offered an excellent opportunity: I received the anonymous letters. I saw that the moment had come,
and I put it to good advantage. The rest you know. I obliged your son to play
such an abject role that my wife, amazed at so much cowardice and truckling,
could not refrain from laughing, and the emotion which she may perhaps have
felt for this great and lofty passion was extinguished in cold contempt and
deserved repugnance.

I have to confess, Baron, that your own conduct was not entirely seemly.
You, the representative of your crown, acted as parental pimp for your
son. . . . Like an obscene old woman, you lay in wait for my wife. . . . You
will agree, Baron, that after all this I cannot tolerate my family having any
relations whatever with yours. . . . I do not care that my wife should continue
to listen to your paternal counsels. I cannot permit your son, after his disgust-
ing behavior, to have the effrontery to speak to my wife and, still less, to tell
her barrack-room puns and to play the role of a devoted and unhappy lover,
whereas he is actually a coward and a blackguard. I am obliged to address
myself to you and ask you to put an end to all these intrigues, if you wish to
avoid a fresh scandal, to which I will certainly not hesitate to expose you. I
have the honor to be, Baron,

                              Your humble and obedient servant
                              A. Pushkin (XVI, 221–22)

The inevitable challenge was issued on 26 January. The duel took
place between d'Anthès and Pushkin on 27 January, at about half past
four in the afternoon on the outskirts of Saint Petersburg. Pushkin was
mortally wounded and, after two days of agony, died on 29 January.

National sorrow at the death of Russia's greatest poet, struck down
by a foreigner, was substantial enough for Benkendorf's department to
be concerned about popular demonstrations. The time and place of the
funeral services were altered to avoid trouble, admission was by ticket
only, and—irony of ironies, since the diplomatic corps was probably

that segment of society in which Pushkin was least popular—the service was attended almost exclusively by members of the diplomatic corps and the court. Pushkin's body was sent from Saint Petersburg to Pskov—at midnight, in order to avoid attention. On 6 February he was buried in the Svyatogorsky Monastery near Mikhaylovskoe, beside his mother.

I have set down the major steps in the drama that ultimately led to Pushkin's death, but interpreting the affair is not simple. Certain facts are still unknown, others disputed. New questions are still being posed, new viewpoints expressed. The reason for this restlessness over Pushkin's grave is not hard to find. Its foundation is wounded national pride. How could a cynical and worthless foreign adventurer bring down Russia's national poet, her Dante, Shakespeare, and Goethe all in one? And there is a different question—a question from the other side. Was d'Anthès as cynical and worthless as he is often said to be? He had four children by Pushkin's sister-in-law. He lived until 1895, a testimony presumably to reasonably good genes rather than moral stature, and became a member of the French senate. The point is that little unbiased scholarly work has been done on d'Anthès's subsequent career. It has been assumed that this young guardsman—insouciant, adept in society, and pleasing to women—fitted the stereotype.and was in fact a scoundrel.

We must bear two things in mind if we are to reach a balanced view of d'Anthès. First, cuckoldry—tragic though its consequences in real life may sometimes be—will nearly always get a laugh, especially in France. Even today, anyone with even cursory experience of French male society will recall the songs and anecdotes that bear witness to the important position occupied by cuckoldry in the French psyche. And Saint Petersburg society of the 1830s, steeped in French culture, shared the tendency to react with mirth to the plight of the cuckold. Nor, certainly in his youth, was Pushkin slow to find amusement in this whole business. Thus if d'Anthès was indeed doing his level best to seduce Pushkin's wife, though this is not in his favor, neither was it at his age and in that society a heinous crime. To take a less cynical view, d'Anthès wrote two letters to his adoptive father early in 1836 that indicate the serious nature of his love for Natalya Nikolaevna.[11] There is no valid reason to doubt his sincerity—at least at the time of writing.[12]

An easier target is presented by d'Anthès's adoptive father, ambassador to the Netherlands Baron Louis van Heeckeren. Heeckeren was a homosexual. No direct evidence proves this, but opinion runs very strongly in its favor. In fact, it was very probably homosexuality that prompted Heeckeren to adopt d'Anthès, but it is quite unlikely that he was an overtly practicing homosexual. Homosexuals at the time were tolerated, but looked at askance. The position of ambassador of the Netherlands was a prominent one, and although after the Pushkin affair Heeckeren was for a while under a cloud, he eventually secured the much-coveted post of ambassador to Austria. It seems unlikely that he would have held these responsible positions if his homosexuality had been grossly indiscreet. Even if Heeckeren was a discreet homosexual, the more important point is that he had a devious, underhanded personality. However, there is absolutely no evidence that he intrigued with malice against Pushkin and his wife before November 1836. On the contrary, in November he and Zhukovsky did everything within their power to avert the duel that for Heeckeren would mean a scandal likely to endanger his career. And they succeeded. What then went wrong?

What in very general terms went wrong was that Pushkin and d'Anthès both remained in Saint Petersburg and both were invited to the same houses, their paths continually crossing. With hindsight it is reasonable to say that only the removal of either d'Anthès or the Pushkin family from Saint Petersburg could have prevented a new clash.

In fact, Heeckeren and d'Anthès had legitimate complaints about Pushkin's implementation of the terms of the November "reconciliation." A basic proviso was that Pushkin would first withdraw his challenge, and *then* d'Anthès would announce his engagement to Pushkin's sister-in-law. But Pushkin immediately nullified this initiative by boasting that d'Anthès would flee the country—i.e., ridiculing his alleged cowardice. It is not surprising, whatever his feelings for Natalya Nikolaevna may have been, that d'Anthès chose to be almost brazenly provocative in his attentions to her: he must at all costs show that he was no coward. And Heeckeren, in his underhanded way, set about undermining Pushkin's and his wife's position.

There was another ground for complaint, Pushkin's refusal after d'Anthès's marriage to Ekaterina to have any social contact with Heeckeren or d'Anthès, in the eyes of society an expression of contempt. One way or another, Pushkin could not or would not leave the matter alone.

We cannot blame Pushkin. Everything that had happened was calculated to rub salt into his wounds. He had received the anonymous letters. His wife admitted that d'Anthès's suit had indeed made an impression on her. He had forced d'Anthès to marry, but d'Anthès was still paying court to his wife. And d'Anthès was being lionized for his gallantry and devotion to Natalya Nikolaevna, demonstrated by his marriage to her sister. On the other hand, as we have shown, d'Anthès and Heeckeren were themselves placed by Pushkin in an invidious position. D'Anthès and Pushkin were on a collision course. The "reconciliation" which the good hearted Zhukovsky had worked to bring about was in fact no reconciliation at all. The animosities remained.

In studying the Pushkin-d'Anthès affair, Soviet scholarship—understandably but regrettably—has manifested varying degrees of paranoia. The impulse to vilify Heeckeren and d'Anthès has at times been irresistible. The November "reconciliation" has been interpreted as a delaying device to have a suit of armor made in Archangel (now Dvina) that d'Anthès would then wear under his uniform. Nicholas I has been accused of masterminding the duel as a means of getting rid of both his "rivals." The doctors who attended Pushkin have been charged with purposely letting him die. Ekaterina has been rebuked for "secretly"—after her arrival in Alsace—converting to Catholicism, when she was married to a Catholic, living in a Catholic country, and raising Catholic children. Even Vyazemsky and the well-disposed Sofya Andreevna Karamzina, daughter of the historian, have been blamed. It is good to report that in recent years many of these wild theories have been dismissed and a more moderate tone has prevailed.[13] But the real lesson to be learned is that it is time to terminate this unprofitable investigation.

One final word. Some of Pushkin's friends failed to realize how serious the d'Anthès affair was for Pushkin. The threat to his family's honor and society's condescending mockery took a terrible toll. It aged Pushkin—one presumes only temporarily—well beyond his thirty-seven years. Anyone who doubts this should walk down Kropotkinskaya in Moscow and visit the excellent Pushkin Museum. Near the end of the tour there is a portrait of the poet quite unlike any of his other portraits. There is no hint of ebullience, of contained energy. Looking out from the canvas is the face of an old, tired, defeated man. The guide will rightly point out that it was painted by an amateur, not a professional, but one is left with a feeling of relief that there was no Rembrandt at hand to capture Pushkin's agony at the end.

Chapter Two

Early Poetry and
Ruslan and Lyudmila

Early Influences and Trends

Pushkin's early verse attempts (up to 1817) reflect fairly faithfully the confused literary currents of the day. The early nineteenth century was a period of rapid cultural change. The dominant influence was still the literature of France of the seventeenth and eighteenth centuries, but new trends were asserting themselves. French classicism, which in the eighteenth century had received a strong admixture of sentimentalism, was beginning to disintegrate. By Pushkin's day the glories of tragedy and the ode were bowing to a preference for comedy, comic epic, and more trivial genres such as the epigram and the madrigal. The Roman and Greek heroes of Corneille and Racine yielded place to nymphs, fauns, shepherds, and shepherdesses; forcefulness was less sought after than elegance; and passion was supplanted by either a wistful melancholy or a cynical and hedonistic eroticism. That is one side of the picture, but there is another.

Even in its seventeenth-century heyday, classicism encompassed comedy, the trivial genres, elegance, and eroticism. Moreover, such eighteenth-century epics—and surely there can be no more classical genre than the epic—as Voltaire's *Henriade* and Mikhail Kheraskov's *Rossiada* were written in response to a growing interest in the culture and history of individual nations or peoples—an interest legitimately regarded as an outgrowth of romanticism. In effect, the seeds of romanticism can be seen in Voltaire. In speaking, therefore, of the dominance in Russia of French classical literature, we must bear in mind the extreme complexity of the situation, demonstrated by the following chronology: James Macpherson's first Ossianic poems were published in 1760; Rousseau, the great precursor of romanticism, died in 1778; Johann Gottfried von Herder published his *Volkslieder* in 1778–79; Goethe's *Werther* came out in 1774; Chateaubriand's *Atala* was published in 1801; and, while Pushkin wrote his first extant verses in

1813, Benjamin Constant's *Adolphe* had appeared four years earlier. Thus several tendencies were simultaneously at work, and the European literary situation was far from clear cut.

For Pushkin, at any rate, the classical and sentimental traditions provided the earliest formative influence. Among French writers he admired Voltaire especially, and also Evariste-Désiré de Parny; among Russian writers he was drawn to Gavrila Derzhavin to some extent, Georgy Zhukovsky, and, most compatible of all at this stage, Konstantin Batyushkov with his Epicureanism. The "hussar" poetry of Denis Davydov was also important. Pushkin's early poems are mostly "occasional pieces," with themes typical of his age and upbringing. The joys of love and drinking occupy a prominent place in them. Anacreon, Eros, and Bacchus are treated sympathetically, the glories of war are compared unfavorably to the delights of love, and the poet flees the loud sounds of the world, the ambitious quest for glory. Solitude in nature, calm, idleness, contemplation, reading, friendship, and love are the things his heart craves, and he hastens to enjoy his Epicurean delights, to gather his rosebuds, for old age and death lie ahead—a thought that scarcely affects the young Pushkin very deeply, although he mentions it more than once.

A lighthearted voluptuousness is evident in some of these early poems. In one, dedicated to a snuff-addicted beauty, the poet wishes he were a piece of snuff, that might roll down her bosom, under her dress; another, describing Zeus' seduction of Leda, concludes with the admonition, "Learn from this example, beautiful maidens; on summer evenings beware of the water in the deep grove."

The epigram was a literary weapon that Pushkin wielded throughout his life. Here is an early example (1814):

> Artist promised us a tragedy
> That would make everyone in the hall howl with pity
> And shed copious tears.
> We awaited this great play.
> And now we've seen it and there's no denying:
> It is impossible to describe its merits,
> Artist really did succeed in writing
> A thoroughly pitiful play.

Pushkin also tried his hand at the more "official" type of poem emerging from the tradition of the eighteenth-century panegyric ode. His "On the Return of the Emperor-Czar from Paris in 1815" is a patriotic outburst, lavish in its praise of Alexander I and his part in the struggle against Napoleon.

In a rather different vein are three imitations of Ossian. These include descriptions of northern nature (caves, rocks, gloom, mists, and moonlight) not found in Pushkin's other poems of the same period. They tell short stories, two of them with unhappy endings. The poems are somewhat stilted and do not evoke a very Celtic atmosphere. Their slight importance lies mainly in the fact that they indicate some interest on Pushkin's part in Ossianic themes, an interest transmitted through Parny.

An important genre for Pushkin was the friendly verse epistle, sometimes humorous, sometimes more serious, even sad. The verse epistle could be written to some anonymous and fictitious addressee, but more often it was destined for a specific friend on a specific occasion. Pushkin wrote several for his schoolmates. The fact that these poems were in effect personal letters gave them an unpretentiousness and stylistic simplicity not characteristic of other genres with which Pushkin was experimenting (e.g., "On the Return of the Emperor-Czar from Paris in 1815"). The fact that simplicity would become one of Pushkin's cardinal poetic virtues lends these early epistles an added significance.

In 1816 a new note emerges in Pushkin's writing, that of melancholy. Up to this year he made references to death, but such thoughts seemed to be superficial, literary rather than personal. In 1816, the year Pushkin turned seventeen, something must have occurred in the life of the adolescent poet. In this and the following year he wrote a series of elegies in which the theme of unhappy love constantly recurs. Now, he tells us, the friendship of his companions no longer brings comfort; his lyre lies idle, he sits in silent sorrow at the feast; he is unable to forget; for him there can be no happiness. This repeated mention of lyres and feasts may strike one as a poetic mannerism—and some of his more melancholy pronouncements may to some people sound exaggerated— but there is no doubt that in these poems of 1816–17 Pushkin was expressing a genuine emotion and that, as a poet, was for the first time using the language of passionate feeling. The short poem, "Desire" ("Zhelanie"), illustrates this mood:

> Slowly my days drag by
> And each instant multiplies in my sad heart
> All the woes of unhappy love
> And stirs up dreams that are madness.

> But I am silent, unheard is my complaint;
> I shed tears; tears are a comfort;
> My soul, the prisoner of longing,
> Finds in them a bitter joy.
> O! life's hour run on, I've no regret,
> Disappear in darkness, empty specter;
> Dear to me is the torment of my love;
> No matter that I die, but let me then die loving.

Meanwhile, the overall influence on Pushkin of such writers as Voltaire, Parny, and Batyushkov encouraged tendencies that were really a part of his own poetic nature: a lively wit; an eye for the *mot juste* and the epigrammatic turn of phrase; careful subordination of emotion to the restraints imposed by intellect and craftsmanship; harmony, measure, and balance as opposed to exaggeration and one-sidedness; a strong feeling for reality; the noble virtue of poetic common sense; concision; and simplicity. These attributes of Pushkin's mature works can be detected in his early writings.

It should be noted that Pushkin's first efforts as a poet coincided with a period of lively debate in Russian literature. During the first two decades of the nineteenth century there was much discussion about the correct path of development for the literary language. The need for development was clear, brought about by the impact of western European culture and by the advent of postclassical literary trends. If Russian literature were to hold its own with other European literatures, it would have to devise methods of expressing concepts and shades of thought and feeling it had never felt the need of expressing before. Furthermore, the eighteenth-century classical literary language of Mikhail Lomonosov and even Derzhavin needed to be brought closer to the norms of everyday speech in order to meet the demands of the early nineteenth century. How were these goals to be achieved? On this question Russian intellectuals divided into two sharply opposed camps.

The traditionalists insisted that innovations should be made by coining new words from Old Church Slavic, the language of the church, which had already profoundly influenced the Russian language and remains even today a productive influence. On the other hand, there were those—and they included the foremost writers of the time—who maintained that the solution lay in borrowing lexically and syntactically from abroad, in particular from French and German. For the former, foreign borrowings undermined the purity of the language; to the latter, words coined from Old Church Slavic appeared clumsy, artificial, and far removed from the norms of everyday speech.

From today's viewpoint the whole issue is quite dead, and it is with difficulty that we can comprehend the intensity of emotion that it once generated. Both solutions, coining and borrowing, were in part adopted. But the traditionalists, though their purist demands were probably beneficial for the development of modern Russian, were on the whole fighting a losing battle. It was the "westerners" who, for the most part, carried the day.

The literary society that served as a focus for the westerners was known as Arzamas. During his lycée days, Pushkin had hoped to be elected a member, and his ambition was fulfilled in the fall of 1817. But for various reasons Arzamas went out of existence in 1818, so that the poet's actual participation in the society was not of great significance. However, the fact that for several years he had been at heart a member of this society, his general alignment with the western group, and the influence of Batyushkov and other westerners were, as we have already noted, significant for his literary development.

Pushkin was installed in Saint Petersburg in September 1817, where his poetry displayed a hitherto untried strain of political liberalism. His "Ode to Freedom" (Volnost), "Christmas Fairy Stories" (Skazki Noël), and "The Countryside" (Derevnya) are the most famous liberal poems of the 1817–20 period. The "Ode to Freedom," written in late 1817, belongs formally to the tradition of the eighteenth-century ode. The ode was most often employed for panegyric purposes, to celebrate or commemorate military victories or such civic events as a monarch's arrival in Moscow or Saint Petersburg, but it was also used didactically—to complain about or warn against civic injustice. Derzhavin had written several odes inveighing against such evils as tyranny and administrative corruption. Alexander Radishchev, exiled to Siberia by Catherine II, had written an ode with the same title as Pushkin's, "Freedom." Consequently, Pushkin was working within a well-established literary genre that left no doubt as to his purpose. Moreover, the poem is linked with the eighteenth-century tradition not only in form but in the political ideas it propounds. It is not rabidly antimonarchical, but is directed against the tyrannical abuse of unbridled power: "Tremble you tyrants of the world! / And you degraded slaves, give ear, / Be strong, take courage and arise!" The poem is particularly severe on Napoleon, "Horror of the world, nature's shame, a rebuke to God on earth," who was sent to scourge France for the lawless execution of

Louis XVI. Louis XVI himself is seen as innocent, but his predecessors, for whose crimes Louis XVI was called to answer, had abused their powers. And in Russia, the tyranny of Paul I led to his assassination. The moral is that abuse of power by the monarch must lead to lawless acts perpetrated by his subjects. The monarch has no absolute, God-given rights, for he must himself answer to Law:

> Rulers! Crown and throne are given
> You not by Nature, but by Law:
> You stand above the people, but
> Above you is the eternal Law.

Only when the monarch is subservient to the Law will he be able to count on the support of a free people amid peace and security. The poem concludes with a warning:

> Learn, O czars, today this lesson:
> Not punishments and not rewards,
> Nor prison roof nor holy altar
> Can save; trust not, O czars, in these.
> Be you the first to bow your heads
> Beneath the sure shield of the Law:
> Then will the peoples' peace and freedom
> Forever stand and guard the throne.

"Christmas Fairy Stories" follows a French tradition of verses written at year's end that satirize the political events of the year. It is a personal attack on Alexander I, for whom Pushkin, for some unknown reason, always felt a strong antipathy. Poland, then under Russian rule, had been granted a constitution, and in his speech at the opening of the Polish Parliament in March 1818 Alexander had promised to extend the constitutional form of government to the remainder of the Russian Empire. Pushkin's short poem, written in December 1818, expresses a widely felt skepticism about the czar's political promises. It also contains an unflattering reference to Alexander's participation in the reactionary Holy Alliance with Prussia and Austria.

"The Countryside" (1819) is an attack on the institution of serfdom. It opens with an idyllic description of the countryside. Here, far from the vulgar crowd and the aberrations of the city, the poet happily seeks solitude, peace of mind, truth, and inspiration. But then amid this

beautiful scenery he is horrified to observe scenes of violence and deg-
radation: here the peasant is deprived by force of the fruits of his labor;
here gaunt Slavery, bent over the plow and lashed by whips, drags itself
to the grave along furrows belonging to a pitiless owner; here no one
dares even to hope; here young girls grow up beautiful only to satisfy
the miscreant's whim; here young boys are taken from their father's
home to serve unhappily in the owner's household. The poet wishes
ardently that his voice could move men's hearts and wonders, in conclusion, whether he will ever see "the people unoppressed, and slavery
banished at a wave of the Czar's hand."

We can see that Pushkin's mood at this time was not consistently
rebellious. Although "The Countryside" is an emotional critique of
serfdom, it is to the czar that Pushkin looks for a solution. Supposedly
Alexander I, on reading this poem, asked to have conveyed to Pushkin
his thanks for "the noble sentiment that inspired his work." Again, the
"Ode to Freedom" may legitimately be interpreted as an attack, not on
monarchy as such, but on the tyrannical abuse of monarchical power.
But there was, on the other hand, the highly personal "Christmas Fairy
Tales." It was the stimulus for Pushkin's involuntary transfer to the
south.

Ruslan and Lyudmila

A little more than one month before he left Saint Petersburg, on 6
May 1820, Pushkin completed *Ruslan and Lyudmila,* a comic epic consisting of six cantos, written in freely rhymed iambic tetrameters. The
story, set in the time of the ancient Kievan dynasty, tells of the abduction of Ruslan's bride, Lyudmila, by a magician, of Ruslan's adventur-
ous quest for her, and of his eventual success in recovering her. It was
probably started while Pushkin was still in the lycée, but the main
work on it was done during his Saint Petersburg years (1817–20).[1] An
examination of the plot shows that the principal narrative ingredients
were culled from two literary traditions, the Russian epic (*bylina*) and
the fairy tale. But the general bent of the poem is neither heroic nor
folkloristic: on the contrary, heroism and fairy tale magic are consistently ridiculed and subjected to irony. *Ruslan and Lyudmila* harks back
to the tradition of Voltaire's *La Pucelle* and to the Italian Renaissance
poetry most eminently represented by Ludovico Ariosto's *Orlando Furioso.*[2]

Pushkin's decision to try his hand at a comic epic was made partly
in response to the pressures of the Russian literary scene at that time.

Everywhere in Europe the advent of pre-romanticism coincided with a heightened national self-consciousness and thus an increased interest in the national past. Symptomatic of this interest was a newfound enthusiasm for folklore. There was also great enthusiasm for the creation of a national epic. Among the Arzamas group there existed a conscious desire to produce a national epic.

But interest in a national epic did not make it any easier to write one. Batyushkov attempted a poem on Ryurik, the Scandinavian founder of the dynasty that ruled Kiev and, later, Muscovy. But Batyushkov's muse was not of epic caliber, and he conceded resignedly: "Clearly, when I die, I shall still be pregnant with my *Ryurik*."[3] Equally ill-suited to the epic task was Zhukovsky's introspective sentimentalism: his plan for *Vladimir*, taking its title from one of the first great rulers of Kiev, a truly national theme, remained no more than a plan.[4] Thus the problem remained unsolved. Pushkin chose not to rise to the challenge. His response, dictated by his admiration for Voltaire's witty skepticism, was to write a comic epic that had little to do with nationalistic epic aspirations and even poked fun at Zhukovsky's otherworldly, mystically inclined Romanticism. *Ruslan and Lyudmila* is, in fact, partly a friendly polemic aimed at Zhukovsky. Several incidents and characters are taken from Zhukovsky's projected *Vladimir*, and in his fourth canto Pushkin recapitulates ironically the plot of Zhukovsky's *Twelve Sleeping Maidens*, casting vague doubts on their chastity and introducing in his own poem, as contrast, twelve maidens who were the reverse of chaste.

But the significance of *Ruslan and Lyudmila* is certainly not limited to the negative achievement of making it virtually impossible for a serious epic to be written. On the contrary, *Ruslan and Lyudmila* is a brilliant masterpiece in a vein and genre in which Pushkin excelled. Zhukovsky was wise enough to recognize this by giving to his young rival a portrait of himself with the inscription: "To the victorious pupil from the vanquished master on that most important day on which he completed *Ruslan and Lyudmila*. Good Friday, 26 March 1820."

Unfortunately, *Ruslan and Lyudmila* is sometimes treated by Russian critics as Pushkin's first step toward a poetic rapprochement with the people, the *Narod*, as "the young poet's first attempt to create a national poem (*poema*)" (Nazarova, 221). This is completely false. Certainly it is not difficult to identify various components of Pushkin's narrative as deriving from the Russian epic or fairy tale traditions. To maintain, however, that these components lend the poem a national or folkloristic character is to fail completely to understand their poetic function. A

given incident can in one context be regarded as "popular," while in
another context the same incident may have quite a different impact.
The epic and the fairy tale normally presuppose a certain ingenuousness,
a degree of naïveté, real or assumed, whereas the comic epic—which
takes lightly what the epic and fairy tale take seriously—normally pre-
supposes a degree of sophistication. The use to which Pushkin puts his
epic and fairy tale elements is precisely the highly sophisticated use to
which they were put in the comic epic of Voltaire or Ariosto. Also, the
epic and the fairy tale tend to be oriented toward the outdoors. The epic
hero of chivalry may feast beneath a roof and sleep, sometimes, in bed;
but his main activity, apart from single combat and ordinary battlefield
duty, seems to consist in pricking endlessly over plains and through
forests. The fairy tale may be situated at the hearth, but it is insistently
aware of the surrounding woods from which sprites are wont to intrude
on human habitation.

In *Ruslan and Lyudmila* knights do indeed dutifully prick over the
plains, but the whole poem is oriented toward the indoors, toward the
drawing rooms of Saint Petersburg, toward the young girls of Saint
Petersburg society, and toward Pushkin's male friends in the sense that
he shares with them his pleasure in the poem's erotic passages and in
the effect that these passages are allegedly calculated to have on the
young female hearts of Russian society. Just as *Orlando Furioso* acquires
its tone from the sophisticated men and women of the court at Ferrara
to whom it is addressed, so the entire orientation of Pushkin's poem is
determined by his audience. His dedication runs as follows:

> For you, the rulers of my heart,
> For you, you beauties, you alone,
> I have in hours of golden leisure
> Recorded with a truthful hand
> The fantasies of times gone by;
> Accept, I beg, this flippant work!
> While I, demanding praise of none,
> Am gladdened by the hope, sweet hope,
> That, fluttering with love, some maid
> May perhaps take a stealthy look
> At these my sinful tales in rhyme.

The dedication immediately sets the tone of the entire work.

One important feature of *Ruslan and Lyudmila* is the author's tendency to interrupt the narrative with digressions, a feature he shares

with Voltaire and Ariosto. In its simplest form the digression is merely a mechanical device enabling the author to temporarily abandon his narrative at a point of high suspense and switch to another episode: "But now, my friends, what of our maid? / Let's leave these heroes for a while; / I will return to them quite soon. . . ." But clearly the author's digression has a very wide range of possibilities. It can involve the author's relationship with the reader, the author's attitude to his characters, his attitude to life, and his personal experiences. Through the digression, the author can in fact create a whole new focus for the events he describes and stamp on his work the imprint of his own subjective poetic personality. Pushkin was later (in *Eugene Onegin*) to exploit more fully the possibilities of the digression, but his mastery of the technique is in evidence as early as *Ruslan and Lyudmila*. The dedication just quoted conveys something of the flavor of these digressions. Here is one more example:

> Ah me, how sweet my princess is!
> Her character has great appeal:
> She has feeling, she is modest,
> And faithful to her wifely love,
> And slightly flighty . . . What of that?
> That makes her all the more delightful.
> New charms she constantly reveals
> Which captivate our willing heart;
> Say: can Lyudmila be compared
> To stern, severe, austere Delphira?
> The one was given by fate the grace
> To charm our hearts and hold our gaze;
> Her smiles and the sweet things she says
> Kindle in me the flame of love.
> The other's skirts belie the truth:
> More apt would be mustache and spurs!
> Blessed the man for whom at eve
> In some deserted trysting place
> Lyudmila mine all eager waits,
> Prepared to tell him of her love.
> But blessed too, believe me, he
> Who from Delphira runs away
> Or, even better, never knew her.

One function of this type of digression is clearly to give a contemporary dimension to events that purportedly belong to the legendary past.[5]

Ruslan and Lyudmila opens in a conventional setting of the Russian epic: Vladimir, prince of Kiev, is presiding at a feast. The feast celebrates the wedding of his daughter, Lyudmila, to Ruslan. The feast is gay, but not so the amorous Ruslan, who "Impatient tugs at his moustache, / While every second seems an hour." Equally unhappy are Ruslan's three unsuccessful rivals: Rogday, bold warrior; Farlaf, a loud and boastful coward; and the passionate Ratmir. At last the feast is over and the bride is led to her bridal chamber. Ruslan's long-awaited moment is at hand: "Love's gifts are readied, and the clothes / That jealous shield Lyudmila's charms / Fall to the lush carpet-strewn floor. . . ." But at this point there is a flash and a crash and, lo, Lyudmila is gone, snatched away by some mysterious, magic hand. The angry father summons his court and promises Lyudmila and half his kingdom to the man who rescues her. Ruslan and his three rivals ride out together, then separate to begin their search. Various adventures befall them. One of the more amusing involves Ratmir, who arrives toward dusk at a castle inhabited by twelve beautiful maidens. He is made welcome, disrobes, and receives a fragrant Russian bath at the hands of the semi-nude maidens, in the course of which his desires are so stimulated that he forgets Lyudmila. In a voluptuous scene reminiscent of Ariosto, Ratmir is visited that night by one of the maidens. He remains for a while in the castle with his delightful temptresses, but is eventually rescued from these seductions by his love for a pure shepherdess. He becomes a fisherman and settles down to a contented pastoral life with his one true love.

Lyudmila's ravisher is the evil magician Chernomor, who carries her through the air to his enchanted castle. But his advanced age renders him incapable of working his vile will, though that does not prevent Pushkin from giving an amusing and fairly intimate description of Chernomor's lascivious but unavailing efforts.[6]

Meanwhile, guided by a benevolent old magician, Finn, Ruslan is making his adventuresome way toward the imprisoned Lyudmila. Finn's life story, which he relates to Ruslan, is an entertaining episode. As a shy youngster herding sheep in the Finnish Northlands, Finn falls in love with the beautiful Naina. Eventually he brings himself to declare his love, but Naina rejects him: "Shepherd, I don't love you!" Driven by grief, Finn becomes a Viking marauder: for ten years he and his bold seafaring companions fight, kill, and loot. He returns home full of passion, pride, and plunder. But Naina responds with indifference: "Hero, I don't love you!" For Finn there is one last resort—to live in the depths of the forest and master the arts of magic in order to obtain power over Naina. For many lonely years he pursues his studies. When at last he is ready, he pronounces the incantation and invokes the spirits:

> And in the forest dark
> A thunderbolt crashed down to earth,
> A magic whirlwind shrieked and wailed,
> The ground shook, quaked beneath my feet—
> And lo, before my eyes appeared
> Gray-haired, decrepit, an old hag,
> With wildly gleaming sunken eyes
> Hunchbacked, her senile head awag. . . .

Finn has failed to take into account the effect on Naina's charms of the forty years of his apprenticeship in magic. The old hag is none other than Naina. Alas, Finn's magic arts have prevailed and only too well, for Naina is aflame with passion. Finn relates:

> A ghastly grin contorts her mouth,
> While in sepulchral, croaking tones
> The ugly crone declares her love.
> How much I suffered you can guess!
> Shaking I stood, with downcast eyes;
> Coughing and wheezing on she went
> Mouthing her noisome passion's plea:
> "Yes, now I've learned to know my heart;
> I understand, true friend, that it
> For passion's tender joys was born;
> My senses now awake, I burn,
> I am consumed with love's desires . . .
> Come let us clasp each other close . . .
> Oh, darling, I grow faint with love . . ."

Finn flees Naina's clutches, pursued by accusations and threats.[7]

Aided by Finn, Ruslan eventually overcomes Chernomor and rescues Lyudmila. He survives a treacherous attack from Farlaf, who is acting under Naina's directions—for she too has learned the arts of magic. He saves Kiev from its besiegers and lives happily with his bride.

Looking back on *Ruslan and Lyudmila* in 1830, and recalling its generally favorable reception, Pushkin remarked, "No one even noticed that it is cold."[8] If by "cold" Pushkin meant that his poem arouses a relatively narrow range of emotions—not including those that tug deep at our heartstrings—then he was right. But therein lies the peculiar charm of *Ruslan and Lyudmila*. Pushkin carries us with him into an unreal and delightful poetic world of cheerful unconcern. He employs the techniques normally associated with this particular genre: wit, irony, bathos, occasional buffoonery, and eroticism. And, in keeping with the tradition and its essentially realistic character, he subjects to gentle ridicule such "serious" matters as chivalry, hand-to-hand combat, sorcery, abduction, passion, and love. But the reader's delight derives only in part from seeing these things exposed to the shafts of Pushkin's wit; it stems more from the fact that these normally serious things are as it were without gravity in the fantasy world that Pushkin has created.[9]

Ruslan and Lyudmila is a poem of lightness and fun, an escape from reality rendered beautiful by the perfection of its poetry. In a sense it is "cold," limited in emotional range, and less ambitious in its appeal to the human spirit than many of Pushkin's subsequent works, but it succeeds fully in what it sets out to do, and in its own modest way is as fine as anything he ever wrote.

Chapter Three

The Southern Poems and *Gavriiliada*

Byronism and the Southern Poems

Byron was probably the dominant influence in European letters around 1820. To some this may come as a surprise; we are apt to forget that no less a writer than Goethe held Byron in high esteem. It is true that his reputation was later to undergo eclipse, but in the last three decades or so his star has risen again. It is today mainly his later works—*Beppo,* and above all *Don Juan*—that arouse admiration, whereas it was his earlier works, *Childe Harold* and the "eastern tales," that first brought him fame in the eyes of Europe. The reasons for this have little to do with literary merit. They lie, rather, in the fact that Byron exploited two strong cultural preoccupations of his contemporaries: their interest in a certain type of personality, and their eagerness for the exotic and the primitive. Just as Goethe's *Werther* had once shaken Europe and produced a rash of suicides precisely because it was so perfectly in tune with the mood of the times, so Byron's early work was successful precisely because it touched exactly the right chord for Byron's day and age. In this sense Byronism was more than the mere total of Byron's early writings; it summed up an entire outlook on life.

Byronism was not, of course, new with Byron. It embodied the profound disquiet, the melancholy, the *Weltschmerz* of the romantic age. It spoke with the voice of liberal protest against tyranny. It questioned the accepted values of a hypocritical and corrupt society. And to an age mesmerized by the figure of Napoleon, it offered, in place of mediocrity and conformism, the appealingly exciting spectacle of the Byronic hero. Byronism thus focused a number of widespread dissatisfactions and aspirations; the *Weltanschauung* it represented became closely associated with the name of the British poet because it was so clearly expressed in some of his writings and because it appeared to many of his contemporaries to be personified in his life and character.

To attempt a brief description of the Byronic literary hero is to court
the danger of oversimplification. Nevertheless, this hero, as he appears
in the appropriate works of Byron, displays the following principal
characteristics: he is proud, aristocratic, highly individualistic, and romantic; he is profoundly disillusioned by life; he feels in conflict with
and superior to society; although his conduct may be antisocial and he
inspires awe and fear in others, he possesses an underlying nobility of
character; he seems marked by Fate and has suffered some irreparable
misfortune in the past (an unhappy love affair, an unspecified injustice),
as a result of which his view of life has become warped, his emotions
atrophied; he brings tragedy to the woman who loves him; and he is
portrayed against some primitive, exotic background.

Two examples, both relevant to this study of Pushkin, must suffice.
In *The Giaour,* the first of Byron's eastern tales, the hero had at some
time in the past fallen irrevocably in love with the beautiful Leila. Her
being a member of Hassan's harem did not deter the hero, and when
Leila responded to his love, she was duly killed by Hassan. The hero
then killed Hassan. At poem's end he is living in a monastery and
wearing monk's clothing though apparently an unbeliever. For the
monks he is an object of awe and fear:

> Dark and unearthly is the scowl
> That glares beneath his dusky cowl:
> The flash of that dilating eye
> Reveals too much of times gone by. . . .
> But sadder still it were to trace
> What once were feelings in that face. . . .
> The close observer can espy
> A noble soul, and lineage high. . . .

In *The Corsair,* the hero Conrad is leader of a pirate band:

> That man of loneliness and mystery,
> Scarce seen to smile, and seldom heard to sigh;
> Whose name appalls the fiercest of his crew. . . .
> He cared not what he softened, but subdued;
> The evil passions of his youth had made
> Him value less who loved—than what obeyed.

He has been the victim of man's duplicity: "His heart was formed for
softness—warped to wrong, / Betrayed too early, and beguiled too

long. . . ." His one redeeming feature is his love for Medora, whom he must now leave behind on the pirate island. Seyd is expected to attack and, to anticipate this, Conrad and his men set fire to Seyd's palace, gallantly saving the lives of the harem inmates. Seyd counterattacks. Conrad and his men are overwhelmed by superior numbers, and Conrad is made prisoner. One of the harem women, Gulnare, who is "Extreme in love or hate, in good or ill . . . ," falls in love with him, kills Seyd, and escapes with him, though she knows he cannot love her since he loves Medora. Conrad is appalled by her crime, and returns to the island only to find that Medora is dead. He disappears.

These "Eastern tales" with their talk of pirates and harems, melodramatic language, and the exaggerated character traits of the heroes may not entirely engross the modern reader. Byron himself did not take it seriously. But for Pushkin in 1820 this was heady stuff, and the appeal of the Byronic hero was strong.

In some respects Pushkin came to Byron prepared. Byronism was not altogether a new graft, rather an organic development within him. Something of the Byronic mood can be discerned in the melancholy outpourings of Pushkin's 1816–17 elegies (Tomashevsky I, 644–46). And in 1820 the course of his personal life made him particularly receptive to Byronism. The dissatisfactions of Saint Petersburg life—including, it is often thought, an unhappy love affair—had induced in Pushkin that pessimistic frame of mind that is an essential part of the Byronic outlook. The Russian poet's liberalism caused him to look on Byron with sympathy. His exile—Byron too was in a way an exile—had caused him suffering, made him feel he had suffered injustice, and created the feeling of a rift between himself and society. He was visiting the Caucasus and the Crimea, which rivaled in their exoticism Byron's Eastern Mediterranean. He was confronted with the living example of one of the Raevsky sons, Alexander, who had taken the Byronic mantle and imitated Byron's manners and personality. And he was encouraged by the Byronic enthusiasms of various other members of the Raevsky family. Everything, in fact, conspired to create a Byronic mood. There was, finally, one further factor which should not be overlooked: for Pushkin—always a craftsman, always interested in new genres—Byron's themes and techniques opened up entirely new poetic horizons, and the Russian poet embraced eagerly the chance of investigating them.

The Prisoner of the Caucasus (Kavkazsky plennik), the first of the

"southern" poems, was written during the latter half of 1820 and early
1821. Composed mainly, like *Ruslan and Lyudmila,* in free-rhyming
iambic tetrameters, it consists of a dedication, two "parts," and an
epilogue (777 lines altogether). The mood of the author is made clear
from the start, in the dedication to N. N. Raevsky, one of General
Raevsky's sons and a good friend to Pushkin from his Saint Petersburg
days. Pushkin speaks of his "exiled lyre," of "love's painful dream," and
of the "sad days of separation." He sees himself as "innocent," the
"victim of calumny" (calumny is twice mentioned), and he talks of
"betrayal." Gloom, a sense of persecution, and feelings of self-pity pre-
dominate: "Early I knew sorrow, persecution suffered early." In fact,
the author identifies very closely, as we shall see, with his melancholic
hero.

The story is simple. At the outset the wild Circassian hillsmen of the
Caucasus are sitting around in their village talking, as always, of war,
horses, and women. Their talk is interrupted by the return of a Circassian bringing in an unconscious Russian prisoner. The Russian revives
and remains in the village, in chains. He awakens the love of a Circassian maid and for a time appears to respond to her untutored, passionate
advances. But then his past proves too strong for him. Haunted by a
previous unhappy love, he loses his emotional spontaneity and cannot
return the love of this child of nature. She understands his predicament
(the initial language barrier between them appears to break down as the
poem proceeds and, presumably, as the Russian extends his stay in the
Circassian village). For a while the hero is left to his solitude. Then,
one night, the maid comes to him, saws through his chains, and bids
him flee. Greatly moved, the Russian begs her to flee with him. But:

> No, Russian, no!
> Bitter for me what once was sweet;
> Life I have known, have felt its joys.
> And all has vanished, without trace.
> Can it be so? You loved another!
> That one go seek, and find, and love. . . .
> Farewell! Forget my pain and grief,
> Give me your hand—for the last time.

After a last embrace the hero swims the river to freedom. As he climbs
the far bank, he hears a splash behind him and a groan. True to her
violent nature, and to the romantic tradition, the Circassian maid has
drowned herself.

The Prisoner of the Caucasus contains some excellent descriptions of nature and the Circassian way of life. These passages exemplify the antiurbanism, the delight in nature's more exotic, wilder aspects and the tendency to glorify human primitivism that are so typical of the romantic outlook. The Circassians are depicted as more generous, more cruel, and more passionate than their civilized, decadent, and corrupt contemporaries: whatever the vices and virtues of these primitive hillsmen, their emotions are uninhibited, wholehearted, and instinctive. This picture stands in direct contrast to the character of the civilized hero, on whom the poem focuses.

The Fountain of Bakhchisaray (Bakhchisaraysky fontan), the second southern poem, was begun in the spring of 1821, the main work was done in 1822, and the final revisions were made in the fall of 1823. The poem, consisting of 578 lines, is once again written in freely rhymed iambic tetrameters. In this work also the background is exotic, and the hero finishes in a state of apathy induced by an ill-starred love. The main differences in plot, compared with *The Prisoner of the Caucasus,* are that the women (here there are two of them) play a larger role and that the traits of the Byronic hero have been attached not to a "civilized" European, but to a Tatar Khan—to someone, therefore, who is himself part of the exotic background.

As the poem opens Girey, the Tatar Khan, broods in menacing and sorrowful silence in the midst of his servile court. He has fallen in love with Maria, a Polish girl recently captured by the Tatars, but Maria knows nothing of passion, and has no feeling for Girey. Awed by his love, the fearsome Khan will not force his attentions on Maria; he even permits her to sleep apart from the other women and the eunuch who guards her is not allowed to enter her room. Meanwhile Zarema, a passionate Georgian girl who had, until Maria's arrival, been Girey's favorite, is neglected and bitter. It is night. Zarema steals past the sleeping eunuch to enter Maria's room, wakes her, and pleads with her to restore Girey's love. After telling Maria of her former happiness, Zarema goes on:

> And then, Maria, you appeared,
> Since then, alas, his soul's obsessed;
> Only one vile desire is his. . . .
> I know that you are not to blame.
> Then listen: I have beauty too;
> In the whole harem you alone
> Can bring misfortune on my bliss;

> But I for passion's joys was born,
> You cannot love as I can love;
> Why then should beauty cold as yours
> Mislead his weak and errant heart?
> Give me Girey, for he is mine. . . .
> By scorn, entreaties, sorrow, tears—
> I care not how—dismiss Girey. . . .
> But listen and beware: if I
> Must use my dagger, then beware!
> The Caucasus was once my home!

Some time elapses. Maria is dead. We do not know exactly how she met her end, but it was undoubtedly at Zarema's hand, for Zarema was drowned by the guards on the same night Maria died. Girey, neglecting his harem (as does Hassan in *The Giaour*), once again departs to fight wars, but his heart is broken. Returning home, he erects a fountain in Maria's honor. The narrator concludes by revealing that he has himself visited Bakhchisaray. It made him think of the khans, their warlike exploits, their feasts, their voluptuous pleasures, their harems. It seemed to him that the shadow of a maid flitted through the palace. Was it Maria? or Zarema?

> Another's charms, as great as theirs,
> Still grace this Earth; her I recall,
> And toward her my heart takes flight,
> I grieve in exile, long for her. . . .

"The Gypsies" (Tsygany) was begun in January 1824 in Odessa, and completed (apart from one passage) in Mikhaylovskoe in October 1824. Strictly speaking it straddles Pushkin's southern exile and his northern exile, but it was conceived in the south, the bulk of the work was done in the south, and in genre it clearly belongs with *The Prisoner of the Caucasus* and *The Fountain of Bakhchisaray*. Like them, it is written mainly in freely rhymed iambic tetrameters. It consists of a number of paragraphs or sections and an epilogue (569 lines in all). But it differs from its predecessors in one important respect. While *The Prisoner of the Caucasus* and *The Fountain of Bakhchisaray* contained a certain amount of dialogue inserted in the narrative, in *The Gypsies* the proportions are reversed: a certain amount of narrative is inserted in the dialogues. The paragraphs or sections referred to above can in many cases be likened to short dramatic scenes; in *The Gypsies* Pushkin was in fact feeling his way toward the dramatic genre, which he would shortly attempt full-scale.

As may be inferred from the title, the exotic background is here provided by a band of Gypsies roaming the plains of Bessarabia. Zemfira, a young Gypsy girl who lives with her elderly father, brings home a Russian, Aleko, who wishes to join the Gypsy band. He is, it seems, wanted by the law, and he suffers the spiritual torments usually associated with the Byronic hero. He nevertheless fits in fairly well with the wandering Gypsies, forgetting the past. His task is to lead a bear on a chain and sing while Zemfira collects money from the audience. He loves Zemfira, and lives with her and her father. Here is part of a dialogue revealing Aleko's negative attitude toward civilization:

Zemfira.	Tell me, my friend: don't you regret
	All you have left behind for good?
Aleko.	What did I leave behind?
Zemfira.	You know:
	Your country's people, city life.
Aleko.	I've no regrets. Could you but know,
	Could you but feel how city life
	Imprisons, stifles, warps the soul! . . .
	What did I leave behind? Deceit,
	Betrayal, prejudice's voice,
	The persecution of the mob—
	Or glory, triumph, crowned with shame.
Zemfira.	But there are mighty mansions there,
	And many-colored carpets too.
	And games and merriments and feasts,
	And maidens clad in rich attire.
Aleko.	Such noisy pleasures have no worth,
	Empty is pleasure without love.
	You are far better than those maids
	Without their costly rich attire. . . .

This harmonious life lasts about two years, after which Zemfira grows tired of Aleko and takes a lover. Aleko, seeing Zemfira's growing indifference, turns moody and morose. The following exchange between Aleko and Zemfira's father reveals the vast difference between the Gypsy and the "civilized" man in their approaches to the problems of love and infidelity:

Old Man.	Tell me, crazed youth, why all the time
	You sigh and sorrow as you do.
	Free are our people, clear the sky,
	Our women's beauty is well known.
	Weep not: such grief will bring your ruin.
Aleko.	Father, Zemfira loves me not.
Old Man.	Take courage, friend: she is a child.
	'Tis foolish thus to rend your heart:
	Your love is heavy with your grief,
	But women's love is mirth and play. . . .

The old man goes on to tell Aleko how years before Zemfira's mother had left him to run off with a Gypsy from another band:

Aleko.	Why did you not pursue in haste
	The cunning and ungrateful wench?
	And thrust a dagger in her heart?
	Bring death to those who helped her flee?

This is in effect what happens. Aleko surprises Zemfira and her lover in the night and stabs them to death. Dawn finds him still sitting at the scene, dagger in hand. The old man banishes him from the Gypsy band with the following words:

> Leave us, proud man. Away, be gone.
> We are wild people without laws.
> We punish not with pain or death.
> Your blood, your groans we do not need;
> But we can't brook a killer here. . . .
> You were not born for freedom's ways. . . .
> Begone, and peace be with your soul.

And the Gypsy band moves out over the steppe, leaving Aleko behind.

It is not difficult to detect Byron's influence in the Southern poems. Pushkin is clearly indebted to him for certain features of situation and plot. The characters of Pushkin's and Byron's heroes also have much in common: a certain emotional impotence, disillusionment caused by some past mishap, a feeling of having been betrayed, and a sense of estrangement from society. The violent, passionate natures of the Circassian maid and of Zarema also owe something to Gulnare. Finally, in narrative technique the two poets reveal definite similarities, notably in their tendency to concentrate on the highlights of a story using dramatic scenes or confrontations between characters.

There are, at the same time, some clear differences between the two writers. Pushkin's heroes tend toward apathy and passivity, while Byron's have to a greater extent translated their disillusionment into energetic and destructive action. It is true that Aleko commits a double murder and that in his delight in the thought of revenge he is reminiscent of the Giaour. Still, throughout most of the poem his passivity is emphasized, and leading a bear on a chain is not really a fitting occupation for one of Byron's heroes. In their general lack of dynamism Pushkin's heroes come closer to the nebulous figure of Childe Harold than to either the Giaour or Conrad. This difference in character is reinforced by a contrast in descriptive techniques; while Pushkin gives almost no physical descriptions of his heroes, Byron does, and frequently portrays them in action.[1]

Pushkin's attitude toward Byronism and the Byronic hero did not remain constant during his southern period. His initial infatuation emerges in the subjectivity of *The Prisoner of the Caucasus.* By the time he wrote *The Gypsies,* Pushkin had learned to survey the Byronic hero with objectivity. The view has frequently been advanced that in *The Gypsies* Pushkin "dethroned the Byronic hero" and "overcame Byronism" (Tomashevsky, I, 644–46). The passage normally cited in support of this view is the speech in which the old man condemns Aleko and banishes him from the Gypsy band. But this is to interpret Pushkin's poem too narrowly. *The Gypsies* is, it is true, a poem of ideas. It is a demonstration (which Chateaubriand, also clearly an influence here, had already offered in his *René*) of "civilized" man's inability to return to some pristine golden-age society. But it is more than that. There is in "The Gypsies" a sense—which was to become very much a part of Pushkin's mature outlook—of man's inability to escape his fate, of a certain tragic inevitability in man's destiny. Pushkin exposes, if you will, Aleko's egotism and violence. But is he then applauding Zemfira's promiscuity? And was her father, simply because he was a primitive Gypsy, any the happier at his betrayal by Zemfira's mother? On the contrary. *The Gypsies* is *not* a demonstration of the superiority of the primitive to the "civilized." Rather it expresses Pushkin's awareness of the fragility of human happiness, an awareness he expressed in the epilogue:

> But even you, nature's poor sons,
> Cannot lay claim to happiness!

And in your tattered tents you dream,
Like other men, tormented dreams.
Wandering through the steppes, you feel,
Like other men, misfortune's blows.
Everywhere passions wreak their ills,
And against Fate there's no defense.

In *The Gypsies* Pushkin did not "overcome" Byronism; he broadened its theme by giving to the rather narrow problem of the Byronic hero a wider application, a more universal dimension.

One other widely held misconception arising from the change between 1820 and 1824 in Pushkin's attitude to Byronism merits comment. To speak of "overcoming" Byronism is to assume that Pushkin was in 1820 completely overwhelmed by Byronism and that he gradually succeeded in emancipating himself from it. This would be at best no more than a partial truth, and a misleading one. Pushkin was affected by Byronism, not engulfed by it. It represented only one side of his outlook on life. The Byronic poem was never a complete reflection of his poetic personality any more than it was of Byron's poetic personality. The Byronic poem was for Pushkin a new genre, and like other genres it imposed a number of conventions and restrictions. One was the deliberate elimination of humor, which is completely absent from the southern poems. Yet it is clear from other works written during the same period that Pushkin's sense of humor had not abandoned him: *Gavriiliada* was written in 1821, the same year in which *The Prisoner of the Caucasus* was completed; and *Eugene Onegin,* influenced by Byron's very different later works, *Beppo* and *Don Juan,* was started in 1823 while Pushkin was still working on *The Fountain of Bakhchisaray.* Notwithstanding the breakdown of the rigid classical distinctions between genres, Pushkin remained all his life very much aware of genre, that is, of what facets of his poetic personality could appropriately be exposed in a given type of writing. Consequently, the reader should be wary of any attempt to link the poet's outlook with individual works too closely.

It is not easy for today's critic to assess the merits of the southern poems. We live in an antiromantic age which is nevertheless in many ways indebted to romanticism, and we resent any suspicion that we may still be enmeshed in its toils. Certainly the naive exhibitionism of the Byronic hero is alien to our taste. The temptation to smile at some of Byron's utterances has already been mentioned. It is well to remember, however, that in the hands of a master like Pushkin, such sweeping lyrical outpourings have about them a certain clarity, simplicity, and even grandeur. What is wrong with them is simply the context in which they occur, the Byronic poem designed to magnify the image of the Byronic hero. Separated from this rather juvenile background and treated on their own merits, many lines and passages turn out to be poetry of a high order.

And yet Pushkin's very craftsmanship at times renders him a disservice. One cannot escape the impression that it is in fact the perfection of his verses that make them on occasion an imperfect vehicle for the expression of raw emotion. For this the choice of meter—or Pushkin's use of the meter—should, perhaps, bear the responsibility. The relative shortness of his lines, their unvarying length, the high degree of regularity in their stress patterns, the fact that syntactic units and syntagmas normally coincide with the unit of the line, and the strongly felt exact end rhymes all tend to make of the iambic tetrameters of the southern poems an adroit tour de force. However, their very neatness argues against depth of feeling. The iambic tetrameter was, of course, entirely appropriate for the light irony of *Ruslan and Lyudmila*. This is not to say that its function should be limited to irony and humor. Pushkin himself had already used it in an entirely different context in his "Ode to Freedom," and the versatility of this meter is clearly demonstrated in such Pushkin masterpieces as *Eugene Onegin* and *The Bronze Horseman*. But against this we should remember that Pushkin's iambic tetrameter later developed a general flexibility which was only beginning to be in evidence in the southern poems. While, then, Pushkin's sense of form, artistic judgment, and dexterity as a writer enabled him to produce some excellent verse, these same qualities—in Pushkin's works in iambic tetrameter—are responsible, on occasion, for lines and passages which seem somehow too pat for the weight of emotion they were intended to carry.

In my opinion the southern poems—judged in their entirety as works of art—should not be ranked too high among Pushkin's achievements. In this Pushkin himself would most probably have concurred, at least as far as the first two are concerned. Of *The Prisoner of the Caucasus* he wrote jestingly, "The character of the Prisoner is a failure, that proves that I do not qualify as the hero of a romantic poem." Again dubbing the Prisoner a failure, he relates how Nikolay and Alexander Raevsky and he had enjoyed many good laughs at the expense of the Prisoner. *The Fountain of Bakhchisaray* he regarded as "weaker" than *The*

Prisoner, although he remained satisfied with the dramatic quality of the scene in which Zarema confronts and threatens Maria, but here again amusement—provoked by a melodramatic description of Girey in battle—is mentioned.[2] The most generally accepted view of the southern poems is that the first two are weak, whereas *The Gypsies,* which marks the "overcoming" of Byronism, is among Pushkin's masterpieces. I would not rate *The Gypsies* that high. If certain features of the first two southern poems provoked laughter, there are quite naive passages in *The Gypsies,* such as Aleko's "exposure" of the evils of city life or his extolling of the joys of vengeance:

> Oh no! If o'er the sea's abyss
> I found my enemy asleep,
> Why even there, I swear it, I
> Would have no mercy on the villain;
> Unblenching, with my foot I'd thrust him
> Defenseless down into the waves;
> His sudden horror as he woke
> My savage laughter would deride,
> And long I'd hear in mirth and jest
> The sweet sound of his rumbling fall.

Pushkin himself has pointed the way to a proper critical evaluation of the southern poems. In labeling *The Prisoner* a failure, he attributed success to "a number of elegiac and descriptive verses" (XI, 145). This sort of selective approach seems most fruitful. While none of the three southern poems can, I believe, be judged an unqualified success, none of them can be ignored; they continue to be read and reread with pleasure. The reason for this lies not so much in the conception of the works themselves as in a number of felicitous verses that, better than the poems in which they appear, retain a lasting appeal.

Gavriiliada

Written in 1821 in Kishinev, *Gavriiliada* has nothing in common with the southern poems or with Pushkin's Byronism. It is a reversion to the eighteenth-century, anticlerical tradition of Voltaire and Parny, and is extremely blasphemous in its handling of the sensitive topic of the Annunciation of the Virgin Mary. The poem was allegedly provoked by Pushkin's mild pique at being obliged, as a civil servant under General Inzov, to observe the fasts and participate in the services prescribed by the Orthodox Church for Lent and Easter. It reflects also Pushkin's dislike for the often hypocritical pietism that prevailed in administration circles during the later years of Alexander I's reign. It should not, however, be regarded as a serious declaration of principle, inspired by militant sentiments and propagandistic aims characteristic of Pushkin's French predecessors. It was, rather, in the words of Vyazemsky, a "delightful prank."[3] Given the close ties between church and regime and the official distrust of anything smacking of atheism, there could be no question of publication; *Gavriiliada* circulated in manuscript form among Pushkin's friends and acquaintances.

It goes without saying that readers' reactions to *Gavriiliada* will be affected by their views of Christian doctrine. To many the poem may appear to be in poor taste, and Pushkin himself was in later years reluctant to be reminded of his authorship.

Gavriiliada is written in freely rhymed iambic pentameters with a caesura after the fourth syllable, a choice of meter dictated by the tradition within which Pushkin was working. Though only 552 lines long, it is composed in the mock-epic style, as is indicated by the title and sub-title ("A Poem in One Canto"), as well as various typically epic accoutrements.

The poem opens with a description of the quiet life of Joseph and Mary. Joseph, an elderly, "inefficient carpenter," works day and night, and completely neglects the charms of his still virginal wife: he "lived like a father with the innocent maid, / Provided her with food—and nothing else." Meanwhile, God has "in his profound wisdom" decided to bless and reward Mary. Surrounded by the heavenly throng, He appears in a vision and addresses Mary:

> Most beautiful of our dear, earthly daughters,
> Of Israel the youthful hope and joy!
> I summon thee, aflame with burning love,
> To share my glory. Harken to the call.
> Make ready for a fate not yet revealed,
> The bridegroom comes, draws near unto his slave.

The vision fades, but not before Mary's attention has been drawn to the imposing figure of the Archangel Gabriel standing among the heavenly throng, his blue eyes fixed upon her. Mary awakens:

> But from her memory the wondrous vision
> And Gabriel's charming figure did not fade.

> She wished indeed to love the king of heaven,
> The words he spoke were pleasing to her ear,
> And filled her with humility and awe—
> But somehow Gabriel took her fancy more.
> Thus the slim figure of some adjutant
> Finds favor, maybe, with the general's wife.
> So fate decrees; there's nothing we can do,
> As all men, wise or foolish, are agreed.

Back in heaven, meanwhile, God experiences the pangs of frustrated love:

> No joy the Creator found in his Creation,
> And heavenly prayer delighted not his ear;
> He busily composed his psalms of love
> and loudly sang: "Mary I love, I love,
> My immortality means nothing now . . .
> Where are my wings? To Mary I will fly
> And on her beauteous breast I will repose!"
> And so on . . . phrase on phrase on phrase; the Lord
> Leaned to a colorful and Eastern style.
> He summoned then his favorite Gabriel and
> To Gabriel explained his love in prose.

And Gabriel "Reluctantly became the faithful servant / Of heaven's king—in earthly terms his pimp."

However, Satan is aware of God's intentions:

> He goes to work. The Almighty sat meanwhile
> Up there in heaven in sweet despondency;
> Forgot the world that He was wont to rule—
> Without his rule it went on just the same. . . .

Mary, meanwhile, is in her garden, sad and lonely, afflicted by thoughts of Gabriel. Satan appears before her in the guise of a beautiful serpent. He is so submissive that Mary, although aware of his identity, is induced to listen. Satan proceeds at some length to give his version of the Adam and Eve story. He had not ruined Eve, he says: he had saved her; he had introduced Adam and Eve to the voluptuous joys of passion. Mary's imagination is fired by his erotic descriptions. Suddenly the serpent disappears, to be replaced by a handsome young man:

Prone at her feet, not uttering a word,
Fixing on her his wondrous shining gaze,
With eloquence he supplicates, entreats,
And with one hand he proffers her a flower,
The other hand rumples her simple blouse
And hastily beneath her vestment steals
And the light fingers playfully caress
Her hidden charms . . . The marvel of it all!
For Mary this is, oh, so subtly new.
But lo, her virgin cheeks light with a flush,
A crimson that is not the blush of shame.
A languid warmth and an impatient sob
Cause her young breasts to rise and fall—and rise.
No word she speaks; but she can stand no more;
Scarce breathing now, her languid eyes half-closed,
She bows her head toward the expectant Satan,
Screams: "ah!" . . . and falls full length upon the grass.

At this point, or shortly afterward, Gabriel arrives and drives Satan away after a hard-fought battle won by a blow aimed deftly at the most vulnerable of places. The victorious Gabriel then addresses to Mary a parody of the "Ave Maria," of which the punch thought is that even more blessed than the fruit of her womb will be the father of that fruit. He presses her hand, kisses her, touches her breast, and again Mary succumbs:

What shall she do? What of her jealous God?
Be troubled not, my beauteous maidens fair.
O women, you who know love's ins and outs,
You know full well the wiles that can deceive
The vigilant observance of the groom,
The expert vigilance of the well-wishers,
That cover up a pleasant little lapse
With all the trappings of sweet innocence.
The errant daughter from her mother learns
The lesson of submissive modesty.
And on the first and all-decisive night
She feigns false fears and pains that do not pain;
And on the morrow, feeling better slowly,
Gets up, can hardly walk, is languid, pale.
Elated the proud spouse, relieved her mother,
And soon once more the old flame's back again.

Gabriel flies to God to report that all is ready. God prepares. Mary lies
dreaming of Gabriel. Then suddenly:

> A sweet, enchanting dove flies in her window,
> Above her flips and flaps its wings and flutters,
> And sings its little winsome birdlike songs,
> Then suddenly between her legs flies in,
> Alights upon the rose and trembles there,
> Claws, turns around, and claws again, again,
> Works with its feet and with its little beak.
> Oh, this is God! Mary has understood
> That this the dove is an Almighty guest;
> Her knees drawn tight, the Hebrew maid cried out,
> Began to sigh, to tremble, and to plead,
> To weep. But no, triumphant is the dove,
> In love's hot heat he quivers and he chirrups,
> Then falls into light sleep, by love undone,
> resting an idle wing across the rose.

> He's flown away. All-weary, Mary thinks:
> "What furious pranks and happenings are these!
> One, two and three—how eager they all seem.
> This has been quite a day, I must admit:
> In one and the same day I fell a prey
> To Satan and to Gabriel and to God."

God recognized the result of this affair as his own. Gabriel continued
to pay visits to Mary. The author concludes with a prayer, initially
addressed to Gabriel, to aid him in his courtship of a certain Elena.
Otherwise he will seek help from Satan.

> But time still passes by, and slowly time
> Will ring my head with silver, by and by,
> And then before the altar I will stand:
> A fitting marriage and a fitting wife.
> Oh Joseph, be my consolation then.
> I pray you, yes, I pray you on my knees,
> Preserver, guardian-saint of cuckolds all,
> I pray you then to cast on me your blessing.
> Grant unto me the blessed gift of patience,
> Grant unto me, again and yet again,

> Sweet sleep at night, and in my spouse full trust,
> A family at peace, love of my brother.

Readers of *Ruslan and Lyudmila* will recognize in *Gavriiliada* the same use of bathos, achieved mainly through stylistic switches from the biblical to the erotic, and of the author's digressions, which here again serve as a focal point for the entire poem and which lend the narrative a contemporary and sometimes personal dimension. Peculiarly effective in terms of Pushkin's artistic intent is the fact that Mary's seduction by Gabriel is shorter and easier than her initial seduction by Satan, while her submission to the dove's clawing endeavors resembles shoulder-shrugging resignation. Those who seek depth of feeling or thought in *Gavriiliada* will be disappointed, but its scintillating wit and flawless artistry make this poem in its own way a minor masterpiece.

Chapter Four

Boris Godunov, Count Nulin and *Poltava*

Boris Godunov

Boris Godunov, an historical drama or tragedy in twenty-three scenes,[1] was started in November or December 1824 and finished in November 1825. In *Boris Godunov* we encounter a new and important influence—that of Shakespeare. Some critics have maintained that Shakespeare's influence emancipated Pushkin from Byronism. This is inexact. The mere fact that *Eugene Onegin* was begun in May 1823 in Kishinev indicates clearly that Pushkin had been for some time in the process of discarding his earlier Byronism.[2] In this process, further-more, the influence of the later Byron of *Beppo* and *Don Juan* had played its part.[3] Shakespeare's influence was no less significant for all that; it opened up hitherto unexplored avenues of creative work, facilitated Pushkin's emergence as a skilled dramatist, helped him formulate his ideas on the techniques of characterization, stimulated his theories on the development of the Russian theater, and stimulated his lifelong interest in the evolutionary processes of Russian history and history in general. Not that Shakespeare should be credited with all these developments. The prime factors here—as in the case of Byron's influence—were Pushkin's own expanding intellectual horizons and inner needs. The direction and form these developments took, however, owe much to Shakespeare.

Pushkin's interest in Shakespeare was not fortuitous. Shakespeare's influence had been on the rise in Germany before Goethe's *Götz von Berlichingen* (1773), and had become a European phenomenon. For the preromantic *Sturm und Drang* followers and for the romantics his appeal was inevitably strong; many of his plays dealt with the English histori-cal past, and his dramatic techniques offered a refreshing example to writers and theorists who felt that the established principles of French classicism were overly restrictive.

In writing *Boris Godunov* Pushkin made a conscious effort to give a new direction to the development of the Russian theater. As he later expressed it, "I am firmly convinced that the popular rules of Shakespearean drama are better suited to our theater than the courtly customs of Racine's tragedy" (XI, 141). The principles of French classical drama had been imported into Russian literature in the eighteenth century—notably in the tragedies of Alexander Sumarokov—and although their influence had diminished, in the 1820s it remained a sufficiently dominant force for Pushkin to feel the need to attack them. *Boris Godunov* dispenses with two of the three classical unities (time and place), preserving only the unity of action. It follows Shakespeare in introducing crowd scenes, thus discarding the classical tradition in which only characters of princely or noble origin appear on stage. As in Shakespeare's plays—and contrary to the tradition of classical tragedy—moments of high drama are interspersed with comic scenes—though not, always successfully. The language of *Boris Godunov* displays the wide stylistic range of Shakespeare's writing, as distinct from the unbrokenly high-flown language of French tragedy. Pushkin also alternates, as did Shakespeare, between verse and prose. His verse, like Shakespeare's, is in mainly unrhymed iambic pentameters, interspersed with occasional rhymes. His chief concession to the French syllabic tradition is this retention of the caesura after the fourth syllable.

Shakespeare's characterization techniques had a considerable influence on Pushkin. On two occasions the Russian expressed himself so clearly on this score that his words are best left to speak for themselves. "How amazing Shakespeare is!" he wrote in 1825, while still at work on his tragedy. "I can't get over it. How petty by comparison with him is Byron as a tragedian! Byron, who created only one character. Byron distributed among his heroes various traits of his own character; to one he gave his pride, to another his hatred, to a third his melancholy, etc., and thus from one integrated character, gloomy and energetic, he created a number of insignificant characters; that's not tragedy at all" (XIII, 197). While Pushkin considered Byron lacking as a result of his egocentricity, he later compared Molière unfavorably with Shakespeare for the limitedness and unrealistic consistency of his characters: "The characters created by Shakespeare are not, as with Molière, personifications of a specific passion or vice. They are living beings, full of many passions and many vices; changing circumstances bring out before the spectator the diversity and many-sidedness of their characters. Molière's Harpagon is miserly—and only miserly; Shakespeare's Shylock is mi-

serly, enterprising, vindictive, fond of children, witty" (XII, 159–60).
Pushkin saw in Shakespeare's characterizations objectivity, breadth,
diversity, and psychological verisimilitude.

The action of *Boris Godunov* is based on historical events that took
place between 1598 and 1605 and deals with the question of who shall
sit upon the throne of Russia. The problem of succession arose in 1598
when the death of Fyodor Ivanovich ended the long-established Ryurik
dynasty. But the origins of the problem go back a few years earlier, and
a brief summary is necessary for an understanding of the play. Ivan the
Terrible died in 1584. Though married eight times in all, Ivan had had
only three sons. Of the two sons by his first marriage the older, favorite
son and heir apparent, Ivan, had been killed by his father in a fit of
temper provoked by a dispute about the seemliness of the clothing worn
by the son's pregnant wife in the presence of her father-in-law. The
throne thus passed in 1584 to the second son, Fyodor, who was sickly,
devout, and ill-suited to temporal rule. The third son, Dimitry, was
by Ivan's seventh marriage. Should Fyodor die childless, the young
Dimitry would have had a claim, albeit far from strong, to the throne.
When in 1591 Dimitry died under mysterious circumstances, some
said that the nine-year-old boy had killed himself with his own knife
during an epileptic fit, but others held that he had been murdered—on
the orders of or with the approval of Boris Godunov, a nobleman who
had, as a result of Fyodor's incompetence, effectively taken into his own
hands the reins of government.

The question as to whether Boris was in fact guilty will probably
never be resolved. He has been defended on the grounds that it would
have been foolish to risk murder when at any time Fyodor might acquire an heir (his wife had had several miscarriages). But all the indi-
cations were that this would not happen. Boris, therefore, could stand
to gain by Dimitry's death. Karamzin, whose *History of the Russian State*
was Pushkin's main source, took the view that Boris Godunov *was*
responsible for the murder, and Pushkin treats Boris as guilty.

Fyodor died childless in 1598 and Boris, already the effective ruler
of Russia, became the logical successor to the throne. He accepted it
with seemly reluctance and after some delay occasioned by a sort of tacit
power struggle between the boyars (noblemen), who wished to limit
the powers of the monarchy, and Boris, who hoped to continue the
Ryurik tradition of absolute rule and to found his own hereditary dynasty in the Ryurik manner. From this struggle Boris emerged triumphant. But, though an able ruler, he was not destined to reign in peace.

A succession of pretenders arose, each claiming to be the dead Dimitry. The first of these was a fugitive monk, Grigory Otrepev, who secured Polish backing and marched on Moscow, aided and abetted by many dissident Russian nobles. As the false Dimitry advanced, defections from the Russian side increased. At this point Boris Godunov died and, unimpeded by any further opposition, Dimitry entered Moscow at the head of a basically Polish army and was crowned (1605). However, Dimitry's Western ideas and Polonophile tendencies aroused the antagonism of the Russian boyars, and a year later he was murdered. The country was now plunged into chaos—a period known as "The Time of Troubles"—and it was not until 1613 that the various pretenders were finally eliminated, order restored, Polish intervention turned back, and a new dynasty established—that of the Romanovs, who survived to 1917.

The story begins in Moscow in 1598. Boris agrees, with the apparent hesitation and seemly reluctance already mentioned, to become czar. He addresses the Patriarch and assembled boyars:

> Most reverent Patriarch, you boyars all,
> My Soul is bared before you: you have seen
> How I now undertake this so great power
> With, in my heart, humility and awe,
> How heavy are these bonds I lay upon me! . . .
> Boyars, I look to you for aid and succor.
> Serve me as you once faithfully served him [Fyodor]
> When I still shared your labors, one of you,
> Not yet elected by the people's will.

The boyars assure him of their loyalty. The next incident occurs five years later, in 1603, and lays the groundwork for the emergence of the Pretender who is destined to threaten Boris's rule. The scene is a cell in the Chudovo Monastery, where a young monk, Grigory, is asleep. His aged colleague, Father Pimen, is writing by the light of a lamp, putting the finishing touches to a historical chronicle. Grigory awakes. He tells Pimen his dream:

> I dreamed I saw steep stairs up-spiraling,
> Led to a tower; and from this height I looked,
> Below lay Moscow like some ant-heap spread;
> Upon the square below the people surged,
> Pointed their fingers up at me and laughed,

And I felt overcome by shame and fear—
And, falling headlong, wakened from my dream . . .
And three times now I've dreamed the selfsame dream.
Is this not strange?

Grigory envies Pimen for his adventuresome youth spent as warrior
and courtier, fighting and feasting, since from adolescence he has
known only the monastic life. Pimen comforts him, saying he had
indeed experienced many of this world's pleasures, but true bliss has
been his only since the Lord brought him within the walls of a monastery. Now, however, Russia has fallen on evil days and, in response to
Grigory's question, Pimen relates how the murderers of the boy
Dimitry repented before their execution and proclaimed Boris responsible for their crime. If he had lived, Dimitry would have been the same
age as Grigory—nineteen. The murder of Dimitry on Boris's orders will
be the final episode in Pimen's chronicle. Left alone then, Grigory
reflects:

Boris! Boris! Before you all things tremble,
And no one dares to even call to mind
The cruel fate of that poor hapless infant.
Yet meanwhile in this dim, secluded cell
A hermit monk writes down the loathsome truth:
Just as God's judgment you shall not escape,
Nor shall you 'scape your judgment here below.

Grigory, declaring himself to be Dimitry, flees to Poland, enlists the
support of the Poles and of Russian dissidents, and marches on Moscow.
Boris's reign has been darkened by famine, Boris himself is saddened
by the death of his daughter's betrothed (for which some people blame
him), plagued by his conscience (for thirteen years he has dreamt of the
murdered Dimitry), and weary of the burdens of rule. He is seen con-
soling his daughter and talking to his son, Fyodor. The boyars are
uneasy, insecure—and alert for news from Poland. The false Dimitry
emerges as enterprising, bold, intelligent, educated, diplomatic in his
handling of people—and susceptible to feminine beauty. After leaving
Kraków, he has halted his forces at Sambor and is staying in the house
of a certain Mnishek, whose beautiful and extremely ambitious daughter, Marina, has captivated him. Dimitry has a nighttime rendezvous
with Marina, at which he declares his love, but Marina wants to hear

only of his plans for capturing Moscow. This upsets the Pretender, who desperately wants to be loved for himself:

> Do not torment me, beautiful Marina,
> Don't tell me that it was my rank that won you,
> Not I myself . . .
>   Enough! Enough!
> I will not share with the departed dead
> A mistress that belongs to him by right.
> Be gone deceit and falsehood! I shall tell
> You the whole truth; know then that your Dimitry's
> Long dead and buried—nor shall quit his grave. . . .

And he tells Marina who he is. Marina treats him with scorn. After several exchanges the Pretender retorts proudly:

> The shade of dread Ivan has called me son,
> Spoke from the grave and named me his Dimitry,
> Roused to revolt the nations round about me,
> And marked Boris my victim. Shame on me
> That I, who shall be czar, should bow my head,
> Humble myself before your Polish pride. . . .

He bids her farewell, saying that she will perhaps regret her unwillingness to share his destiny.

> *Marina.* Czarevich, wait. At last your words
>   Are those not of a stripling, but a man. . . .
>   Win Moscow, in the Kremlin mount the throne,
>   Then send your envoy who shall speak your suit.
>   But God's my witness, till your feet have trod
>   Those steps ascending to proud Moscow's throne,
>   Until Boris is routed and cast down,
>   I shall not heed nor hear your words of love.

Dimitry moves his forces on into Russia, and Boris prepares to counter the threat. We witness part of a battle scene in which Dimitry is victorious. We see Dimitry after a defeat bemoaning his dead horse, but still confident. In Moscow an atmosphere of terror, repression, and intrigue prevails. We see Boris in conversation with his ablest lieutenant, Basmanov. Boris is not misled by his recent victory. He knows that Dimitry has reassembled his scattered forces and that his own army is ineffective. He proposes to put Basmanov in command. Summoned to receive some foreign visitors, Boris leaves, telling Basmanov to await his return. But a minute later Boris is carried back on stage, stricken with a mortal sickness:

> Go all from hence—I wish to talk alone
> With the Czarevich. (*All leave.*) Death approaches me;
> Embrace, farewell, my son: for shortly now
> You shall begin to reign . . . O God, my God!
> Soon must I stand before Thee—with no time
> To do my penance, purify my soul.
> And yet, my son, to me you are more dear
> Than is salvation; let God's will be done!
> A subject I was born, and should have died
> In deep obscurity, a subject still;
> But I attained the highest power of all . . .
> Don't ask me how. You are without guilt,
> And you shall rule by right, while I alone
> Will answer to my Maker for my deeds. . . .

The dying czar warns Fyodor of the extent of the threat posed by the Pretender and advises him—among other things—to put Basmanov in charge of the armed forces. The Patriarch, Boris's wife and daughter, and the boyars enter. Boris makes them swear loyalty to his son, and the last rites begin.

In the following scene Basmanov, now in charge at the front, decides to betray Fyodor, Boris's son. Although Dimitry's troops are little better than a rabble, Basmanov fears the treachery of his own men, for defections have been numerous and many cities have welcomed Dimitry without resistance. In the penultimate scene Pushkin (an ancestor of the poet) pleads successfully with the Moscow crowd to transfer its loyalty to the Pretender. In the final scene, outside the Kremlin, several boyars thrust through the crowd and enter the Kremlin. There is a commotion within and cries, after which one of the boyars appears on the threshold to announce:

> Men and Women! Maria Godunova [Boris's wife] and her son
> Fyodor have taken poison. We saw their dead bodies.
> (*The crowd is horrified and silent.*) Why say you nothing?
> Shout: long live Czar Dimitry Ivanovich! (*The crowd is silent.*) END.

Boris Godunov rated high in its author's affection, and rightfully occupies a distinguished place in Russian letters. Those unacquainted with the original will have to take on faith that it contains poetry of a very high order. There is, however, something about it which is not entirely satisfactory. As Belinsky expressed it, "In none of his earlier works did Pushkin attain such artistic heights and in none of them did he reveal such vast defects as in *Boris Godunov*. This drama was for him a genuine Waterloo, in which he deployed the full breadth and depth of his genius, and nevertheless suffered a decisive defeat."[4] Needless to say, many do not share Belinsky's view. Some critics even exaggerate the merits of *Boris Godunov*. For example: "As Pushkin scholarship has demonstrated, Pushkin's social-historical and social-philosophical realist tragedy was a new phenomenon in Russian and world dramaturgy at that time. . . . However, the criticism of Pushkin's day was incapable of rising to a serious understanding of the innovative character of the dramaturgic system created by Pushkin."[5] Indeed, opinions vary widely as to the play's merits. A critical examination of *Boris Godunov* may help to explain these divergences and to arrive at an understanding of what Pushkin actually achieved.

First, the reader of Soviet evaluations soon realizes that much of the praise lavished on *Boris Godunov* is elicited by the role allegedly played by the "people" (*narod*). For example: "In *Boris Godunov* we find demonstrated for the first time—not only in Russian literature but in Russian historiography—the decisive role of the people in the historical process and the potentiality of a victory by the people over the autocracy."[6] The same critic informs us that the central problem of this tragedy is the role of the people in the historical process.[7] Soviet criticism holds that Pushkin's handling of the people is fundamentally different from Shakespeare's. This may be so. It is, however, noteworthy that in his numerous surviving comments on *Boris Godunov* Pushkin nowhere hints at any intended radical change in his approach to this problem. And on the evidence of the play itself the people—formidable force though it undoubtedly is—appears in a passive role, as something to be manipulated by boyars and Czars. Sometimes quoted as evidence of the people's "decisive role" are the following lines spoken by Pushkin, the Pretender's intermediary, in convincing Basmanov that the cause of Boris's son is a losing one:

> I will be frank: our army is a rabble. . . .
> But listen then, Basmanov, our strength lies

Not in our army, nor the Poles' support,
But in the minds and feelings of the people.

These lines convey, however, no more than what can be found in Shakespeare's plays and what has been shown many times since the beginnings of recorded history: that no ruler or military commander can survive if a sufficient number of his followers defect to the enemy. But the main problem here with the Soviet approach lies not in the interpretation of the historical process, but rather in the fact that Pushkin's view of the people's role—whatever it was, and whatever understanding it may reveal of the historical process—is largely irrelevant to the artistic merits of *Boris Godunov*.

Pushkin's own expressed views on the people, or rather on the "popular" or "folk" quality (*narodnost*) in literature, are instructive. *Narodnost* for Pushkin meant in part the Shakespearean opposite of French classicism with its courtly tradition and polished conventions. As noted above, Pushkin considered "the popular rules of Shakespearean drama" to be better suited to the Russian theater than "the courtly customs of Racine's tragedy" (XIII, 197). But this remark is made specifically in terms of what would be desirable for the Russian theater. It is significant that on other occasions Pushkin finds in Racine as well as in Shakespeare the quality of *narodnost*. Racine, whose stage is peopled exclusively by aristocratic characters, is even cited in the following definition of tragedy, which includes a mention of the people: "What is it that tragedy develops? What is tragedy's goal? Man and the *people*. Man's fate and the fate of the *people*. That is why Racine is great, notwithstanding the narrow form of his tragedy. That is why Shakespeare is great, notwithstanding the unevenness, carelessness, ugliness of his execution" (XI, 419). When it comes to *narodnost*, Pushkin's definition is remarkably broad.

One of our critics, it seems, assumes that *narodnost* consists in selecting themes from our nation's history, others discern *narodnost* in the choice of words, i.e., they take pleasure in the use of Russian expressions in Russian. But it would be difficult to deny Shakespeare's *narodnost* in *Othello, Hamlet, Measure for Measure,* and other plays. Vega and Calderon transport us all over the world, taking the subjects for their tragedies from Italian *novelle* and French lays. Ariosto sings the praises of Charlemagne, French knights, and a Chinese princess. Racine's tragedies are taken from ancient history. But it would be difficult to deny to any of these writers the quality of *narodnost*. . . . Climate, the form of government, religious beliefs give to each people its own particular physiognomy, which to a greater or lesser degree is reflected in the mirror of its poetry. There exists a way of thinking and feeling, a thousand and one customs, beliefs and habits which belong exclusively to any given people. (XI, 40)

Pushkin's approach to *narod* and *narodnost* is, as we see, consistently literary. Further, it lacks the democratic and class overtones that in the latter half of the nineteenth century and in the twentieth century came to be associated with the concept of *narod*. Pimen, who is of noble origin, is as representative of the spirit of *narodnost* as is the poorest and most ignorant member of the masses.[8] Within the thoroughly reasonable terms of the literary definition laid down by its author, *Boris Godunov* may be said to possess in full measure the quality of *narodnost*.

However, *narodnost* may permeate a work, but it cannot be regarded esthetically as an end in itself. Pushkin most often referred to *Boris Godunov* as a "tragedy," and also as a "genuinely romantic tragedy" (XI, 67). "Romantic" or not, it is as a tragedy that it is most often and most profitably considered. The term *tragedy* immediately brings to mind such concepts as "inexorable necessity," "inevitability," "conflict," "fate," and "character" (or the tragic flaw in a person's character that brings about his undoing). It is right that such concepts should be linked with tragedy, for taken together they are not simply arbitrary rules, but the essentials of the tragic mood. However, from Aristotle on there have, naturally enough, been various theories of tragedy, and it would be a mistake to measure *Boris Godunov* by any preconceived set of principles. Nevertheless, the organizing principle of this work must be sought within the general framework of the tragic mood.

In 1831 Ivan Kireevsky wrote, "The shadow of the murdered Dimitry dominates the tragedy from beginning to end, controls the entire course of events, serves as a link between all the characters and scenes. . . ."[9] Much has subsequently been written on *Boris Godunov*, but no one has pinpointed the dominant theme more accurately than Kireevsky. This is first and foremost a play about power, about the evil and futility of ambition, about a man wracked by his guilty conscience. The tragic mood is centered on Boris, a hero of truly tragic stature. He has committed murder and thereby achieved the power he craved, but power has not brought him the anticipated satisfactions. He is weary and troubled.[10] Yet ambition is an essential part of his make-up, and it has not died—it is now merely transferred to his children. In order to see his childred established, to found a dynasty, Boris, plagued by ill-luck and ill-repute and rendered skeptical by his experience of sovereignty, still exercises all his intelligence and skill in government and is even ready to go unshriven to his Maker so long as he can ensure his son's succession. The play's tragedy and irony lie not so much in Boris's death, but in the fact that his great crime was all for nothing: his daughter's fiancé dies and his son is overthrown and killed (though the latter event occurs after Boris's death, it may fairly be maintained that Boris while dying is aware that his son's survival is problematic). The play's dominant poetic mood, recognition of the vanity of power and the evil of ambition, is built up, over and above the focal tragedy of Boris, in many ways: through the intriguing of the survival-minded boyars; the incomprehension of the common people; Pimen's praise of the contemplative life and especially his recollection of how both Boris's predecessors wished to lay down the burdens of power; the Pretender's impetuous willingness to abandon his ambitions for love (Dimitry is adventuresome rather than ambitious); Marina's cold-bloodedness and naked ambition; Dimitry's reluctance to spill Russian blood in war, to say nothing of his sorrow over his dying horse; the grief of Boris's daughter at the death of her fiancé; the feeling of her own and her brother's vulnerability; and the murders that mark Dimitry's successful seizure of power and conclude the play. At the end of *Richard III* (the Shakespeare play with which *Boris Godunov* is most often compared) there is the feeling of a new start, of England's having been liberated from a tyrant and malefactor. *Boris Godunov* offers no such emotional release; the play ends without triumph, on a note of gloom.[11] Such is, I believe, the most fruitful conceptual framework for viewing this tragedy.

Why then this talk of Pushkin's Waterloo? The reason lies, in my opinion, in the play's structuring. The character of Boris is of tragic stature, but he is simply not on stage enough or sufficiently active to solidify his central role as tragic hero (he appears in six scenes out of twenty-three, and his crime was committed before the play opens) and create a focus for the entire plot. Second, there is the matter of Boris's death. This simply occurs. We know that Boris is weary, but one moment he is giving perfectly sensible orders to Basmanov and the next he is a dying man. Not only does the lack of any causal relationship between Boris's death and his problems deprive us of that feeling of inevitability that so heightens awareness of the tragic in literature; its very abruptness makes it seem irrelevant, an alien element introduced out of nowhere and destructive of the mood prevailing at that stage in the play. That mood is one of suspense. For whatever the true facts of history may have been, the artistic development of this drama calls for a more serious confrontation—not necessarily face to face—between Dimitry and Boris. Boris's sudden death not only permits him to escape vengeance in this world, but—by depriving Moscow of a skilled ruler—hands Dimitry a triumph so easy that it is anticlimactic.[12]

If Pushkin failed in Boris Godunov to create a tragic hero or a truly tragic conflict, he was successful in creating a tragic mood: everything in the action and the characters serves to underscore the inevitable tragic consequences of the pursuit of power, and it is in the creation of this thematically unifying mood that Pushkin's very considerable achievement is to be found.

Count Nulin

Count Nulin, a short comic poem (370 lines) in freely rhymed iambic tetrameters, was written, according to Pushkin, in two mornings: 13 and 14 December 1825 (XI,188). It is set in the remote Russian countryside, with the atmosphere of tedious isolation that Pushkin got to know so well in Mikhaylovskoe. The plot parodies Shakespeare's *The Rape of Lucrece,* which Pushkin considered a "rather weak poem." Meanwhile, its true artistic affinities are with the comic verse tale of the Italian Renaissance, of La Fontaine, and—closer in time—with Byron's *Beppo.* Like these literary predecessors Pushkin's poem is characterized by its racy style and sophisticated, amused view of sex.

The poem opens with a lively description of horns, huntsmen, and hounds in front of a country home. The landowner emerges, equipped with such essentials as a knife, a horn, and a flask of rum, and inspects the scene with satisfaction. Meanwhile his wife, in nightcap and shawl, looks through the window, sleepy-eyed and irritated. The husband mounts his horse, shouts to his wife not to wait for him, and rides off.

What does a wife left alone do in her husband's absence? Natalya Pavlovna takes no interest in such household chores as pickling mushrooms, feeding the geese, ordering meals, checking on the barn and the cellar, for she was not brought up according to the old patriarchal traditions, but in a "foreign" boarding school for girls of noble families.

She is bored. Suddenly a passing carriage overturns and Count Nulin enters, limping slightly from his mishap, accompanied by his French servant Picard. He is returning from abroad, where he has dissipated his future income but acquired all the accessories of alien fashion— clothing of all sorts; the "right" books; opinions on the theater, the opera, actresses, the latest bon mots from Paris; and a contempt for all things Russian. he is on his way to Saint Petersburg to display himself and his newfound talents. Meanwhile, it is time for dinner. Nulin joins his hostess,

> And launches into conversation:
> Russia is frightful, he's amazed
> That folks can tolerate this place,
> He misses Paris, yes egad.
> "How's the theater?" "In poor shape.
> *C'est bien mauvais, ca fait pitié.*
> Talma has really gone downhill,
> Mad'moiselle Mars is getting old.
> There's really only Poitier left. . . ."
> "What writer is in fashion now?"
> "Still d'Arlincourt and Lamartine."
> "They're imitated here as well."
> "By Jove! You mean that here as well
> The mind is starting to develop!
> God grant enlightenment to Russia!"
> "How are the waistlines?" "Very low,
> Down almost to . . . well, down to here.
> If I may see your dress, Madame;
> Oh yes . . . the trim, the bows, the pattern;
> Almost exactly like the fashion."
> "You see, we get the *Telegraph*."
> "Aha! Perhaps you'd like to hear
> A most delightful little song?"
> The count begins to sing, "But, count,
> Your food." "I've really had enough."

Enchanted by their scintillating conversation, the two spend a delightful evening together. But it is past midnight and Natalya Pavlovna says that it is time for bed:

> Reluctantly the Count,
> All tenderness and half in love,

> Rises to kiss her hand. Oh no!
> Oh what will coquetry not do?
> The flirt—and may she be forgiven—
> Just barely squeezes Nulin's hand!

They part company. Natalya Pavlovna is undressed by her maid, and Count Nulin by the French servant, who provides him in bed with a cigar, a cigar clipper, a bedlamp, a carafe, a silver glass, an alarm clock, and a Walter Scott novel with uncut pages. The count glances idly through his novel, but is distracted by thoughts of Natalya Pavlovna. He should have pressed his suit, he thinks, but it is still not too late:

> He straightway resolute threw on
> His gaudy, silken dressing gown,
> Knocked over in the dark a chair
> And, with soft expectations filled,
> This modern Tarquin 'gainst Lucrece
> Stole forth prepared to do or die. . . .

> Along the hall the amorous count
> Gropes in the dark and feels his way
> Aflame with ardor and desire. . . .
> Tries the brass door handle—and lo
> Quietly it yields; the Count goes in,
> Looks round: the lamp now burning low
> Casts through the room its feeble light:
> The lady's lying sound asleep—
> Or is her sleeping only feigned?
> The Count draws near, retreats, draws near
> Then flings himself down by her bed.
> And she . . . With great respect I ask
> The ladies of Saint Petersburg
> To picture to themselves the horror
> With which my heroine awakes
> And to decide what she should do.

> She, her large eyes wide open now,
> Looks at the Count—and he meanwhile
> Mouths amorous Gallic platitudes
> And stretches an audacious hand
> Toward the covers. Paralyzed,
> Confused, she lies unmoving . . . then
> Comes to her senses with a start,

And—filled with anger and proud scorn,
And, to be frank, maybe with fear—
She swings with all her might, and on
Our Tarquin's face implants a slap—
And no mean blow it was at that!

At this point her small dog begins to bark, and Count Nulin retreats hastily. Next morning he is embarrassed at having to confront his hostess. But she appears to be secretly amused, and is as charming as on the previous evening. Within a short space of time the Count is again at ease—and half in love again. There is a noise in the hall. It is Natalya Pavlovna's husband returning from the hunt. He greets Count Nulin cordially and invites him to stay. But the carriage has now been repaired, and Count Nulin leaves. After Nulin's departure Natalya Pavlovna tells her husband and the neighbors of his nocturnal exploit. The husband is furious. The one most amused over the incident is a certain Lidin, a neighboring landowner of twenty-three.

This delightful verse tale depends largely for its effect on the variations that Pushkin has worked on Shakespeare's theme: in place of Ancient Rome, contemporary Russia and its benighted countryside; in place of a husband absent in the noble cause of war, a husband away hunting hares; in place of an event that allegedly changed the course of history, a trivial incident that amused the neighbors; in place of a sinister Tarquin, a foppish Nulin; and in place of a faithful wife who succumbed, an unfaithful spouse who repulsed the onslaught—with the help of a hefty slap and a barking Pomeranian. The three main characters are sketched briefly, but with a sure hand: the husband is noisy, hard-riding, hard-drinking, and imperceptive; Natalya Pavlovna is useless, robust, and flirtatious; and, of course, there is the pivotal character of Count Nulin, in whom fatuity, foppery, Gallomania, and a sophisticated veneer go hand in hand with a very human weakness here deprived of its darker implications—if only by the failure of his attempt.

With *Count Nulin* Pushkin proved again—as with *Ruslan and Lyudmila*—that when he turned his hand to the lighter genres of poetry and the lighter sides of human experience, his sense of humor and proportion and his artistic skill almost invariably stood him in good stead. *Count Nulin* is a slender little poem, and its subject matter is frivolous indeed. It is also an unqualified success and deserves a place among the best of Pushkin's masterpieces.

Poltava

Poltava was written in the short space of some three weeks in October 1828. It consists of a sixteen-line dedication, presumed to be addressed to one of the Raevsky daughters, Maria,[13] and three cantos (1487 lines in all). While the meter is familiar—iambic tetrameters freely rhymed—*Poltava* is in one respect experimental: it fuses different genres and linguistic styles. Parts of the poem are stylistically and thematically reminiscent of the eighteenth-century ode;[14] development of the action through dialogue (a technique already used in *The Gypsies*) introduces an element of the drama; one passage suggests the ballad form;[15] and certain other passages have stylistic and lexical affinities with the oral tradition.[16] In structure *Poltava* calls to mind the southern romantic poems, but now the narrator is no longer close as a person to his heroes, and the poem's involvement with history imparts a new epic quality to it. Actually, in plot and conception *Poltava* harks back to a pre-Byronic narrative poem, Walter Scott's *Marmion*: in both *Marmion* and *Poltava* romantic-type heroes are described against a known historical background. The main historical event described in Pushkin's poem is the Battle of Poltava (1709), the turning point in the Russo-Swedish War when the Russians under Peter the Great decisively defeated the Swedes under Charles XII. The main protagonists are historical persons, though the heroine's real name, Matryona, is changed to the more poetic Maria.

The first canto opens with a description of the wealth of Kochubey, a Ukrainian noble. Kochubey's greatest pride is his daughter, Maria, a beautiful and modest young woman who has rejected many suitors. Her elderly godfather Mazepa, who as hetman (military commander) is the leading power in the Ukraine, asks her parents for her hand, but the parents refuse with indignation. The mother tells Maria:

> "No shame! No honor! At his age!
> How dare he? No, while we're alive,
> He shall not perpetrate this sin.
> Supposed to be a friend and father!
> And you, sweet innocent, his godchild!
> What madness! Bent with years, how dare
> He even think to be your spouse?"
> Maria trembled, and her face

> Grew mortal pale, and all her limbs
> Were seized with chill as from the grave,
> And down she fell into a faint.

It is indeed Mazepa whom Maria loves. For two days, weeping and groaning, she will not touch food or drink. On the third night she elopes. The dishonored Kochubey plots vengeance. At this point the personal fates of Maria, Kochubey, and Mazepa are affected by historical events.

> It was that troubled time in which—
> With Peter's genius at the helm—
> Embattled, straining nerve and will,
> Young Russia grew from youth to man.
> And in the arts of war and glory
> Stern master Peter proved; and harsh
> Were the lessons, swift and bloody,
> Dealt by the Swedish champion, Charles.
> But, after long and bloody trials,
> Weath'ring the heavy blows of fate,
> Russia grew strong. Thus is steel forged
> By blows which shatter glass to bits.

The Swedish forces under Charles are threatening Moscow, and the Ukraine is stirring with revolt. Though he feigns inactivity, Mazepa secretly plans to betray Peter and Russia by bringing the Ukraine over to the side of Charles XII. Kochubey informs Peter of this, but his revenge miscarries because Peter believes Mazepa rather than Kochubey. Mazepa arrests Kochubey. Maria does not know that her father is being held in the dungeon of the castle in which she is living with Mazepa.

The second canto consists mainly of dialogues. In the first of these Maria complains to Mazepa that he is neglecting her. Mazepa explains that he is preoccupied with his plans to raise the Ukraine against Peter. He then asks who is dearer to her, her father or her husband:

> *Mazepa.* Now, answer me: if one of us,
>   If either he or I must perish,
>   And you were judge and had to choose,
>   Whom would you name as victim? And
>   Whom would your judgment spare from death?
> *Maria.*   Oh, say no more! Do not torment

	My heart, nor tempt me so.
Mazepa.	Reply.
Maria.	You're pale; the words you speak are harsh.
	Do not be angry. I am willing
	For you to sacrifice all things,
	Believe me. But say no more, your words
	Make me afraid.
Mazepa.	Remember well
	What you have said just now, Maria.

The scene shifts to the dungeon. Kochubey is to be executed the next day. He has already been tortured, and now is tortured again in an effort to discover where his treasures are hidden. His groans reach the ears of Mazepa, who is unable to sleep, wracked by his conscience and fearful of Maria's reaction when she finds out about her father. Next morning Maria is awakened by her mother who comes unknown to Mazepa, hoping that Maria will persuade Mazepa to stay her father's execution. Maria is appalled by what she learns, and the two women rush off. The canto concludes with a description of the execution of Kochubey and his friend Iskra; the two women, tired and dusty, arrive at the scene too late. Maria does not return home. Mazepa sends out riders to search for her, but in vain.

Sorrow does not prevent Mazepa from continuing his intrigues, which he camouflages by pretending to be at death's door. Suddenly Charles swings south into the Ukraine; throwing off all subterfuge, Mazepa rises against Peter. Peter, taking energetic measures to minimize the rebellion in the Ukraine, hurries to meet Charles, and the opposing forces converge on Poltava. It is the night before the battle, and in both camps all is quiet. In one tent, however, a whispered conversation is in progress. Mazepa confides to his friend Orlik that he has made a great mistake in joining Charles:

> . . . No, I was wrong about this Charles.
> He is a brave and ready youth;
> Of course, he boldly leads the way,
> And twice or thrice can win the day. . . .
> But he is not the man to match
> And best the autocratic giant:
> The drums that wheel his regiments,
> He thinks, can change the course of fate;
> Impatient, stubborn, blind is he,

> And thoughtless and conceited too,
> And foolishly he trusts his luck,
> Measures the enemy's new strength
> With memories of past success.
> The hour of his defeat has come. . . .

Orlik suggests that Mazepa can still make his peace with Peter if the battle goes badly, but Mazepa tells him that it is too late. Once during a feast, after Mazepa had said something that offended the czar the latter had pulled his mustaches and threatened him. Mazepa had never forgiven the insult. Let the dawn decide who is to flee.

The dawn comes and the battle begins. The Swedes begin to give ground:

> 'Twas then that Peter's ringing voice
> As though from heav'n inspired called forth:
> "On in God's name!"—and from his tent,
> A throng of favorites flanking him,
> Strides forth great Peter, eyes ablaze,
> His visage striking fear and awe,
> His movements swift, a prodigy
> Of nature, like the wrath of God.

The Russians are victorious. Charles and Mazepa flee. That night, while the fugitives sleep, Mazepa is awakened by Maria. She is thin, pale, tattered, with sunken, flashing eyes and disheveled hair. She is mad; as her mind wanders through her fearful memories, she thinks herself mistaken, for this man is surely not her lover who was so handsome. She runs away, laughing wildly. In the morning the sleepless Mazepa, torn by remorse, follows Charles, abandoning his native land. The poem concludes with a sort of epilogue in which the author reflects that only Peter the Great, of all the strong-willed people participating in these events, truly left his mark on history.

Poltava has always been one of Pushkin's most controversial works. The reaction to its publication in 1829 was mixed, but predominantly hostile. Much of the criticism was of an historical rather than aesthetic nature, having to do with Pushkin's interpretation of historical events, in particular his portrayal of Mazepa, who some considered was in real life motivated by Ukrainian patriotism. The problem of historical accuracy also arose in connection with Charles, who was held to have fared badly at Pushkin's hands, being completely dwarfed by the formidable figure of Peter. To this Pushkin objected that the description of Charles as a madcap and irresponsible boy is voiced by Mazepa, not by the narrator. It must be conceded, however, that the whole tenor of the battle description confirms Mazepa's low opinion of Charles.[17]

It is, in any case, on aesthetic grounds that *Poltava* must be judged. Here, too, opinions have long been divided. Pushkin himself was sensitive to criticisms of this work, which he regarded as "mature" and "almost completely original." He had difficulty understanding how *Poltava* could be so harshly treated while *The Prisoner of the Caucasus,* which he rated far lower, had encountered so enthusiastic a reception. There are, however, valid reasons for finding fault with it. First, Mazepa—however unpleasant his personality in real life may have been—is something of a literary stereotype done in the melodramatic colors of a gothic-novel villain. Then too, the childish business in the second canto when Mazepa tricks Maria into choosing him over her father is a blemish. The battle in the third canto is described in intentionally hyperbolic language, and the larger-than-life portrait of Peter is acceptable within the laudatory tradition of the eighteenth century, but one cannot help wondering why both Charles and Mazepa should at various moments during the battle be "plunged in thought"—unless Pushkin wished to depict them as both vacillating and hesitant in contrast to Peter. In this and other details *Poltava* gives evidence of haste. But its main weakness—and this has been expressed in different ways by various critics from Belinsky on—lies in Pushkin's failure to fuse the personal and the historical, or, one might say, his failure to combine the romantic poem and those elements of plot and style derived from the heroic ode and the epic. In the excellent first canto, the individual fates of Maria, Mazepa, and Kochubey hold our attention, while historical events provide the background; in the third and final canto, despite Maria's nocturnal confrontation with Mazepa the individual fortunes of the protagonists are completely overshadowed by the patriotic theme of the Russian victory at Poltava. This shift of emphasis is aesthetically disappointing. The attempted fusion between the historical and the personal in *Poltava* is, in fact, imperfect.

It is difficult to argue with the Soviet scholar Dimitry Blagoy's contention that *Poltava,* written at the time of the *Gavriiliada* investigation, was designed to be a palatable sop for Nicholas I that might help extricate Pushkin from a dangerous situation.[18] Many critics would disagree with my less-than-enthusiastic assessment of *Poltava*. A recent attempt to salvage it finds within it "a multiplicity of narrative voices" that achieve "unity," but such a contrived construct is unconvincing. Incidentally, the author complains that Blagoy's view "oversimplifies the matter." Not so. Blagoy is never oversimple about anything, least of all this. Either he is right or he is wrong. In my view he is right.[19]

Chapter Five
The Little Tragedies

The "little tragedies" are four in number: *The Covetous Knight (Skupoy rytsar)*, *Mozart and Salieri (Motsart i Salieri)*, *The Stone Guest (Kamenny gost)*, and *The Feast During the Plague (Pir vo vremya chumy)*.[1] They were written in an incredibly short space of time during Pushkin's highly productive autumn of 1830 at Boldino, but (with the exception of the fourth, which is basically a translation of part of an English play) their conception dates back several years, to the Mikhaylovskoe days when Pushkin wrote *Boris Godunov*. Like *Boris Godunov*, the little tragedies are composed in unrhymed iambic pentameters, but unlike *Boris Godunov* they dispense with the regular caesura after the fourth syllable; intonationally, therefore, their lines represent a break with the French *décasyllabe* tradition (already under way in *Boris Godunov*, the caesura notwithstanding). Part of Pushkin's admiration for Shakespeare rested on the breadth and many-sidedness of Shakespeare's characters, and in the little tragedies there is a deliberate striving for this psychological complexity.

The format for the little tragedies came to Pushkin from the now little-known English writer Barry Cornwell (1781–1814), whose "dramatic scenes" may have had perhaps little impact on the essence of Pushkin's works but did serve as models from the standpoint of genre. The little tragedies are indeed "little," ranging in length from 231 to 542 lines.

In the little tragedies the highlights are not always of a dramatic nature, if by dramatic one means decisive action in word or deed. The most impressive passages in these plays have about them a decidedly lyric quality.[2] This is not to say that they do not fit in perfectly with their dramatic setting, but their impact has definite affinities with that of the lyric in that, over and above the action, they hold us with what they have to say about life, a specific problem, or an emotional attitude.

Another quality, characteristic of much of Pushkin's writing and certainly of the lyric poems of his mature age, is the conciseness of his style, his compression of thought. As others have noted, every line is made to count.[3] This compression should be borne in mind; to read these pieces expecting normal theater could be frustrating and blind us to the true qualities of these outstanding works. Whether "tragedies" or "little," the works now under discussion are best thought of as belonging to something other than the familiar genres of the literary tradition.

Pushkin toyed with the idea of calling them "dramatic investigations."[4] This would have been by no means inappropriate, for each of the four pieces holds up, through the voices of the characters involved, a specific problem, dilemma, or conflict of life for examination. This concentration on a single dilemma is at first sight more reminiscent of Molière—with his "personifications of a specific passion or vice"—than of Shakespeare. It is in his depiction of the dilemma's complexities that Pushkin comes closer to Shakespeare. Nevertheless, there is a basic difference between the methods of the Russian and the Englishman. We know already Pushkin's view that Shakespeare's characters are "living beings, full of many passions and vices; changing circumstances bring out before the spectator the diversity and many-sidedness of their characters." Shakespeare, of course, had five acts in which to present the "changing circumstances." The poetic medium chosen by Pushkin—by its brevity—is clearly more restrictive when it comes to characterization. Pushkin's little tragedies, with the exception of *The Stone Guest,* present very few "changing circumstances"; instead they offer conflict-laden situations. Thus the breadth of character sought by Pushkin is achieved by depicting the many complex facets of a problem as seen through the eyes of the character or as inferred from the character's words and reactions.

The Covetous Knight

The Covetous Knight centers on a conflict between father and son over money, which the son desperately needs in order to participate in tournaments and, in general, further his knightly career. The rich but miserly father, the Baron, regards the son as a spendthrift and hoards his wealth, depriving his son. It is generally believed that there was a link between *The Covetous Knight* and the differences over money between Pushkin and his own miserly father. It was probably to deny any such link that Pushkin added the misleading subtitle, *Scenes from Shenstone's Tragicomedy* The Covertous Knight, for neither William Shenstone (1714–1763) nor any other English writer is known to have written such a work.

In the first of the three scenes in *The Covetous Knight,* the son, Albert, laments his predicament to his servant, Ivan. His helmet was broken during his most recent tournament, his horse is limping and he wishes to buy another one. Unfortunately, the Jewish moneylender with whom he has dealt before refuses to lend him any more money, Ivan tells him, unless he can provide security. The Jew enters and Albert both pleads with him and browbeats him in an attempt to obtain money. Is not his knightly word of honor sufficient? His father is rich; surely his father will not outlive him? The Jew replies:

> Who knows? Our days are numbered—not by us;
> The youth who thrives today, tomorrow's dead,
> Laid out, and lo, is to the graveyard borne
> On the stooped shoulders of four aged men.

The baron is in good health, the Jew says, and may live even thirty years more. The Jew then suggests that through an acquaintance he might be able to provide the son with poison to hasten his father's death. Albert becomes furiously indignant, and the Jew beats a hasty retreat. Shaken, Albert calls for a glass of wine, but Ivan reminds him that there is no wine; he has given away his last bottle to a sick blacksmith. Albert asks for water and decides to appeal to the Duke, his father's Lord, to compel his father to treat him justly.

The second scene, set in the Baron's cellar, consists entirely of a 118-line monologue in which the Baron lovingly examines his treasures and expounds on their significance for him. In this scene—undoubtedly the highlight of this short drama—Pushkin's characterization techniques are at their best. This is not a matter of "changing circumstances," or even really breadth of character, but rather, as we shall see, of Pushkin's ability to play devil's advocate. After a first scene in which miserliness is viewed in the simplest terms, from the standpoint of the victimized son, as a thoroughly uncongenial vice, Pushkin now permits us to see from the inside the complicated motivations behind the father's behavior:

> Like a young rake who waits his evening tryst
> With some lewd, profligate, deceiving wench
> Or foolish woman tricked by him, so I
> Have all day waited till I might descend
> In secret to my trusty treasure chests.
> O happy day! Today one handful more. . . .

'Tis but a pittance, true; but in small ways
Do treasures grow. Somewhere I chanced to read
Of how some king once bade his warriors fetch
Handfuls of earth and pile them in a mound,
And a proud hill rose up—and thence the king
Could from the summit happily survey
The vale below, where tent on tent gleamed white,
And the blue sea alive with scudding sails.
So to my cellar here I too have borne
My daily tribute, piece by little piece,
And built my hill—and from its summit I
Can look upon what lies in my domain.
What lies not there? Like some divinity,
I can from here hold sway o'er all the world;
If such my wish, then palaces shall rise;
And in my sumptuous gardens, if I wish,
Will gather sprightly nymphs in loveliness;
To me the Muses will their tribute pay,
Genius' free spirit shall obey my whim,
And virtue shall, sleepless endeavor too,
Stand meekly by, begging of me reward.
One finger lifted, and obediently
Shall bloodied malefactors timid wait
To lick my hand and look into my eyes
To read my will and take their orders thence.
All things obey me, I no thing obey;
I am above desire; I am content;
I know my power; and 'tis enough for me
That I should know it. . . .

His treasure is for the Baron not merely gold. He knows what it
represents in terms of human suffering, crime, deception, tears, en-
treaties, and curses. And then the agonizing thought of his heir comes
to him:

I rule . . . but who will follow in my steps
To rule this realm when I am gone? My heir!
A young and giddy-headed squanderer,
The bosom friend of fellow debauchees!
Scarce I'll be dead, and he will hither come,
Hither beneath these peaceful, silent vaults,
He and his fawning, greedy courtiers.
Stealing these keys from my dead body, he

Will open up these treasure chests—and laugh . . .
He'll squander all . . . But by what right? What right?
Was it at such small cost I made this mine?
Like some lighthearted gambler who in jest
Shakes out the dice and gathers in his gains?
Who knows the bitter sacrifices made,
The passions held in check, the heavy thoughts,
The daily cares, the long and sleepless nights
That this has cost me? Or will my son say
That I knew no desires? Will he say too
That conscience never gnawed into my heart . . . ?
Let him first suffer that hard road to wealth;
Then let us see if the unhappy wretch
Will squander what was won by sweat and blood.
Could I but from unworthy eyes conceal
This treasure vault! Could I but from the grave
Come hither as a ghostly sentinel,
Stand watch upon my chests, and from the living
Preserve my treasures as I can today . . . !

The concluding scene opens with Albert's complaint to the Duke. The Duke is sympathetic, and has already summoned the Baron. As the Baron enters, the Duke orders Albert into the next room. After some moments of courteous conversation, the Duke asks the Baron why his son is never at court. After giving various excuses, the father charges that his son has wanted to kill him and has tried to steal from him. The latter accusation provokes the son, who has been listening from the next room, to burst in and accuse his father of lying. The father throws down his glove and the son picks it up, accepting the challenge, and exclaims, "I thank you. My father's first gift to me." The Duke intervenes to drive the son from the room, but the father collapses and dies, uttering his final words: "Where are my keys, my keys!"

Where lies, we may ask, the aesthetic appeal of this three-scene drama? It ends with the father's death, but this is no climax of the type to be found, for example, in the last act of *Hamlet*. Some commentators have seen a climax in the father's challenge accepted by the son with the remark that this is the first gift he has received from his father, and the allusion here to a somewhat similar episode in Molière's *L'Avare* has been studied. A certain amount of psychological interest—from the point of view of characterization—stems from the son's underlying desire for his father's death, a desire which he has never faced up to until he is provoked by the Jew's suggestion that he poison the Baron, and becomes vehemently indignant precisely because this suggestion echoes his own subconscious wish.[5] But these happenings and psychological insights are sketched in very summary fashion, and do not in themselves justify the high acclaim accorded this drama. In effect, scenes 1 and 3 really do little more than provide a framework for the second scene, the Baron's truly moving monologue. The father's death in the last scene is, it is true, no real climax, but it is significant that his final words evoke the entire second scene and, in particular, its closing thoughts. The second scene, then, is aesthetically the focal point of *The Covetous Knight*; and it epitomizes the lyric essence of the little tragedies. To feel the appeal of the second-scene monologue, one need not be a miser or imagine oneself a miser; one has only to know that success is sometimes obtained at the expense of others and leaves in its wake a troubled conscience, and that worthwhile achievement is usually the fruit of painful endeavor and deliberate self-denial.

Mozart and Salieri

The "problem" of *Mozart and Salieri* is envy (Pushkin appears to have contemplated calling it *Envy*)—the envy of conscientious talent for effortless and unmerited genius.[6] Again, in this shortest of the little tragedies we are struck not so much by the protagonists' breadth of character as by the complicated nature of the problem. Just as in *The Covetous Knight* miserliness was not dismissed as a mere vice, so here Salieri's envy of Mozart is not a simple emotion. It is based on Salieri's outraged sense of justice in the scheme of life and raises a metaphysical question as to the ordering of the universe.

Mozart and Salieri which consists of only two scenes is based on a rumor that on his deathbed Salieri confessed to having murdered Mozart out of envy. The first scene opens with Salieri ruminating alone.

> They say that there's no justice here on earth.
> But there's no justice—this I clearly see—
> No justice either in the heavens above.

He was born with a love of art. He sacrificed pleasure and other pursuits to devote himself entirely to music. First he had sought perseveringly to acquire knowledge and technique. Only when he had mastered these did he begin—diffidently and in secret—to compose.

When the great Gluck opened up new musical horizons, Salieri had abandoned all he had loved and, modestly, uncomplainingly, followed in Gluck's footsteps. At long last his perseverance had brought him renown: he had found tranquil pleasure in his labor and in success, and in those of his friends, coworkers in the service of glorious art. Never had he known envy—until now. Now, he admits,

> . . . I feel envy—deep,
> Tormenting envy. O ye heavens above,
> Is this your justice when the sacred gift
> Of deathless genius is bestowed upon—
> Not upon ardent love, self-sacrifice,
> Not upon labor, diligence and prayer—
> But sent to crown with light a madcap's head?
> Idle reveler, Mozart, that you are!

Enter Mozart. He had been on his way to visit Salieri with a recent composition, but upon passing a tavern he had heard a blind old violinist mutilating one of his arias. He brings the old man in and has him play an aria from *Don Juan*. The excruciating performance amuses Mozart, but Salieri is deeply shocked at Mozart's reaction. Mozart gives the old man some money and sends him on his way. Mozart then plays for Salieri his latest composition, a sad and hauntingly beautiful piece. Salieri exclaims:

> *Salieri.*   . . . 'Twas this that you were bringing;
> Yet on your way you at some tavern stopped
> To listen to this blind violinist! God!
> You, Mozart, are not worthy of yourself.
> *Mozart.*   You think it's good?
> *Salieri.*   What depth that music has!
> What bold invention, perfect harmony!
> You, Mozart, are a god, and know it not;
> But I—I know.

Mozart leaves after agreeing to dine with Salieri at the Golden Lion. Salieri decides to poison him. For years Salieri has had some poison in his possession, which he might use in retaliation for some unforgivable affront. Life has often seemed to him like some "unendurable wound," and he has often sat at the same table as some "carefree enemy" who had insulted him. But though no coward, Salieri has held his hand;

perhaps a worse enemy might come, a more grievous insult. Perhaps he would use the poison on himself, for "Life I love but little"; but he has been deterred by the thought that new gifts may suddenly be bestowed on him:

> And ecstasy, perchance, would be my guest,
> Nights of discovery and inspiration;
> Perhaps some great new Haydn would create
> New marvels in which I could take delight. . . .

But now the hour has come. The poison will be for Mozart—Mozart who never had to acquire his skills by labor, Mozart whose genius was given him by the gods, Mozart who—sin of sins—seems even unaware of his own gifts, who represents discrepancy and contradiction in the established order of effort and just reward that Salieri seeks to defend.

The second scene takes place in the Golden Lion. Mozart is low in spirits. He has written a Requiem at the command of an unknown visitor in black. The visitor has not returned, but Mozart feels haunted by his unseen presence. Salieri recalls how Beaumarchais once told him that, when besieged by dark thoughts, a person should either open up a bottle of champagne or read through *The Marriage of Figaro*. Mozart asks Salieri if there is any truth in the rumor that Beaumarchais once poisoned someone.

> *Salieri.*   I doubt it: he was too much of a jester
> To ply a trade like that.
> *Mozart.*   He was a genius.
> As you and I are. Genius and evil,
> Like oil and water, do not mix. Agreed?
> *Salieri.*   You think so? (*He pours the poison into Mozart's glass.*) Well,
> drink up then.
> *Mozart.*   To your health,
> My friend, I drink and to that loyal bond
> That joins together Mozart and Salieri,
> Two of sweet music's sons.

Mozart then plays his Requiem for Salieri, who is in tears. Mozart ponders:

> If only one and all could feel the power
> Of music! No! It could not be, for then

> The world would cease to turn; none would there be
> To take in hand life's lowly, trivial tasks;
> And all would know that freedom which is art. . . .

Mozart feels unwell and leaves, bidding Salieri farewell.

> *Salieri.*   Good-bye.
> (*Alone.*) You'll sleep a long, long sleep,
> Friend Mozart! But could it be that he's right,
> And I'm no genius. Genius and evil,
> Like oil and water, do not mix? Not true.
> Great Michelangelo—did he not kill?
> Or was that but a fairy tale put out
> By idle tongues, by the dull-witted crowd?

And so Salieri is left with his tormenting doubts.

While no one can harbor doubts as to the author's sympathy for Mozart, Pushkin again plays the devil's advocate with telling effect. Although Salieri's indignation at the blind violinist's faulty playing and Mozart's jesting emphasizes his pedantry in contrast to the ironical playfulness of genius, Pushkin has made a strong case for Salieri, whose sense of injustice also arouses the author's sympathy.

It is not pure chance that *Mozart and Salieri* was completed only three days after *The Covetous Knight.* The problems posed in these two little tragedies are by no means dissimilar. While the settings are very different, the two dramas both depict characters who have acquired something by painful effort and who resent the thought of someone else's acquiring as much or more with no effort at all, and, worse still, without even being aware of the painful effort involved. And this sense of injustice is convincingly pleaded in one case through the mouth of a miser, and in the other through the mouth of a poisoner![7]

The Stone Guest

The Stone Guest is the longest of the little tragedies and the most "dramatic" in the sense that it contains more events, more "changing circumstances" than the other three. At the same time, the problem that preoccupied Pushkin in *The Stone Guest* was one that troubled him in his personal life at the time of writing; consequently, there is in this short drama a strong lyrical, subjective element.

The first of the four scenes comprising *The Stone Guest* opens outside the gates of Madrid. Don Juan is returning secretly from exile, accompanied by his servant, Leporello. The place recalls to his mind a past affair with Ineza, a woman who perished near this spot, presumably as a result of Don Juan's attentions. Ineza was not really beautiful, the Don concedes, but her eyes . . . ! He had wooed her for three months. Her husband was a scoundrel and a harsh man, as Don Juan had discovered—too late. Poor Ineza! But, as Leporello points out to his master, Ineza was followed by other women and there will be still others in the future. The Don agrees and, shaking off his remorse, announces that his first visit in Madrid will be to Laura. A monk passes by who, not recognizing Don Juan and Leporello, tells them that Dona Anna will arrive shortly, as she does every day, to weep and pray in front of the monument she has erected to her late husband, the Commander, killed by Don Juan in a duel. She will talk to no man except a monk, and she is beautiful. Don Juan's amorous curiosity is aroused. Dona Anna enters to pray, but she is so shrouded in her cloak that Don Juan's curiosity remains for the moment unsatisfied. Meanwhile dusk has fallen, and it is safe to enter Madrid.

The second scene opens with Laura entertaining guests. She is an actress who has just finished an absolutely inspired performance. Her guests beg her to sing for them while she is still in her aroused state. She obliges, to their delight; on being asked who composed the words of the song, she informs them the author was Don Juan, "My faithful friend, my fickle-hearted lover." This admission provokes a jealous outburst from the taciturn Don Carlos, who is in love with Laura and whose brother has been killed by Don Juan in a duel. Incensed at Don Carlos's outburst, Laura threatens to have Don Carlos killed by her servants. Swayed not by fear but by love, Don Carlos begs forgiveness, and the quarrel ends. As the guests leave, Laura bids Don Carlos to stay; his passionate fury reminds her of Don Juan. Suddenly there is a knocking at the door and Don Juan enters the room. Laura throws herself into his arms. Don Carlos and Don Juan fight, and the former is killed. Indifferent to the presence of the corpse, Don Juan makes love to Laura.

The third scene takes place, like the first, in the vicinity of the Commander's statue. For some time Don Juan, disguised as a monk, has been coming to this spot every day in order to see Dona Anna. When she arrives, Don Juan addresses her. Dona Anna is surprised to hear such flattering and ingratiating words from a monk. Don Juan reveals to her that he is no monk. He is, he tells her, Don Diego, and he loves her without hope of reward but with a love that has for the first time revealed to him life's value and the meaning of happiness. Dona Anna is afraid that someone will discover them, and agrees to receive him on the evening of the following day, provided he respects her virtue. Dona Anna leaves, greatly agitated. Enter Leporello, who is informed by the triumphant Don that he has obtained a rendezvous. Leporello wonders what the Commander will think of that; the statue, he thinks, looks angry. But there is no stopping Don Juan. Carried away by his success, like a triumphant rival, he issues his invitation: "I, Commander, bid you come tomorrow / To your widow's home, where I shall also be, / And stand at the door on guard. Well? Will you come?" To Don Juan's horror, the statue nods agreement.

The final scene takes place on the following evening. Don Juan tells Dona Anna how happy he is to be alone with her in some place other than at her husband's graveside. Dona Anna is surprised that he can be jealous of the dead. She had not, she reveals, chosen her husband; she had been ordered to marry by her mother; but she cannot listen to words of love, for a widow must be faithful even to the dead. Don Juan skillfully lets slip that he feels guilty toward Dona Anna. Her curiosity is aroused and, induced, in return for his frankness, to forgive him in advance, whatever his crime, she insists that he explain. Don Juan reveals his true identity. Dona Anna almost faints from shock. Don Juan then admits that his reputation as an evil profligate is not altogether undeserved, but he has never loved before. Only now, through his love of Dona Anna, has he been reborn; only now for the first time, loving Dona Anna, has he learned what it is to love virtue. Dona Anna becomes concerned for Don Juan's safety; discovery would mean death. Don Juan responds that he will gladly lay down his life for one moment with her. He also points out that her concern for him surely means that, in spite of everything, she does not hate him.

Preparing to leave, he begs for another meeting, and Dona Anna agrees to receive him again the next day. He also begs for and receives one kiss—a token of her forgiveness! Suddenly they hear knocking. Don Juan leaves but immediately runs back in, followed by the Commander's statue. The statue asks for Don Juan's hand, and they vanish together. Don Juan is killed. His last words are, "Oh Dona Anna!"

The Stone Guest constitutes in many ways a radical departure from its predecessors in the Don Juan tradition. Both the plot and the character of the hero differ significantly from earlier versions by not only Tirso de Molina (which Pushkin probably did not know), but also Molière and Mozart-da Ponte, with both of which Pushkin was familiar. The changes Don Juan underwent at Pushkin's hands are to be explained partly, by the brevity of his play, which made change inevitable, and partly, by the spirit of Pushkin's age, but they were shaped largely by the relationship of the author to his hero and the nature of the problem Pushkin was investigating.

The traditional Don Juan of Molina, Molière, and Mozart was obsessively dedicated to the act of seduction, completely promiscuous, recklessly brave, ruthless, and untroubled by remorse. Some of these characteristics reappear in Pushkin's Don Juan. But it is the manner in which Pushkin's hero *differs* from his predecessors that is revealing, for the differences in character and situation clearly indicate a close relationship between hero and author.

Like his predecessors, Pushkin's Don Juan is cavalierly gay, carefree, and reckless—qualities that, however, appear in several of Pushkin's heroes and that correspond to one of Pushkin's favorite images of himself. Pushkin's Don Juan is, in the approved tradition, physically brave—and that Pushkin undoubtedly was. But, in contrast to his predecessors, Pushkin's hero is a poet. Unlike his predecessors, he is no mere lecher with an unflagging zest for seduction. He is, rather, a connoisseur of women, capable of savoring their individual characteristics and delighting in their differences rather than their sameness. His easy-come, easy-go relationship with Laura is the relationship of a man with a tolerant mistress, far removed from the catastrophe-laden affair with Ineza. His reminiscences of Ineza reveal, further, another aspect of his nature that sets him off from his predecessors; there is something of the poet in his approach to Ineza, in his ability to see what other men miss—the beauty of her eyes—which for him compensates for the mediocre appeal of her other physical attributes. The Ineza affair shows, too, that, contrary to tradition, he is capable—at certain moments—of remorse. Again contrary to tradition, he is willing to devote considerable time to the business of wooing and seducing. He spends three months courting Ineza, and masquerades as a monk for an unspecified period of time to make the acquaintance of Dona Anna. Incidentally, masquerading and lying are basically alien to his nature. While the traditional Don Juan is willing to make use of the dark in order to impersonate another man, to promise marriage, to resort to any device that will enable him to gain his end, Pushkin's Don Juan rejects all such deceits—not so much, one is tempted to feel, on moral grounds, as that his attitude toward women and toward himself impels him to demand that he be loved as himself and for himself. Pushkin's Don Juan is—at least until he encounters Dona Anna—a sophisticated hedonist with a touch of the poet and a touch of the lonely introspective in his nature. All of these characteristics, to a greater or lesser degree, bring him closer to his creator.[8]

If Pushkin's own personality influenced the character of his hero, his personal life had a hand in shaping the plot as well. One minor detail is the transfer of the action from Seville to Madrid. In *The Stone Guest* Don Juan returns secretly and illegally from exile. In 1825 Pushkin had contemplated a similar unauthorized return from exile to Saint Petersburg, the capital of Russia. Since Pushkin *nearly* returned to the Russian capital, his hero must return to the Spanish capital; Madrid, therefore, is substituted for Don Juan's traditional Seville. Seville does appear in a draft of Pushkin's work. The switch to Madrid in the final version can therefore be regarded as deliberate—and a further indication of the poet's tendency to identify with the hero.

A far more important break with tradition concerns the person of the Commander. The Commander is traditionally Dona Anna's father, who is killed by Don Juan while defending his daughter's honor. Pushkin made him the husband. This change may have been dictated by purely artistic considerations, but it was probably also tied in with Pushkin's own feelings. In the fall of 1830 the poet was still only engaged to his future wife. Yet before even possessing her, he was already morbidly obsessed by the thought of one day being replaced by another man. As early as 5 April 1830 he wrote to his future mother-in-law, "God is my witness that I am ready to die for her, but to have to die leaving her a beautiful widow, free to choose a new husband on the day after: this thought is hell." It should also be noted that Dona Anna did not marry the Commander for love but in obedience to her mother, just as Pushkin's wife did. Thus, Pushkin not only infiltrated some of his own personality into his Don Juan, he also put himself in the situation of the Commander. Critics have pointed out that by switching the Commander's role from father to husband, Pushkin was left without a motive for the duel in which the Commander died. But this is an insignificant loss, one more than offset by the added meaning that Pushkin could then give to Don Juan's invitation.

By far the most important manner in which Pushkin's own preoccupations influenced *The Stone Guest* has to do with its central emotional problem. Pushkin's bachelor existence had not been particularly happy, yet at the same time the prospect of marriage caused him considerable misgivings. In the fall of 1830, as he prepared himself for this decisive change in his life, the question of love and happiness was constantly on his mind. Could love bring true happiness? Could love give a value to life that it had never had before? Could a man through love of a woman be redeemed, born anew? These questions are basic to the whole conception of *The Stone Guest.*

One may wonder whether Don Juan's protestations of newfound love, newfound happiness, and newfound redemption are sincere. Are these lofty statements simply ploys to ensnare Dona Anna? She herself is very much aware of this possibility: "Don Juan is most eloquent—I know. / I've heard; he is a skilled and cunning tempter . . ."; and again, "Should I believe / That for the first time Don Juan's now in love! / Or does he seek in me his latest prey?" The thesis that Don Juan was seeking only to add Dona Anna to his list of victims has been maintained, most persuasively by Charles Corbet.[9] Corbet sees Don Juan as a satanic seducer, intent—to the point of sadism—on Dona Anna's total humiliation. He derives, according to Corbet, a diabolic pleasure from revealing to her his true identity as the man who killed her husband. Human motives are indeed mixed, and Corbet's insight on this last point may have a certain validity. However, there is another stronger motive—the need to be loved for what one really is, without the aid of disguise or false pretenses. Henry Kucera has astutely pointed to a parallel situation in *Boris Godunov,* where the Pretender, like Don Juan, is jealous of the dead; he insists on revealing to Marina what he really is—a poor monk. "In both the Pretender and Don Juan," Kucera observes, "one detects the same striving for completeness of love, manifested in their desire to be loved for themselves, in their own identity."[10] This seems to me to give a truer picture of Don Juan's psychology. Yet the doubt remains, a doubt that on the evidence of *The Stone Guest* alone cannot be finally resolved. Each of Don Juan's fine phrases does indeed gain a point for him in his wooing of Dona Anna. Nor was Pushkin naive enough not to know that today's sincerity can become tomorrow's falsehood. Yet belief in Don Juan's sincerity of the moment is important, not merely because of the extrinsic evidence offered by Pushkin's biography, but because without this belief *The Stone Guest* loses much of its point.

Pushkin loved concision; in this case, however, his concision and the ensuing ambiguity have rendered him a disservice. The one weakness of *The Stone Guest* lies in a certain failure to make it absolutely clear to the reader that Don Juan is experiencing feelings that are for him totally new. If the reader were completely convinced of this, if there were less room for ambiguity, then the reader's sympathy for Don Juan at the end would be increased and the sense of tragedy would be heightened. For the tragedy of *The Stone Guest* is to be found, ambiguity notwithstanding, in the irony that Don Juan, who before this has never truly loved, never known true happiness, never set much store by life, and never believed in virtue, perishes at precisely the moment when life has acquired value for him, when love, happiness, and redemption seem within his grasp. It is to be noted that this very question of Don Juan's love for Ineza being replaced by his love for other women who followed is raised in the first dialogue of the first scene between Don Juan and Leporello. Was it to be always so? The ensuing courtship of Dona Anna would seem to offer an answer, albeit not a conclusive one.

According to one interpretation, "Don Juan is really saved—saved by a woman."[11] But this is to impose on Pushkin's work the Christian ethic of the original Don Juan legend. Equally absent from *The Stone Guest* are both the Christian belief in damnation and salvation and the romantic notion of salvation through love of a woman. If Juan had come to believe in redemption, it was redemption here on earth; the love and happiness he thought to have found were to be experienced in this life, not in the hereafter. In place of the Christian ethos *The Stone Guest* offers poetic justice, retribution, the Nemesis of Greek tragedy. Don Juan is, at the very start, revisiting the scene of a crime involving Ineza. He goes on not merely to kill Don Carlos, which was unavoidable, but to make love to Laura with the dead Don Carlos in the room. There is a macabre parallel between the second and the fourth scenes. In the former he consummates his love in the presence of the victim; in the latter, following his callous and sadistic invitation to the statue to play the role of voyeur, we anticipate a repetition of the second scene. Instead, at the most poignant moment in Juan's life, the tables are turned, retribution catches up with him, the dead man—his former victim and now apparently defeated rival—returns to exact his vengeance and destroy the Don. Juan does not really suffer a just punishment meted out by a Christian God; he is, rather, the victim of a pagan Nemesis. When he dies, it is not fear of Hell or hope of salvation that agitates him, but agony at being deprived of life just when life had taken on a new meaning.

The Feast During the Plague

The Feast During the Plague is a fairly accurate line-by-line translation of Act I, scene 4 of John Wilson's *The City of the Plague* (1816), set

during the London plague of 1665. The topic was obviously suggested
to Pushkin by the cholera epidemic then keeping him a prisoner at
Boldino. The scene translated by Pushkin depicts a group of young
revelers who are carousing, although preserving a certain ritualistic dig-
nity, as an act of defiance in the face of death. The threat of nearby
death goads them on, heightens the need for intense emotions, emancipating them from their normal habits and moral standards. They are
driven by fear and by a sort of frenzied ecstasy induced by a consciousness of living on the brink of the grave.

A young man makes a speech in honor of the late departed Jackson
(in Wilson's original, Harry Wentworth), who only two days ago was
regaling them all with his keen jests and merry anecdotes. Let Jackson's
death not bring sadness to the feast. He proposes a toast to Jackson,
and they drink. The Master of Revels then proposes that Mary sing
them a sad, slow song from her own part of the country—deliberately
sad, so that afterward they may readdress themselves to merriment with
even greater zest. Mary sings a song (Pushkin here departs from the
original) describing a village in prosperous days. Now church and
school are empty, the fields untended; only the churchyard is full as the
victims of the plague are brought in. If, Mary continues, an early grave
is to be my fate, you whom I loved so much, do not come near the body
of your Jenny. Leave the village and, when the plague is past, visit my
poor dust, but even in heaven Jenny will not abandon her Edmond. The
Master of Revels thanks Mary for the song. Mary wishes that she had
never sung it outside her parents' cottage and bemoans her lost innocence. Louise upbraids Mary for playing on people's sympathy. At this
point the hearse passes; Louisa faints and is revived by Mary. The Master of Revels is then asked to sing a song, a hymn in honor of the
plague. Here again Pushkin departs from the original with one of his
most famous lyrics:

> There is an ecstasy in battle,
> And on the edge of the abyss,
> And in the raging ocean's might
> Mid threat'ning waves and darkling storm,
> In the hurricanes of Araby,
> And in the foul breathing of the Plague.
>
> All, all that threatens us with death
> Brings to the heart of mortal man

Some unexplained delight—the pledge,
Perchance, of immortality.
And happy he who in the storm
Can find and feel these awesome joys.

And so to You, O Plague, our praise!
We shall not fear the tomb's deep dark,
We shall not tremble if You call!
Our sparkling goblets one and all
We raise, and quaff the fragrant wine,
Perchance, the fragrance of the Plague!

A priest enters who remonstrates with the revelers. They bid him leave. He reminds the Master of Revels:

Art thou that groaning pale-faced man of tears
Who three weeks since with sobs embraced thy mother's corpse,
And wailed
With ragelike grief above her grave?
Or do you think she would not weep,
Weep even in heaven, could she behold her son
Presiding o'er unholy revelers. . . .

The Master of Revels refuses to leave; he is held here by self-contempt and

By despair, by awful memory,
By the consciousness of my wrong-doing,
By the horror of that empty silence
Which greets me at my door,
And by the newness of these mad delights,
And by the blessed poison of this cup,
And by the embraces (Lord forgive me)
Of this lost creature, lost but dear to me.

Let the old priest go in peace, he says, but cursed be he who follows him. The priest reminds him of his dead wife. The Master forbids him to mention the name of one who had "Once thought my spirit lofty, pure, and free / And on my bosom felt herself in Heaven." The priest leaves and the feast continues, but the Master of Revels broods.

The connection between death and the need for intense emotion that reasserts the awareness of living and seeks to cram a maximum of expe-

rience into a short span that may at any time be abruptly ended has
been observed before—in times of war, plague, and disaster. It is not
new in literature with either Pushkin or John Wilson. And the format
used to present this phenomenon was, with the exception of the two
songs, of Wilson's choosing rather than Pushkin's. Not too much,
then, should be made of the underlying dilemma exposed in this short
scene. But neither should the fact that *The Feast During the Plague* was
basically a translation obscure the poignancy of the situation, the beauty
of Pushkin's verse, or yet the choice of theme, which was Pushkin's,
and which links with the main themes of the other three original small
tragedies.

Chapter Six

Eugene Onegin: A Novel in Verse

Origins

Pushkin started work on *Eugene Onegin* in May 1823, while still in Kishinev. The poem was virtually complete in the fall of 1830, except for one short but essential passage that the author did not supply until October 1831.[1] Thus *Eugene Onegin* was more than eight years in the writing, and even after 1831 Pushkin thought of returning to his poem. It goes without saying that Pushkin did not work uninterruptedly on *Eugene Onegin*; it was often laid aside in favor of new endeavors, and there were frequent periods of idleness. But to no other work did Pushkin devote a comparable portion of his life nor, it is safe to assume, a comparable amount of thought. This makes *Eugene Onegin* particularly deserving of attention.

In its final form the poem consists of eight cantos, although Pushkin also wrote parts of two further cantos. One of these, now generally known as "Onegin's Journey," describes the hero's travels through different parts of Russia and gives the author's impressions of life in Odessa. The other, very fragmentary, appears to be the beginning of a sequel to *Eugene Onegin* proper. The hero, the surviving fragments suggest, was in this canto to have become involved in the Decembrist movement. Pushkin burned one copy of this canto (1830), and the surviving fragments have been deciphered from his notebooks, where they were found in crudely coded form. On the basis of these fragments alone it can be confidently stated that its politically sensitive subject matter would have made this canto totally unacceptable to the censors and would have had very unpleasant consequences for the author.[2] Apart from these two omitted cantos, a number of passages Pushkin eventually discarded have survived, and his notebooks contain many textual variants that provide interesting insights into the creative process. Worth mentioning also in this connection is the fact that Pushkin originally published the sixth canto as "End of Part I," a certain indication that he at one time contemplated writing twelve cantos; indeed,

some scholars wonder whether *Eugene Onegin* was not so much completed as abandoned.[3] But for all these variants and vacillations, most
of them normal enough in the work of any writer, the final version as
approved by the poet is our concern here.[4]

Each canto or chapter, as Pushkin preferred to call them, contains
between forty and fifty-four stanzas, and each stanza (except those few
that are incomplete) consists of fourteen lines with a regular rhyme
scheme. (Only four passages do not conform to this pattern: the dedication, a song sung by peasant girls, and two letters, one from the
heroine to the hero, one from the hero to the heroine.)

A detailed analysis of the characteristics of the "Onegin" stanza lies
beyond the scope of this discussion, but the following points may be of
interest. (1) The "Onegin" stanza is composed in four-foot iambics,
Pushkin's preferred meter at the time of writing, and alternates between
masculine and feminine rhyme, that is, eight- and nine-syllable lines.
(2) The rhyme scheme is as follows (small letters for masculine and
capital letters for feminine rhymes): AbAbCCddEffEgg. (3) *Eugene
Onegin* was one of the first and one of the few occasions when Pushkin
used a regular stanzaic arrangement for anything beyond a lyric or short
poem—the idea was most probably suggested to him by Byron's use of
the Italian *ottava rima* in *Beppo* and *Don Juan.* (4) Although fourteen
lines naturally call to mind the sonnet, the "Onegin" stanza is basically
new—the final rhymed couplet, which lends itself so well to the epigrammatic or bathetic ending, was probably also suggested by Byron
and by the *ottava rima* in general, with its similar "homestriking final
couplet."[5]

We have noted that Pushkin preferred, in publishing *Eugene Onegin,*
to use the term *chapter* rather than *canto* (though in his letters he casually
speaks of *cantos* quite often), and this preference is consistent with the
subtitle, *A Novel in Verse.* The fact that Pushkin chose to refer to his
work as a *novel* is important for the literary historian, but unfortunately,
it has generated a great deal of misplaced emphasis in critical studies of
the poem. *Onegin* has been hailed as the first genuine Russian novel and
the first great work of Russian realism.[6] Such pointless claims are encouraged by the well-known fact that at that time the novel was the
up-and-coming literary form; it was destined to dominate the nineteenth century, and was (to cite only Balzac as an example) to prove
itself an admirable vehicle for social analysis. Thus, to treat *Eugene
Onegin* as a novel in the normally accepted sense enables the critic to
thrust it forward in time and to seek in this masterpiece virtues of a

sociological order that have nothing to do with its aesthetic merits. Pushkin's perfectly justifiable decision to call his work a novel is best seen in the light of the conscious efforts of contemporaries to break down the rigid classical distinctions between genres and, specifically, of their tendency to speak of narrative poems as *tales* or *stories* (as witness Byron's "oriental tales"). Furthermore, *Eugene Onegin* does have very definite affinities with the novel, especially, where subject matter is concerned, with such sentimental-romantic novels as Rousseau's *La Nouvelle Heloise* and Benjamin Constant's *Adolphe*.[7] Although the subtitle of Pushkin's work is an interesting fact of literary history, let us guard against the misplaced emphasis to which this has given rise, and let us also bear in mind that *Eugene Onegin* is inconceivable without the stanzas and verses in which it was written.

Actually, the stimulus to the writing of *Eugene Onegin* came from another novel in verse, Byron's *Don Juan*, or rather from its first two cantos. On 4 November 1823, Pushkin wrote to his friend and fellow poet Petr Vyazemsky, "I am writing, not a novel but a novel in verse—a devil of a difference. It's in the genre of *Don Juan*." The "novelty" of *Don Juan* consisted precisely in its unification of prose and verse genres, which had most often existed in separation. "The real model of *Don Juan*," Elizabeth Boyd notes, "is the picaresque novel, the great catchall of narrative and reflection, subject to no law but the author's desires."[8] At the same time, *Don Juan* is also linked with an English verse tradition going back to Chaucer, and with the French and Italian tradition of the *conte* and the comic epic going back through Voltaire and La Fontaine to Francesco Berni, Ariosto, and Luigi Pulci. The "genre" of *Don Juan* is thus a hybrid that interweaves a number of strands from the literary tradition. Of these strands, the two most immediately evident are the comic epic and the novel, genres that had expanded to embrace most of the others.[9] In *Eugene Onegin* the picaresque element is lacking. But with this qualification, much of what has just been said about *Don Juan* can be applied to *Eugene Onegin*. *Eugene Onegin* is no less hybrid than *Don Juan*, combining several genres, primarily the sentimental novel and the comic epic.[10]

The Work

The events described in *Eugene Onegin* are nearly contemporary. The young hero has received a superficial education, speaks French, dances the mazurka, bows gracefully: "What more can you expect? Society decided that he was clever and very charming." His real *forte* is the art of seduction. His typical Saint Petersburg day includes a drive, a gourmet dinner, the ballet, a ball. But society life brings Onegin no happiness; he suffers, like Childe Harold, from spleen and melancholy, from the *mal du siècle*.

The death of Onegin's uncle makes him owner of a country estate. Installed in his old-fashioned home, Onegin—partly to pass the time—improves the lot of his serfs by putting the estate on a quit-rent basis. The change pleases the serfs, but strikes neighboring owners as a dangerous precedent. They decide that Onegin is a crank and leave him to his own devices—to Onegin's relief. His one friend is Vladimir Lensky, a romantic, idealistic youth who has just returned to his estate from the university at Göttingen. Lensky writes poetry about sublime feelings, about parting and sorrow, about life's mystery, and about love. Lensky confides to Onegin his love for Olga, the younger of two sisters from a neighboring estate. "Ah, he loved as in our time people no longer love; he loved as only the poet's crazed soul is still condemned to love," the narrator remarks with irony.

Olga is modest, obedient, cheerful, simple, and charming. She has blue eyes, a sweet smile, flaxen hair, graceful movements, a pleasant voice, a slender figure, everything—but, the narrator says, "Take any novel and you will surely find her portrait. It is very charming. I myself once found it most appealing, but I have grown immensely tired of it. Allow me, reader, to tell you about her older sister."

The older sister, Tatyana, is, unlike Olga, not really beautiful. She is pale, retiring, sorrowful, silent, and shy. She seems a stranger even to her own family. As a child she did not know how to show affection to her parents. She did not play with the other children, sew, or play with dolls, but would sit all day dreaming at the window. Her heart was captivated by the fairy tales told by her nurse. She loved to sit on the balcony watching the dawn come up, and from an early age was an avid reader of the sentimental novels of Richardson and Rousseau which were more real to her than the life going on around her. There is a time for young girls to fall in love: Tatyana's time has come, and she falls in love with Onegin.[11]

"Tatyana, sweet Tatyana," the narrator commiserates with his heroine, "I shed my tears with yours; you have surrendered your fate into the hands of a fashion-conscious tyrant. You will perish, dear one." Tatyana decides to write to Onegin. Here the narrator feels it necessary to defend her against criticism: she is neither coldhearted nor an experienced coquette adept at manipulating men, but is straightforward, loves with all her heart, and is naively trusting.

"I am writing to you," Tatyana's letter begins. "What more can I say? I know that it is now in your power to punish me with your contempt." If he had never come, she would never have known him and she might have become another's faithful wife and a virtuous mother. But no! She could never have given her heart to another! She belongs to Onegin; that was predestined, the will of heaven; she had recognized him at once. Perhaps all this is self-deception, but she entrusts her fate to him and begs for his protection: "I end my letter, I'm afraid to read it through. I am dying of shame and fear. But I am protected by your sense of honor, to which I boldly entrust myself."

Anxiously Tatyana waits for a reply. But the days pass—and she hears nothing. Then one day suddenly there is the sound of galloping hoofs: it is Onegin. But the narrator lacks the strength today to continue.

As the fourth chapter opens, the narrator reflects on love and the art of seduction. The less we love a woman, the more we attract her, and the easier it is to work her destruction. But Onegin had been genuinely moved by Tatyana's letter and for a moment had felt something of his onetime ardor; but he did not wish to deceive Tatyana.

In the garden the two stand face to face. Onegin addresses Tatyana, "You wrote to me, don't deny it. I have read the confessions of your trustful soul, the outpourings of your innocent love, and I was moved by your sincerity." Her letter, he tells her, reawakened feelings long dormant, and he will repay her by being as straightforward as she. If he had wanted to settle down to married life, he would certainly have chosen Tatyana as his wife, and been happy—as far as possible. But he is not made for happiness. The years cannot be rolled back, and he cannot change or renew himself, but he loves her with a brother's love and perhaps more tenderly than that. She will fall in love again, he assures her, but she must learn to restrain herself, for not everyone would understand her as he has, and inexperience can be a woman's undoing. Thus Onegin concludes his lecture.

The pangs of her unrequited love cause Tatyana to grow sickly. After describing her wretched condition, the sympathetic narrator declares himself relieved to turn his attention to a happier love affair, that between Lensky and Olga. How Olga's shoulders have improved, Lensky tells Onegin, and her bosom is magnificent! But he had forgotten; next Saturday is Tatyana's name day, and Onegin is invited. Onegin objects that there will be a crowd of people, but Lensky assures him that there will be just the family, and Onegin agrees to go.

The fifth chapter opens with a description of winter, a season Tatyana loves. Tatyana is "Russian in soul" and believes in the omens and fortune-tellings of Russian folklore. For instance, on Twelfth Night an unmarried girl may see her future husband in the mirror, and Tatyana, upon going to bed, places her mirror under the pillow.

She dreams a strange dream: she is walking across a snow-covered clearing when her way is barred by a dark, menacing stream. The only way across is on two poles frozen together, and Tatyana hesitates. Suddenly a bristling bear emerges from a snowdrift and offers her his sharp-clawed paw. Trembling, Tatyana leans on the paw and crosses the stream. As she continues the bear follows her. Not daring to look behind her, she quickens her pace, but the bear is still there, and she plunges on through the deep snow and into the forest in panic. A long branch clutches at her throat and she loses her earrings, one of her shoes, her handkerchief. As she hurries on she is afraid even to lift her skirt—and still the bear is behind her. She falls exhausted in the snow. The bear picks her up and carries her off, unresisting and scarcely conscious, to a hut; there is light in the window, and the noise of shouting comes from inside. The bear tells Tatyana: "Here is my relative [*kum*], warm up in his place for a while," and sets her down near the door. Coming to her senses, Tatyana sees that the bear has disappeared. Inside there are the sounds of shouting and of clinking glasses. She looks through a chink in the door and, to her amazement, sees a company of weird monsters around the table. One has horns and a dog's head, another the head of a cock; there is a witch with a goat's beard, a stiff, proud-looking skeleton, a dwarf with a tail, a beast that is half crane and half cat, a lobster mounted on a spider, a skull on a goose's neck, and a windmill dancing and waving its wings. But still more amazing, Onegin, the leader of the company, is also seated at the table. Onegin rises and opens wide the door, and Tatyana, who wishes to run but cannot move, is revealed to the gaze of the monsters. The monsters laugh wildly and, pointing at Tatyana, all shout, "Mine! Mine!" But Onegin responds menacingly, "Mine!"—and the monsters disappear. Onegin gently draws Tatyana into a corner and, laying her on a rickety bench, puts his head on her shoulder. Olga and Lensky enter suddenly; Onegin, eyes flashing, curses the unbidden guests. The argument grows more heated, and suddenly Onegin seizes a long knife and plunges it into Lensky. There is a chilling scream—and Tatyana awakes in horror to find that it is now daylight. The dream's ominous nature fills her with dark foreboding.

But now it is her name day, and the guests arrive for the party, many of them to spend the night: they are described satirically with allegorical names in the eighteenth-century tradition. Lensky and Onegin arrive late, and the guests, who are already at table, make room for the two friends—right opposite Tatyana. Onegin is in a vile mood. He had had doubts about coming, but Lensky had assured him that there would be only the family, and now it turns out that there are all these uninteresting guests. Worse still, Tatyana seems on the point of fainting from embarrassment and emotion, and he cannot abide such displays. He swears he will get back at Lensky for all this.

With dinner over some guests play cards, while others dance. Onegin waltzes with Olga, sits with her, talks to her, then waltzes again. People are amazed, and Lensky can scarcely believe his eyes. When it is time for the mazurka, once more Onegin dances with Olga, his tender whisper and the pressure of his hand on hers bringing a blush to her face. Lensky waits for the mazurka to end, then invites Olga for the cotillion, but she can't!—she has already promised Onegin! Lensky, inveighing against feminine deceit, calls for his horse and gallops off in anger; only a duel, he thinks, can settle his fate.

Despite his feeling of guilt at ·having foolishly upset Lensky, and notwithstanding his reluctance to duel, Onegin allows himself to be guided by how others may interpret a refusal and accepts the challenge. He kills Lensky.

My friends—the narrator addresses his readers—you pity the poet, struck down in the springtime of his eager hopes. Where are his noble aspirations, his passionate desire for love, his longing for knowledge, his hatred of evil, his poetic dreams? Perhaps he was born to better the lot of mankind or, at least, to win glory. His now silent lyre might have sounded through the ages. Or, perhaps, the poet's lot would have been more ordinary: the ardor of his soul would have passed away with his youth; he would have abandoned the muses; lived in the country, married, been happy, and a cuckold; had gout at forty; have drunk, eaten, suffered from boredom, grown fat, grown sick; and finally died in his bed, surrounded by children, wailing womenfolk, and doctors. The narrator reflects on his own fate. The years are turning his mind to prose, driving away the frolicsome rhymes that his pen no longer pursues with the eagerness of past days. His springtime has passed, and there is no return, for soon he will be thirty. Let him bid a friendly farewell to youth.

It is spring as the seventh chapter opens, but spring brings no joy to the narrator. His strength is not renewed as nature is renewed by the seasons. Nevertheless, spring is the time to go to the country, and he invites the reader to accompany his muse to the place where Onegin lived last winter and where, for a while, Olga and Tatyana wept over Lensky's grave. But things have changed. Onegin has gone; Olga, "inconstant to her sorrow," has fallen in love again, married, and departed with her husband to join his regiment; and Tatyana, bereft of her sister and mourning Lensky, still tormented by her love for Onegin, is left alone in her sorrow.

On an evening walk Tatyana, buried in her thoughts, comes unawares to Onegin's house. After some hesitation she asks if she may enter, and the housekeeper shows her the rooms. She sees his study with its books, a portrait of Lord Byron, and a small cast-iron figure of Napoleon. Two days later she is back to visit his study again. She weeps for a long time and then begins to look over the books. She is struck by something strange in Onegin's taste and, as she reads, eagerly now, a new world opens before her. Onegin has little fondness for reading in general, but there are, Tatyana discovers, a few exceptions: works by Byron and certain novels that "depict fairly faithfully the modern age and contemporary man with his immoral, self-loving, and cold soul, overly given to dreaming, his embittered intellect seething in futile activity." Tatyana pays particular attention to the passages Onegin has marked, and slowly starts to understand better the man whom fate has condemned her to love. She wonders if he is not some sort of imitation, some parody of Byron or Childe Harold.

Some time later the reluctant Tatyana is taken to Moscow, and a husband is found for her.

The opening stanzas of the last chapter trace the progress of the narrator's muse on his journey through life. The muse first started to appear to him in his lycée days, when she sang of childish delights, the glories of Russia's past, and the tremulous dreams of his heart; and the first outpourings of his muse were kindly received by the world. Next, over a glass of wine his muse had sung of noisy feasting and loud argument, and among his young friends of past days he had felt pride in her singing. But he had left these friends behind, and his kindly muse had accompanied him in his distant travels, bringing him solace in the mountains of the Caucasus and on the shores of the Crimea. In remote Moldavia his muse, forgetting the glitter and revelry of the capital, had visited with him the humble tents of wandering gypsies. Suddenly all had changed, and the muse appeared in his garden in the guise of a provincial maiden, with sad thoughts in her eyes and a French novel in her hands. Now for the first time he brings his muse into society and with jealous timidity gazes on her wild charms. She watches with quiet pleasure the serried ranks of aristocrats, officer dandies, diplomats, and proud ladies, the dresses glimpsed as they pass by, the snatches of conversation, the slow procession of guests moving forward to greet the young hostess, the dark clothes of the men framing the bright colors of the ladies, the well-ordered rhythm of distinguished conversation, the coldness of self-assured pride, and the blend of rank and years.

But who is this who stands silent, alien, and apathetic among this select group? It is Onegin. Suddenly there is a stir in the crowd. A lady, followed by an important general, approaches the hostess. The lady is calm, unpretentious, simple, perfectly comme il faut; men and women, old and young, approach her with respectful affection. Onegin is thunderstruck. The princess (for this is now Tatyana's title) makes a few conventional remarks and leaves Onegin standing tongue-tied. He returns home astounded by the change in Tatyana—and hopelessly in love. Day after day he follows her in society, hoping in vain for some special sign of recognition, but Tatyana's poise is unshaken; she hardly notices him. He grows pale and sickly. The doctors advise him to take the waters, but he will not leave the city. He still hopes stubbornly, and finally writes her a passionate letter.

He foresees, he writes, that his letter may offend her and make him an object of ridicule. He recalls his former indifference; how mistaken he was, how severely is he punished now. But he can no longer restrain himself. The die is cast; he is in her power and submits to his fate.

There is no answer. Onegin writes a second and a third letter. Still no answer, only, when he meets her, Tatyana's icy reserve. Once more Onegin withdraws from society. He reads voluminously, indiscriminately, and without concentration. He almost goes mad; he almost becomes a poet. But spring arrives and revives him. The recluse leaves the study where he has spent the winter and dashes to Tatyana's house, to fall at her feet. Finally, after a long silence, she begins to speak.

Enough, she says, bidding him rise; she must talk to him frankly. She recalls how, on the garden path, she had once listened meekly to

Onegin, but today it is her turn. She had been younger and, perhaps, better then, and she had loved him, but he had answered her love with a stern lecture. A humble girl's love had been no novelty to him, but she will not blame him; he acted honorably, and she is grateful. But now he pursues her; she wonders if this is not because of her prominent position in society and because her surrender would flatter his vanity. He must leave her alone. She loves Onegin (why deny it?), but she belongs to someone else, and she will be faithful to her husband forever.

She leaves the room. Onegin stands stricken. Just then Tatyana's husband enters. So, the narrator suggests, let us leave the hero at this bad moment—leave him forever. Long enough we have followed him through the world; let us congratulate each other as we reach the shore—it was high time (isn't it true?) a long while ago! And in a bantering tone the author-narrator takes leave of his readers. He bids farewell also to Onegin, ("my strange companion"), to Tatyana ("my true ideal"), and to his work. Blessed is he who early left life's feast, without draining its wine cup to the dregs, without reading life's novel to the end, able to part company in a trice, even as now the author parts company with his Onegin.

Responses

Eugene Onegin has been called "the story of a twice-rejected love"— Tatyana's love for Onegin, and Onegin's love for Tatyana.[12] Indeed, the symmetry between the two incidents is striking. First Tatyana writes a letter to Onegin, and Onegin rejects her love in a monologue that (since Tatyana does not interrupt) itself has something of the character of a letter.[13] In the last chapter the process is reversed; Onegin writes and Tatyana delivers the rejection speech, again without interruptions from the listener. The parallelism between the two situations is underlined by certain similarities in the letters; formally, both stand out from the rest of the work by their being written in freely rhymed paragraphs of varying length rather than in the "Onegin" stanza. Furthermore, the content of the two letters is developed along roughly the same lines; each writer fears the other's contempt, and both claim to be writing with reluctance, *à contre-coeur*. While Tatyana complains about not see-ing Onegin, Onegin complains that his meetings with Tatyana in so-ciety do not allow him to vent his feelings, and both conclude by putting their fate in the hands of the other. The symmetry is reinforced by the behavior of the two protagonists. In the first encounter Onegin is poised, while Tatyana is gauche and tongue-tied; later the roles are reversed. This reverse parallelism of the two Onegin-Tatyana confrontations has a very real significance.[14] In one sense, it is possible to think of *Eugene Onegin* as "the story of a twice-rejected love." It can be seen as a tragedy of mistiming: if only, we are tempted to speculate, Onegin had perceived in the early Tatyana what he came to love too late in the married Tatyana, then everything might have ended happily. But Pushkin's poem clearly is not simply a tragedy of blindness. Something more needs to be said about the underlying motivations of the two principal characters.

First, Tatyana. Why did she choose, of all people, Onegin to fall in love with? Almost anyone else, it seems, would have been more suitable than the self-centered, aimless Onegin; she fell in love without knowing anything of Onegin's character! But in the poetic world of *Eugene Onegin* such reflections are unsubstantial. Surely the point is that Tatyana did not have a choice—or had very little choice—and she did know about Onegin one very important thing, namely, that he was "different." Tatyana's sensibilities and romantic expectations have been fostered by her reading of sentimental novels. Furthermore, she is at exactly the right age to fall in love. But she cannot fall in love with the average young man whom she meets in the countryside, for there the gap between romantic daydream and prosaic reality is too wide. The principles of romantic love demand of Tatyana, among other things, not only that she love once and for all time a specific and predestined person, but also that this person be special, be unique. Into this pattern of expectation the unfamiliar Onegin fits admirably, and to these principles of love Tatyana submits—inevitably. It is significant that Tatyana's letter is not only a declaration of love but also a call for rescue from a milieu that, she feels instinctively, can never bring her happiness: "I am here alone, no one understands me, my mind cannot bear the strain, and I must perish in silence." That Tatyana's falling in love with Onegin is indeed a "mistake" is made very clear by the author's comments and by what follows, but it is a "mistake" that could not have been avoided and that cannot be remedied. Tatyana's love for Onegin is not simply a case of faulty judgment, it is a tragic inevitability.

In the final chapter Tatyana rejects Onegin; she still loves him, but she will remain faithful to her husband. This denouement, which leaves Tatyana to her part in society as a faithful wife, has been seen as a realist element in Pushkin's poem, in that it appears to constitute a break from the romantic tradition exemplified by such novels as Rousseau's *La Nouvelle Héloise* and Benjamin Constant's *Adolphe,* where the heroines are destroyed. However, this view—though it does indeed point up a valid distinction—must be treated with reserve. Tatyana neither dies of pneumonia (*Adolphe*) nor drowns (*La Nouvelle Héloise*). She plays the role of a prominent and fashionable society hostess, and is the pride of her fond husband, but her great love for Onegin remains a permanent burden in her life. To overemphasize the maturing of Tatyana's character, her strength, her sense of duty, and her "constructive" approach to life's problems (as much criticism tends to do) is, I believe, to misinterpret the author's artistic intent and to disregard Tatyana's own sad words as she dismisses Onegin: "But happiness was so possible, so close! But my fate is already decided." She has had her one small chance at happiness (not really a chance at all) and it is gone—forever.[15]

The main outlines of Onegin's character are clear enough and have been frequently noted. He is an early example of a long series of Russian male heroes who, because of their inability to conform to the philistine norms of Russian society or carve out for themselves an independent and productive way of life, are often referred to as "superfluous people"—treated, depending on the critic, as objects of pity or censure. Onegin is also undoubtedly an example of a certain type of person (common in European life and literature in the latter half of the eighteenth and first half of the nineteenth centuries) who suffered from romantic melancholy, *mal du siècle, Weltschmerz.* He has affinities with such literary figures as Werther, Adolphe, and Childe Harold.

But to define Onegin as a "superfluous man" or a Russian Childe Harold tells us little of the author's attitude toward him or of his function in this work. Onegin does not cut a very admirable figure: his assumption of his own superiority is based on no achievement whatsoever; his rejection of Tatyana, though honorable enough in itself, does not particularly endear him to the reader; he kills Lensky in a duel that he knows he should have stopped; his choice of reading makes Tatyana wonder if he is not a "parody"; and he pursues Tatyana when she is a married woman. Would it not, therefore, be true to say that in the character of Onegin the Childe Harold type, which had once appealed to Pushkin, is condemned? Such a view has been frequently expressed, and there is a good deal to be said in its favor. Pushkin had come to recognize the sterile negativism of the Childe Harold approach to life, and he was at pains to distinguish between himself and his hero (as Byron, too, had sought to distinguish between himself and Childe

Harold). But there is a difference between objectivity and antipathy— or, better, between objectivity and lack of understanding. For the truth is that Pushkin understood Onegin only too well; he was not immune to Onegin's sickness. Pushkin's very reluctance to have himself identified with Onegin is in itself an indication of their closeness, and a side glance at certain works he wrote during the same period (e.g., his 1825 "A Scene from Faust") will show that the character whose spontaneous emotional reflexes are atrophied by self-analysis remained a preoccupying problem for Pushkin. It is one thing to be intellectually aware of the inadequacies of an attitude to life; it is something very different to free oneself of its emotional commitments and penalties. To say that Onegin was Pushkin's disguised alter ego would be a gross oversimplification; however, recognition of the fact that he represents an important facet of the poet's most intimate emotional experience is essential to any true understanding of the entire work. Pushkin realized poetically—and we have to accept this—that Onegin's predicament was in fact insoluble. Indeed, his conduct was not very admirable, but his poetic function in *Eugene Onegin* rests on the premise that his actions were in reality no freer than Tatyana's and that Onegin, no less than Tatyana, was predestined to misery.

The question is sometimes asked whether, in the final chapter, Onegin really is in love with Tatyana or whether his ego is simply tempted by the thought of conquering this poised and socially prominent woman. Tatyana herself, in rejecting Onegin, speculates shrewdly on the latter possibility. But the whole point of the episode lies in the fact that both hypotheses are true. Onegin grows pale and sick and is certainly in love; however, a surrender on the part of Tatyana would not have solved Onegin's problems. His problems lie not in his ability or inability to love Tatyana, but in his whole negative approach to life. Not only in the field of love, but in all other fields, he is incapable of constructive effort. Deep down he prefers to be ironically detached rather than wholeheartedly committed to any undertaking and the effort it requires.

No discussion of *Eugene Onegin* would be complete without mention of an important secondary character, Lensky. He is immature and inexperienced, and the author has no hesitation in making him a target for his irony. Yet Lensky, like Onegin, represents a facet of the author's emotional experience. Lensky's naive idealism was something Pushkin had himself at times experienced and with which, in spite of his irony, he could still sympathize. Also, from the standpoint of plot, Lensky has several significant functions: his enthusiastic idealism serves as a foil to Onegin's world-weariness; his death drives Onegin and Tatyana farther apart (his death is mentioned both in Onegin's letter to Tatyana and in her spoken reply to Onegin), and also frees Olga to marry someone else—an event that, notwithstanding the author's lack of interest in Olga, is essential to the work's conception. For Olga's marriage and her easy forgetfulness (a completely nonromantic trait) set her apart from the other main characters, who all display in some form that extreme vulnerability to life's trials characteristic of the romantic: Lensky is happy for a while in his illusions, but is cut down before he can come to grips with reality; Tatyana believes for a time that she has a chance of happiness, but then realizes she is doomed; and Onegin, who initially denies the possibility of happiness, deludes himself later into believing that he simply failed to recognize his chance. These people had no chance of happiness, or what chance they seemed to have was missed and, once missed, irretrievable. Olga, on the other hand, after losing her fiancé, remakes her life with an almost callous imperviousness.

Two secondary characters provide a further comment on the question of romantic love, Tatyana's nurse and Tatyana's mother. The nurse, a peasant woman, was married off with never a thought of love. The mother, a member of the landowning class, had thoughts of love, but they had to be put aside, as she was married against her will. Yet these two women lead productive and reasonably happy lives.

But no discussion confined to plot and characters can adequately convey the feelings evoked by a reading of *Eugene Onegin*. The events in which the characters participate do not determine the overall aesthetic impact of the poem: they constitute *one* vitally important, but not *the* decisive, factor. Any work of literature is made up of various elements, all of which—be their significance greater or smaller in what may be termed the work's "aesthetic hierarchy"—have some function in terms of the whole. While some of these elements may be so unobtrusive as to escape the analyst's eye, others will inevitably attract attention. One such element in *Eugene Onegin* is the metaphor of the revolving seasons, which is used to emphasize the irrevocable passage of time.[16] And among such elements, clearly, of great significance in this "hierarchy" is the plot, the entire composite linkage of events and characters. But over, above, and beyond the plot there is another, higher element: the author-narrator's poetic personality. That personality is not simply one of several component elements; rather it binds together all the others.

It pervades the entire work and gives it a whole new focus, a whole new dimension.

The author's poetic personality is expressed mainly through the narrator's digressions. Not only do the digressions provide, structurally, the connecting chain that links the various elements of the narrative together, they also enable the author to maintain an unbroken commentary on the plot. He can with his sympathy reinforce the feelings of his characters, for example, when he commiserates with Tatyana; or by his detachment and irony dissociate himself from their feelings, as when he ironizes at the expense of Tatyana's mother. Events and characters are thus seen not only directly but also through the prism of the author-narrator's emotions. Moreover, the author does not confine himself to commenting on the plot. On the contrary, he may be stimulated by the events of the plot to relate his personal experiences and to convey his subjective feelings toward life in general. Thus, there is a two-way flow of causes and effects. The relationship between the author-narrator and the plot has been aptly expressed in the following comment: "The originality of *Evgeny Onegin's* structure consists therefore, in our view, in the fact that in this work not only do the digressions, which indicate the author's presence, perform a function in terms of the characters and events of the novel, but also the characters and events perform a function in terms of the digressions."[17] In effect the characters, like all other elements of the work, are subordinated to the author-narrator's poetic personality, and this constantly felt presence is aesthetically the work's unifying and organizing principle. In this sense, *Eugene Onegin*, notwithstanding its affinities with the novel and the comic epic, may justifiably be labeled a lyric poem and be said to have a lyric author-hero (Lo Gatto, 30). For the reader's most basic emotional reactions are stirred not by the doings of Tatyana, or Onegin, or Lensky but by the poetic personality of the author, the poetic personality of Pushkin.[18]

What, in conclusion, is the fundamental theme of *Eugene Onegin?* The definition "the story of a twice-rejected love" covers only one aspect of the work. Love was for both Onegin and Tatyana merely one facet of their problems. Furthermore, if our insistence on the aesthetically dominant role of the author-image is correct, then no explanation that takes into account solely the good or evil fortunes of the protagonists can be considered a complete answer. *Eugene Onegin* cannot be treated simply as one more unhappy love story, although the theme of unrequited love is important and is a valid part of a larger answer.

One approach is to regard *Eugene Onegin* as a poetic analysis of that spiritual sickness loosely associated with romanticism. The three main protagonists are, in their different ways, products of the romantic age, as is the putative author-hero. But to label *Eugene Onegin* an analysis of romantic ailments is to run at least two risks. There is, first, the danger—invariably incurred in mentioning a literary movement—of losing sight of the very specific qualities that make the work what it is. Second, we run the risk of unjustifiably dating a work, the significance of which is not limited to one country or one period. Thus, while the subject matter of *Eugene Onegin* is undoubtedly derived from romanticism, its treatment is peculiarly Pushkin's own and one, furthermore, that transcends romanticism in time and place. This approach does nevertheless yield valid insights to be borne in mind as we seek a larger answer.

It may be fruitful in this attempt to point out that the mood of *Eugene Onegin* becomes increasingly somber as the work progresses. One critic has remarked: "*Don Juan* begins in fun, but it ends in bitterness and sadness" (Boyd, 31). The same, roughly speaking, can be said of *Eugene Onegin*. The first chapter gives little indication of what is to follow or of the mood that prevails at the poem's end. For the first chapter—talk of spleen and melancholy notwithstanding—is "fun," while the sum total of *Eugene Onegin* is not. A shift in mood or several shifts in mood occur. This is of primary significance in determining the fundamental theme.

The transition in *Eugene Onegin* from "fun" to "sadness" is conveyed in several ways, not least in the comments of the author. But it is most easily traced in the events of the narrative. In the first chapter the reader is told in a lighthearted vein of Onegin's upbringing, his superficial education, his social prowess, his dandyism, his cynical attitude to women, even of his "spleen." None of this weighs very heavily. But in the second chapter a definite change takes place with the introduction of Tatyana. The author, whose attitude to Onegin and Lensky has been on the whole detached and ironical, adopts a more respectful tone in speaking of Tatyana; even her naïveté and her penchant for sentimental novels are handled without irony. In the third chapter Tatyana falls in love and writes her letter, an imprudent act that the author takes pains to explain and defend. With Tatyana lovesick, the flippancy of the early stanzas is gone. But the reader is not unduly disturbed. Even Onegin's kindly rejection of Tatyana in the fourth chapter comes as no surprise. But in the fifth chapter a darkening of the poem's mood is produced by Tatyana's bad dream, whose function is to prepare the reader for the tragic turn of events to come (Cizevsky, 256–59). Clearly a parallel is intended between the monsters seated round the table in the dream and the guests at Tatyana's name-day party, and in the dream Onegin kills Lensky just as he will shortly do in real life. With Lensky's death a further change takes place. It is not so much that the mood becomes more somber; rather it is the feeling that something irreparable has happened. Death allows no return.

But it is not death alone that allows no return: life does not, either. This entire work—and not just the steps in the narrative—is from the outset dedicated to the proposition that time moves inexorably forward, with no second chances, no putting right of past mistakes. Even in the lighthearted first chapter the narrator looks back to the pleasures of the ballet, of the ball, to the little foot he saw caressed by the waves, the little foot he held in his hand. If, he speculates, he were to return to Saint Petersburg, wouldn't the ballet be drastically changed? He no longer feels about balls as he once did. And the moments of the little feet are gone forever. He looks back, therefore, with the knowledge that the past cannot be recaptured. A similar function is performed by the metaphor of the seasons; the seasons revolve and come again, but man is not made new. Not only that, but just as once he thrust his forebears from the stage, so will the coming generation no less relentlessly thrust him from that same stage. Finally the symmetry of the work, noted above, is also a part of this message of passing time: symmetry there may be, but nothing is really the same.

This realization brings us close, I believe, to the poem's unifying sentiment. It is a feeling of deep sorrow unmitigated by redeeming hope, presented soberly, at times ironically, always with restraint and balance. This sorrow is produced by the very thought of no return, the recognition that years past have been wasted and that, alas, what lies ahead will be worse and not better than what lies behind.

Chapter Seven

The Little House in Kolomna, *Angelo,* Fairy Tales in Verse, *The Bronze Horseman,* and Prose Writings

The Little House in Kolomna

The Little House in Kolomna (Domik v Kolomne) is an unpretentious and slender work consisting of forty octaves (it is written in *ottava rima* in the manner of *Beppo* and *Don Juan.*) The influence of Byron has been noted frequently and justifiably, both with regard to the southern poems and to *Eugene Onegin.* Nowhere, however, is it more in evidence than in this small work, written during the highly productive autumn of 1830 in Boldino. Pushkin's digressions and their connection with Byron's works have already been pointed out, but nowhere does Pushkin more completely reflect the Byronic digression than in this poem, where digressions, as in *Beppo* and *Don Juan,* lack the calculated precision shown in *Ruslan and Lyudmila* and *Eugene Onegin.* They can be described more as loose, meandering thoughts that give the impression that the author is genuinely unable to concentrate on the topic at hand. This new and significantly more freewheeling quality of the digressions is to be attributed almost certainly to two things, Pushkin's improved knowledge of English and his consequent recognition of the possibilities of the noncaesural iambic pentameter for comic verse and its inevitable digressions (Pushkin at one time read *Don Juan* almost exclusively in Amédée Pichot's French prose translation.)

The Little House in Kolomna starts, in rambling fashion, with Pushkin's thoughts on using the caesura after the fourth syllable in the iambic pentameter. This is, in effect, Pushkin's manifesto of emancipation from the caesura—an emancipation already noted in connection with the little tragedies. Along with meter, the caesura, and his former preference for the caesura, Pushkin discusses the business of rhymes, which are seen as soldiers lined up in array. After this lengthy preamble, the poet gets down to the business of his slender story. In Kolomna there is a widow living with her daughter. The two sew and indulge in other feminine activities at their window. The daughter, though simply dressed, attracts the attention of passing guardsmen. Mother and daughter have been looked after by an elderly cook who, however, now dies. The mother bids the daughter find another cook to replace her. The daughter brings back a cook, who stipulates no fixed wage—which is very pleasing to the mother—and installs herself in the house. The cook proves highly inefficient. The dishes are broken, the meals are overcooked and oversalted. Nevertheless, they keep her because she is cheap. On Sunday, the mother and daughter go, as is their habit, to church. Suddenly the mother is afflicted with suspicions: she wonders if the cook may not be stealing. Returning home early from the service, she discovers the cook shaving. The cook leaves without explanation and without demanding any pay. The daughter returns somewhat later from church and is "horrified" to hear what has come to pass. The moral of this story, according to Pushkin, is that one should not try to hire a cook cheaply or for nothing, and that someone who is born a man should not put on skirts, because sooner or later he will have to shave. This is a real "nonsense" poem, and as Pushkin says in his concluding lines, "There is nothing more that can be squeezed out of my story." The problem with *The Little House in Kolomna* is that the story is too fragile; this genre requires something like a *Decameron* twist, which is certainly not supplied by the shaving cook. All in all, it is not a success.

Angelo

Angelo is the only one of Pushkin's longer poems to be written in six-foot iambs (with a caesura after the third foot.) Divided into three parts with a total of 535 lines, it is an adaptation of Shakespeare's *Measure for Measure,* with some changes (Marina is here Angelo's wife, whom he has put aside because her reputation was touched—wrongly— by the breath of scandal). Highly compressed, as is evident from the number of lines, the work has been stripped of everything that is not central to Pushkin's main artistic goal, the delineation of Angelo's character, which clearly fascinated Pushkin. In expressing his preference for Shakespeare over Molière, Pushkin, we remember, called attention to Shakespeare's breadth of characterization in contrast to the consistency and narrowness of Moliere's creations, "personifications of a specific passion or vice." Shylock was on these grounds rated superior to Harpagon, as was Angelo to Tartuffe:

In Molière the Hypocrite runs after his benefactor's wife—hypocritically; assumes the guardianship of an estate—hypocritically; asks for a glass of water—hypocritically. In Shakespeare the hypocrite pronounces sentence with a self-satisfied severity, but justly; he justifies his cruelty on the well-reasoned grounds of administrative expediency; he tries to seduce innocence with powerfully persuasive sophisms, not with a comic mixture of piety and gallantry. Angelo is a hypocrite—because his public acts and statements are at variance with his secret passions! But what depth this character possesses! (XII, 160)

Pushkin's interest in Shakespeare's approach to characterization and the complicated nature of human psychology provides a link between *Angelo* and the little tragedies. *Angelo* has, further, the same terseness and elimination of all "nonessential" elements as the little tragedies. It differs from the latter in that it is not a drama. Although it contains (like *The Gypsies* and *Poltava*) passages of dialogue, *Angelo* is basically a verse narrative.

Angelo is something of a problem for the literary scholar. It was rated very low by most of Pushkin's contemporaries. On the other hand, D. S. Mirsky thought that "*Angelo*, if not a masterpiece of the highest order, is for the student of Pushkin and of his last manner [Mirsky has in mind Pushkin's wish to write impersonally and objectively] one of his most interesting works."[1]

The events presented in *Angelo* can be summarized very briefly. The Duke of an Italian city has been too kindhearted in his enforcement of law and order, and it is difficult for him to suddenly turn the tide. The Duke therefore provisionally gives the reins of government to Angelo, "a man experienced, not new in the art of governing, austere in his way of life." The Duke departs. Under Angelo, law enforcement immediately becomes stricter. One of the laws that has not been enforced under the Duke prohibits fornication, which has been taking its ordinary course. Among the first victims of the new austere regime is the young patrician Claudio, caught fornicating with Juliet, the woman he intends to marry. Claudio must suffer the death penalty, but begs his friend Lucio to ask his sister Isabella to intercede on his behalf. Isabella, who is on the verge of becoming a nun, pleads with Angelo for mercy. Angelo conceives an immediate lust for Isabella and makes her an obvious proposal—which, incidentally, Isabella is very slow to understand. Isabella conveys this ultimatum to her brother, Claudio. Her brother is much concerned with Isabella's virtue but is not reluctant to see her lose it if only this will enable him to live. Isabella is outraged by her brother's lack of moral fiber, but forgives him and still loves him. The Duke, who has meanwhile been masquerading as a monk and has overheard the conversation between brother and sister, then finds a solution: Mariana, the wife whom Angelo has put aside because of false rumors about her behavior, will replace Isabella at the nocturnal tryst. The tryst is successfully consummated, but Angelo nevertheless orders the execution of Claudio. He is confronted and exposed by the Duke. Not lacking courage, Angelo asks that he be executed as soon as possible. The Duke forgives him.

Angelo is a rather depressing piece of writing by virtue of the view it offers of human nature. At the outset there is a certain Byronic lightness of touch; there is irony and the assurance that none of this should be taken too seriously. But then the atmosphere changes with the realization that Claudio will die, and this becomes a matter of life or death. The trouble—from the point of view of appreciation—is that the discussion between brother and sister, although well enough motivated, does not move the reader very deeply; he expects an easy way out. To oversimplify, the plot becomes more like a game of chess than a moving drama. Angelo's courage, expressed at the end in his request for death, does come through; as Pushkin would have wished, Angelo's "breadth" of character when he breaks his word to Isabella must be recognized. But the real impact, if any, of this narrative poem must be sought in Pushkin's demonstration of the fact that words mean nothing and principles change from one minute to the next: the brother who would fight for his sister's honor is willing to have her sacrifice that honor if only he can live!

George Gibian, in an illuminating comparison of *Angelo* with *Measure for Measure,* has shown convincingly that Pushkin, not so much by omissions (inevitable in so brief a poem) as by changes from Shakespeare's original, has revealed what he admired more and what less in Shakespeare's play. Citing several changes (e.g., the transfer of the action from Vienna to "happy Italy"), Gibian speaks of Pushkin's "lightening the mood." He finds in *Angelo* a Chaucerian quality.[2] All this is valid, but it is precisely the Chaucerian opening that renders more sordid what follows. And what follows is told so briefly, with the characters sketched in so laconically, that the reader has no time to grasp their motives and actions. It is not, therefore, that the "immorality" of the story and characters offends; if this were so, then much of Boccaccio, Chaucer, and Pushkin would be offensive. It is, rather, the semijocular opening leading abruptly to a revelation of human nature at its least appealing—without the reader's sympathies being involved—that creates a certain distaste for humankind. To say this is not necessarily to diminish the value of *Angelo*; it is to interpret it in the darkest of colors.[3]

Incidentally, the problematic nature of *Angelo,* in particular the chiaroscuro quality here noted, is undoubtedly due at least in part to the fact that this piece's subject matter lay far closer to home for Pushkin than is apparent on the surface. It reflects his thinking on the potential dangers of unlimited power, specifically his anxieties occasioned by Nicholas I's attentions to his wife. *The Golden Cockerel* and *The Bronze Horseman,* both reflecting very similar personal issues, were written at the same time.

The Tale of the Czar Saltan

The *skazki* (usually rendered in English as fairy tales in verse) reflect two of the artistic preoccupations of Pushkin's later years, his striving during the 1830s for impersonality and objectivity and his increased interest in folk poetry. He completed four *skazki: The Tale of the Czar Saltan* (Skazka o tsare Saltane, 1831); *The Tale of the Fisherman and the Fish* (Skazka o rybake i rybke, 1833); *The Tale of the Dead Princess and the Seven Heroes* (Skazka o mertvoy tsarevne i o semi bogatyryakh, 1833); and *The Tale of the Golden Cockerel* (Skazka o zolotom petushke, 1834).[4]

Much of Pushkin's interest in folk poetry dates back to his 1824–26 stay in Mikhaylovskoe, when he heard and wrote down folk tales and poems recounted by his nurse, Arina Rodionovna, and others. In this period his ear became attuned to the folkloristic turns of phrase and intonational patterns he was later to introduce into his own creations.[5] However, in his own *skazki* Pushkin did not faithfully reproduce what he had heard at Mikhaylovskoe. Rather, he incorporated what he had heard into his tales, making use of it where appropriate. He did not consider himself bound by the Russian oral tradition. On the contrary, he felt free to turn to literary sources, including non-Russian sources such as the brothers Grimm and Washington Irving.

This does not mean that his verse tales lacked a truly Russian quality. In order to understand this, we may recall Pushkin's views on *narodnost* discussed above in connection with the writing of *Boris Godunov*. His view of *narodnost* was not a narrow one. He had the confidence to take what he wanted where he found it; it would be no less original, no less Russian for that.

Of all Pushkin's works, the verse tales probably lend themselves least to interpretation for the non-Russian reader. This is because their content is slender indeed; they make no claim to profundity of thought, and there are few theories or ideas in them to be discussed. Their merit rests on their formal perfection, the rhythms, rhymes, repetitions, and variations that are bound to elude the non-Russian ear. For this reason little can be done in translation to convey the real merit of Pushkin's *skazki*. We shall recapitulate only one verse tale, the one generally regarded as his most perfect.

The Tale of the Czar Saltan is written in four-foot trochees, with rhymed couplets alternating between masculine and feminine (i.e., alternating 7- and 8-syllable rhymed couplets), arranged in stanzas or paragraphs of varying length. It consists of 996 lines.

As the tale opens, three sisters are spinning at their window. Each speculates on what she would do if she were czarina. The first would prepare a feast for the whole world; the second would weave an enormous cloth:

> "And if I should be czarina,"
> Said the third of the three sisters,
> "I would bear a warrior-son,
> Bear him for my lord, the czar."

This answer delights the czar, who has been listening from behind the door:

> "Thrive and prosper, lovely maiden,"
> Spake he, "Thou shalt be czarina,
> Thou shalt bear a warrior-son
> 'Ere September's days are done."

And to the other two sisters:

> "One of you shall work the loom,
> And the other be the cook." . . .
> And no time at all he tarried,

On that very eve he married:
At the marriage feast Saltan
Sits with his czarina young. . . .
Raves one sister in the kitchen,
At the loom the other's weeping,
And they both great envy feel,
Envy feel against the bride.
And meanwhile the young czarina,
No long time at all she tarried,
That first night she was with child.

Czar Saltan then goes off to war. At the appointed time a magnificent
boy-child is born. The czarina sends off a messenger to inform the
father, but the envious sisters, with the help of a scheming old woman,
Babarikha, have the messenger intercepted, and a false messenger
reports to the czar:

The czarina has brought forth
Not a daughter, not a son;
Not a mouse and not a frog,
Some strange beastie she has borne.

The czar, mortified, wants to hang the messenger, but relents and sends
him back with a written order to await the decision he will make on
his return. The cunning women get the returning messenger drunk and
substitute a different order:

Czar Saltan his nobles orders:
Secretly, with no delaying,
The czarina shall be cast
With her offspring in the deep.

Reluctantly the nobles obey the order. Mother and child are committed
to the sea in a cask, which then washes up safely on the shore of a
deserted island. The child, who has been growing "not by the day, but
by the hour," has the strength to break it open. On the unknown
seashore the boy shoots and kills with an arrow a hawk that was
attacking a swan. The swan then, "in the Russian language," hails the
czarevich as her savior, tells him that the hawk was no hawk but a
magician, that she is no swan but a maiden, and that she will repay his
good deed.

Mother and son lie down to sleep. When they awake, they are bewildered to see before them a magnificent city. They are hailed by the citizens. The son is crowned and rules over the city under the name of Prince Gvidon.

A ship sails by. The sailors are amazed to see that a fine city has sprung up on a familiar island. They put in and are welcomed by Prince Gvidon, who asks what cargo they have been trading and whither they are bound. They have been around the world and are now on their way to "the kingdom of the glorious Saltan." The Prince tells them:

> Travel safely, goodly men,
> On the sea, upon the ocean,
> To the glorious Czar Saltan;
> And to him my greeting give.

Prince Gvidon watches from the shore in sorrow as the ship departs. Suddenly the swan appears and asks him why he is sad. He would like to see his father. The swan transforms him into a mosquito. He flies and catches up with the ship, and is thus able to visit his father's city. His father, surrounded by the three scheming women, is sad. He asks the sailors what they have seen beyond the seas, and they tell of the miraculous new city and of Prince Gvidon's greeting. Czar Saltan wishes to visit the city but is dissuaded by the women, who tell him of even greater wonders more worthy of a visit. The mosquito in anger bites one of his aunts on the right eye and flies away. The incident is repeated twice more. Saltan again wishes to visit the new city, but on the first occasion he is again dissuaded by the scheming women. Finally, however, he rebels:

> "What am I? A child or czar?"
> Says Saltan in earnest now:
> "Go I shall!" He stamped his foot,
> Walked away and slammed the door.

He sails his fleet to Gvidon's island, is reunited with his wife and son, embraces his beautiful daughter-in-law (the swan who was in reality a princess), and pardons the three wicked women. There is a feast, after which Czar Saltan is put to bed half-drunk, and everything ends happily.

In mentioning the difficulty of conveying to the non-Russian reader the beauty of Pushkin's *skazki*, we should note that Russian critics, while justifiably abundant in their praise of them, have very little to offer beyond generalizations on the exact nature of their aesthetic qualities. The truth is that the *skazki* offer us art at its most "playful" and at its best. The *skazki* are better read than discussed, and better still read aloud.

The Bronze Horseman

The Bronze Horseman (Medny vsadnik), completed in Boldino in the fall of 1833, is written in freely rhymed iambic tetrameters and consists of an introduction and two parts, 481 lines in all. It is rightly regarded as one of Pushkin's greatest masterpieces. It is also one of the most tangled webs Pushkin ever wove, composed of so many strands of a personal, literary, and political nature, so many facets and angles, that it is not surprising that commentators have differed widely in their interpretations of the poem, or at least in their view of where its main emphasis lies.

The poem takes its name from Falconet's equestrian statue of Peter the Great that stands in Saint Petersburg near the banks of the Neva. The historical incident around which the poem centers is the flood that devastated Saint Petersburg in November of 1824, but the introduction, consisting of ninety-six lines, begins many years before that. Peter the Great is seen standing on the site of what was to become Saint Petersburg, looking out over the desolate waters of the Baltic. The broad Neva River—on it a single small craft—flows past. He sees only marshland and forest, with here and there a poor Finnish hut. A fateful thought comes to him: here shall be founded a city, whence Russia will threaten the haughty Swede and "open a window onto Europe." One hundred years passed, and from the dark woods and marshlands arose a prosperous, proud city, "the beauty and wonder" of the north. Where formerly the lonely Finnish fisherman cast his dilapidated net from the marshy shores into the unknown waters, the lively banks are now crowded with mighty towers and palaces. Ships from the ends of the earth dock at its rich wharves, and the Neva flows between walls of granite. Famous are the lines:

> Before the new capital's bright blaze
> Dimmed is ancient Moscow's star,
> As before the new czarina fades
> The aging widow of a czar.

Here the theme of Saint Petersburg is interwoven with the narrator's thoughts of his own activities and impressions. He loves Saint Petersburg's austere harmony, the majestic flow of the Neva, "the transparent dark, the moonless gleam" of its "pensive heights," when in his room he writes and reads without a lamp. He loves the motionless air and the frost of Saint Petersburg's cruel winter, the sleds running along the banks of the broad Neva, the rosy flushed cheeks of the young girls, the glitter and stir and conversation at the balls, the sparkling wine and the blue-flaming punch of the bachelor parties. Then his thoughts turn away from more intimate personal impressions to embrace a larger, civic theme—the military reviews, the perfect precision of infantry and cavalry, the victorious standards tattered in the fray of battles, the boom of cannon announcing the birth of a royal son or a new Russian victory. He concludes this paean of praise:

> Thrive, Peter's lovely city; stand
> Unshakable as Russia stands.
> Even the elements subdued,
> May they with you be reconciled. . . .

And then an abrupt change! A terrible event came to pass, which is still fresh in the narrator's memory. He will tell about it, and "sad will be my story."

Part I opens on a cold, dark, rainy, windy day in Saint Petersburg, when the Neva is raging "like a sick man on his bed." It is late as young Evgeny returns home. Let us call our hero Evgeny, the author suggests, since his pen was once on good terms with that name. The family name doesn't matter; it was once famous in the annals of Russian history, but is now forgotten. Evgeny undresses and goes to bed, but he is kept awake by his thoughts: he is poor, but hopes by hard work go gain a modest share of financial independence and honor; he envies those unintelligent idlers who have life so easy. He thinks too of the rising river. If the bridges go down, he will be separated for two or three days from his Parasha, who lives on one of the islands in the Neva. He sighs deeply and, like a poet, starts to dream. Marry? Well, why not? It will be difficult, of course, but he is young and healthy. And in his mind Evgeny creates a picture of simple domestic happiness.

Next morning Saint Petersburg is flooded (the description of the flood is among the most famous passages in Russian poetry). Everywhere there is chaos and destruction. Sad and troubled, the late czar Alexander I emerges onto his balcony and says, "Even czars cannot

master God's elements." Pensively, with eyes full of sorrow, he gazes
on the catastrophe. Meanwhile, Evgeny has sought refuge from the
flood by seating himself astride a marble lion near the statue of Peter
the Great. Evgeny is hatless and pale. He is in mortal fear, not for
himself, but for Parasha and the little house in which she and her
mother live, and where the flood is raging with terrible intensity:

> They are there,
> Widow and daughter, his Parasha,
> His cherished dream. Could what he sees
> Be but a dream? Or is all life
> An empty dream and nothing more,
> Heaven's cruel mockery at earth?

The nearby statue is oblivious to Evgeny's torments:

> With his back turned toward Evgeny,
> High, mighty and unshakable,
> Towering above the raging flood,
> There proudly rides with arm outstretched
> The idol on the horse of bronze.

As part II opens the Neva is gradually subsiding, leaving behind
death and destruction. Evgeny hires a boatman to take him over to
where Parasha lives. With difficulty they reach the shore. The scene is
unrecognizable: houses are twisted, collapsed, and strewn about by the
flood; bodies lie as though on a battlefield. Evgeny rushes to Parasha's
house, to find it gone. He walks round and round, talks to himself
aloud, and suddenly, striking his forehead with his fist, starts to laugh.

Very quickly life returns to normal. In their "cold callousness" people walk the streets as before, civil servants return to their offices, and
hucksters resume trading, trying to recoup their losses at the next man's
expense. A minor court poet sets about describing the flood in "immor-
tal verse."

But as for "my poor, poor, Evgeny," his mind gives way before the
horror; his ears are filled with the rebellious roar of the Neva and the
wind. He does not return home, and his room is rented to someone
else. By day he wanders around, sleeps by the wharves, and feeds on
what may be thrown to him through a window; his clothing is in rags,
children cast stones at him, coachmen whip him if he gets in their way,

but Evgeny seems not to notice. He lives until summer again turns to autumn. Then one night he awakens and remembers the full horror of his experience. He starts to walk about, to look around him, and there—"There proudly rides with arm outstretched / The idol on the horse of bronze." He trembles, and his mind grows terribly clear. He recognizes the place, the lions, the square, and that one whose bronze head rises immobile in the darkness, the man "by whose fateful will a city had been founded beneath the sea."

> How awesome in the mist is he!
> And 'neath that brow what thought is hid!
> What strength lies in that man contained!
> And in that steed what fearsome fire!
> Where are you galloping, proud steed?
> Where will your steel hooves come to rest?
> O mighty ruler of man's fate!
> Was it not thus that o'er the abyss
> On high with bit of iron you made
> The Russian steed to prance and rear?

Evgeny walks around the statue and confronts face to face the "ruler of half the world." Then, clenching teeth and fists, he hurls defiance at the statue, turns, and flees headlong. It seemed to him that the face of the dread czar suddenly flamed with anger and turned toward him. As Evgeny flees through the streets of Saint Petersburg, he hears the Bronze Horseman riding after him. From that night on, whenever Evgeny chanced to go through the fatal square, he would raise his battered hat, keep his eyes lowered, and pass well to the side.

The poem concludes with the mention of a small deserted island, where a fisherman sometimes puts in to cook his humble meal or where a civil servant might take his boat on a Sunday outing. On this island a small house had been washed ashore by the flood, and last spring was removed by barge. It was empty and completely demolished. On its threshold they found "my madman, and there they buried his cold corpse 'in God's name,'" that is, a pauper's burial.

In this work Pushkin displays a complete mastery of technique. While employing the same meter throughout, he changes his style to conform to various moods, situations, and personalities. The majestic sonority of the lines describing Peter the Great and the might of Saint Petersburg are in marked contrast with the abrupt, jerky rhythms and

frequent enjambments that perfectly convey all that has to do with
Evgeny: his humble dreams, his ineffectual actions, his harassment, his
panic. The poem contains a wealth of brilliantly devised images that
serve mainly to personify inanimate objects, in particular the Neva and
her raging waters, and to intensify the sensation of constant movement
and unrelenting restlessness pervading so much of *The Bronze Horseman*.
Then, too, there is the skillful use of onomatopoeia, which permits the
reader to hear the echoing hoofbeats as the Horseman pursues Evgeny.
The questions of style in *The Bronze Horseman* are innumerable, and have
been dealt with exhaustively by a number of critics.[6]

In its complexity the poem lends itself to a variety of interpretations.
We have, on the one hand, the affirmation of Peter's achievements and
Russia's proud destiny; on the other, the story of an unremarkable
young man who lost his fiancée in a flood and went mad. Since Saint
Petersburg was founded, it would seem, not in compliance with the
logic of nature but in defiance of nature, at the bidding and through
the iron will of a dictator who was the embodiment of Russia's destiny
and historical "mission," the poem clearly has as its theme the sacrifice
of the individual to "historical necessity." This has been frequently
noted, but it tells us little of the poem's unifying aesthetic principle.
It is this principle that we must seek to establish, or at least approach
more closely.

What, to begin with, was Pushkin's personal attitude to the dilemma of historical necessity and the welfare of the individual?
Pushkin's objectivity, his ability to see many conflicting sides of a
problem and to hold the scales in even balance, is a commonplace of
Pushkin scholarship. But a closer look at the poet's subjective reactions,
in this case as in others, helps to render the work more meaningful.[7]

One stimulus to the writing of *The Bronze Horseman* came from the
great Polish poet Adam Mickiewicz. Mickiewicz, then an involuntary
guest of the Russian Empire, had become friends with Pushkin on the
latter's return from exile in 1826. Mickiewicz had been allowed to leave
Russia in 1829. There had followed the 1830–31 Polish uprising, during which—as we know—Pushkin took a strong anti-Polish stand.
After the defeat of the Poles, Mickiewicz wrote a cycle of poems (the
most important of which were "The Statue of Peter the Great" and
"Oleszkiewicz") attacking the Russian autocracy, the lack of freedom in
Russia, and the purposelessness of the vast Russian imperial mechanism. Pushkin's *The Bronze Horseman* is, in one of its aspects, a rebuke
to Mickiewicz. Where Mickewicz saw Asiatic inertia and aimlessness,

Pushkin saw, embodied in Peter, dynamism and destiny. Critical though he was in many ways of his native land, Pushkin did not share the views of such thinkers as Petr Chaadaev, who saw Russia as having contributed nothing to civilization and, in effect, lying beyond the pale of history and historical progress. Pushkin believed in Russia—although with gritted teeth. Thus the passages, mainly in the introduction, praising Saint Petersburg and Peter's achievements, are perfectly sincere. In style and content they reflect the eighteenth-century tradition of the laudatory ode. At the same time Pushkin's attitude to Peter the Great was ambivalent. He was aware of the brutal methods the tyrant had employed to achieve his ends. Peter had used the "iron bit," forcing Russia to rear up on its hind legs; he had, other things apart, sacrificed over 100,000 Russian lives to the building of the strategically placed and beautiful city of Saint Petersburg.

Against the background of these political evaluations Pushkin sets Evgeny's story. Evgeny is the victim of Peter's city, the prototype in Russian literature of a series of characters, found in Gogol, Dostoevsky, and others, who are driven mad by the oppressive atmosphere of the "unnatural" city of the north. But it was not merely acute powers of social observation that enabled Pushkin to depict this emerging type: Pushkin was himself a victim of Saint Petersburg. And in Evgeny there is a great deal of Pushkin.

Evgeny, like Pushkin, came of formerly illustrious but now impoverished stock. The fact that in the final version of the poem Evgeny, contemplating marriage, dreamed "like a poet" might be dismissed as a piece of irony, but an earlier draft shows Evgeny actually writing verse (V, 445). Far more important than these superficial similarities between author and hero is the fact that Evgeny's sense of injustice and persecution, as well as of his own impotence, was Pushkin's own.

Andrey Bely, using quotations from Pushkin's letters to his wife and from his diary, has demonstrated convincingly that Pushkin's own pent-up feeling of imprisonment was expressed in *The Bronze Horseman*. Pushkin was Nicholas's prisoner, as Evgeny was Peter's victim. Bely has also pointed out that the lyric beginning "God grant that I not lose my mind" (discussed here on p. 147), although of uncertain date, was written at about the same time as *The Bronze Horseman*.[8] In *The Bronze Horseman* Pushkin, as was often his wont, concealed his most intimate feelings under the cloak of objectivity. This fact tells us a good deal about Pushkin. More important, it gives us a whole new perspective on the poem. It renders Evgeny's misfortune, his madness, his defiance, and his irrational fear immeasurably more poignant and terrifying than they would otherwise be. Pushkin's own misery, transmuted into artistic terms, is the aesthetic unifying principle of *The Bronze Horseman*. This would not be so were it not for the fact that, as so often with Pushkin, the poet's personal emotions strike a deep chord in the hearts of others.

There is another aspect to *The Bronze Horseman*. Even the inadequate recapitulation above suffices to show a similarity between the scene at the poem's opening and that at the end. In both scenes desolate nature, unmarked by man's hand, predominates; even some of the same lexical items are employed. Could it be that after all nature will triumph? As the czar on his balcony remarks sadly, "Even czars cannot master God's elements." Is this, perhaps, the thought, the unspoken wish of the poet, that the "unnatural" and oppressive Saint Petersburg shall perish?

It has often been said of great works of literature that they lend themselves to varying interpretations from one generation to another. *The Bronze Horseman*, written in 1833, seems to have a clear message for the second half of the twentieth century, when millions of small individuals are confined in large cities, suffer from the indifference of their surroundings, rise up in their ghettos in sometimes irrational anger and hurl defiance, and are consumed by irrational anxieties and fears—the more terrifying because they are not fully understood.

Prose Writings

Pushkin, along with some of his contemporaries, realized early in his literary career that Russian prose had lagged far behind Russian poetry in its achievements. Furthermore, the flowery characteristics of much Russian poetry had infiltrated prose. As early as 1822 he comments, "Voltaire may be regarded as an excellent example of sensible style. . . . Precision, tidiness, these are the prime matters of prose. It demands thought and more thought, brilliant expressions are of no use; poetry is another business. . . . Whose prose is the best in our literature? Karamzin's: this is no great praise."[9] Pushkin's intense interest in Vyazemaky's translation of Benjamin Constant's *Adolphe*, which he greatly admired, was motivated not only by the undoubted merits of the French original, but by Pushkin's feeling that Constant could point the way to what Pushkin felt was lacking in Russian literature: "metaphysical"[10] language, as he termed it, by which he appears to have meant the language of abstract thought and of psychological analysis.

In this connection Pushkin's thoughts were turned not only inward, to the needs of Russian literature, but outward, to the scene of world literature on which, he felt, Russian literature could win its right of citizenship only through prose. Thus Pushkin approached the problem of Russian prose writing—just as he approached the problem of the Russian theater—with definite theoretical views on the needs of Russian literature and the correct path to be taken. As his remarks on Voltaire indicate, Russian prose should be simple and to the point. It was essential that Russian literary prose be sharply distinguished from poetry, that it should cast off the influence poetry had hitherto exerted on it, should free itself from its Cinderella position, and establish itself in its own right. These theoretical views he sought to implement in his own work.

Pushkin himself was from his early days a master of Russian prose, as can be clearly seen from his letters. We should not forget that letter writing in Pushkin's day was, even when the letters were intended for private consumption, still considered something of a literary genre. The clarity, precision, and punch of Pushkin's letters show that he was quick to acquire deftness and authority in wielding his native language. However, in the field of strictly literary prose Pushkin was slow to make a start. His first serious attempt at literary prose dates to 1827, when he wrote his unfinished *The Moor of Peter the Great*.[11] His first completed prose works were written in 1830 at Boldino. But once started, Pushkin's prose output increased steadily, and during the 1830s he wrote considerably more in prose than in verse. In the following comments we discuss briefly three of *The Tales of Belkin* (Povesti Belkina), *The Queen of Spades* (Pikovaya dama), and *The Captain's Daughter* (Kapitanskaya-dochka).

The Tales of Belkin consists of five short stories purportedly related to and then retold by the late Ivan Petrovich Belkin. These are *The Shot* (Vystrel), *The Snowstorm* (Metel), *The Stationmaster* (Stantsionny smotritel), *The Undertaker* (Grobovshchik), and *The Lady Turned Peasant* (Baryshnya-krestyanka). They were all written in the fall of 1830 at Boldino. In these unpretentious tales Pushkin rigidly follows the principles outlined above on the necessity for drawing a sharp distinction between prose and verse. The style is clear and concise, bereft of all ornamentation—to the point of austerity. The syntax is straightforward and lean; there are few subordinate clauses and few epithets. The narrative proceeds logically and rapidly, with no attempt at psychological analysis and very few comments from the narrator.[12]

There is one aspect of *The Tales of Belkin* likely to elude the modern reader, which also has to do with Pushkin's views on literature. *The Tales* tend to lightly parody then-existing fashions in prose. This may be intentional, but it also follows naturally from the fact that Pushkin's age was in literary matters more down-to-earth than its predecessors were. Such parody as may be claimed—and not too much should be made of it—is achieved by taking a staple literary situation and adding a new twist to expose the artificiality of the literary cliché involved. Pushkin's "twists" point invariably in the direction of common sense. For example, *The Stationmaster* is a rebuttal of the sentimentalist fallacy that poor girls are by nature innocent, that they are ensnared and deceived by rich young men, and that the results of their seduction or abduction are bound to be catastrophic. In a way Pushkin is polemicizing with Karamzin's *Poor Liza*. But such polemical aspects of *The Tales* may well have little importance for today's reader and should not, in any case, be exaggerated. For this reader then, they will fall into perspective as straightforward, lightweight anecdotes, well told, with a touch of irony, and without great literary pretensions.[13]

The hero of *The Shot,* Silvio, is a sardonic, "demonic," pseudo-Byronic character of about thirty-five. By his personality he dominates the young officers (Silvio is a civilian) whose company he keeps in the small town where their regiment is stationed. One night he is insulted at the gambling table by a newcomer, but to everyone's amazement, although he is an excellent shot, Silvio refuses to challenge the young officer. No one would have suspected Silvio of cowardice. And indeed the reason behind his inaction lies elsewhere. Six years earlier Silvio had received a slap in the face. He had been at that time a hussar, the hardest-drinking and most pugnacious in the regiment. But when a new officer joined the regiment—a youthful, intelligent, handsome, gay, brave, high-born, immeasurably wealthy, openhanded count, Silvio's primacy was challenged, and he sought the occasion for a quarrel. The brilliant newcomer's success with women—particularly one with whom Silvio was involved—was the last straw. A remark from Silvio at a ball, a slap, and both men drew their sabers. Separated momentarily, the two were in place and ready to duel at dawn the next day—the young officer arrived late with his cap full of cherries, which he was eating. After discussion, the rivals drew for the first shot. Silvio's opponent won the draw, fired first, and put a bullet through Silvio's cap. His life was now in Silvio's hands, but Silvio could not be satisfied with killing a man who seemed not to care for life but continued to eat cherries and spit out the pits. At Silvio's suggestion that his rival leave and take a meal, the latter agreed, saying that Silvio would be entitled to his shot at any time he chose. Because of this incident Silvio retired from the regiment to bide his time, and refused to duel with the drunken young officer who insults him at the beginning of the story.

The time for Silvio's revenge comes when his carefree rival gets married. Silvio arrives at the estate of his hated rival, the now married Count, and claims his shot. The Count, no longer indifferent, in love with his wife, asks Silvio to fire quickly, but Silvio hesitates and insists they again draw lots. Once more the Count wins. He fires and misses. How had he allowed himself to be persuaded to draw lots again? What dishonor! Silvio starts to take aim, when suddenly the Countess bursts in. The Count assures her that it is only a joke. Silvio continues to take aim, and then—when the Count begs him to fire quickly—Silvio, with the Countess at his knees, refuses! "I am satisfied," he says, "I have seen you looking bad; I have witnessed your timidity; I made you take the first shot, this is my satisfaction. You will remember me. I commit you to your own conscience." Silvio was later killed fighting for the Greeks against the Turks, but he had his revenge!

The Snowstorm is a designedly improbable story. The heroine, Maria Gavrilovna, has been brought up on French novels and is consequently in love. Her hero, Vladimir, is a poor army ensign. The parents are opposed to a match, and the young couple decides to elope. Maria Gavrilovna is, according to plan, put in a sledge and brought to the church. On his way to the church her hero loses his way in the countryside in a snowstorm. Maria Gavrilovna returns home and falls feverishly ill. Her parents decide that love is the cause and that she should marry her beloved. She recovers, but Vladimir, in spite of the parents' willingness, refuses to enter the house. He leaves for the army to take part in the 1812 campaign, and dies. Maria Gavrilovna's father also dies. She inherits his property, moves, and is besieged by suitors whom she rejects. The 1812 campaign now being victoriously concluded, she—in spite of her fidelity to Vladimir's memory—falls in love with a wounded veteran, Burmin, colonel in the hussers, and he with her. However, both are restrained in their courtship by something undivulged. The problem, it turns out, is that both are married. On the fateful night when Vladimir failed to appear, Maria Gavrilovna, without seeing the groom, had married someone else! That someone had been the then irresponsible Burmin, also lost in the storm. The problem is therefore no problem: they are already married!

The Stationmaster, as noted above, tells of the abduction of a poor girl, the stationmaster's daughter Dunya, by a rich young man—in this case a hussar. Dunya is a flirt, and the hussar abducts her with her full consent. The post station of which the father is master boasts pictures of the story of the prodigal son, and the fallen returning sinner clearly forms a pseudoideological background to the work. When Dunya does not return, the father falls ill. Upon recovering, he follows Dunya to Saint Petersburg "to bring home his sheep that has strayed." The hussar, Minsky, receives him after some delay, begs his forgiveness, tells him that he has no intention of returning Dunya, and gives him some money. Somehow the stationmaster finds himself on the street. In conventional disgust he spurns the money, throws it away, has second thoughts and returns, only to find that it is gone! He makes one more unavailing attempt to penetrate Dunya's new "home," and is ejected. He returns to the station, becomes an alcoholic, and dies. Some time later a fine lady with a six-horse carriage and three children arrives at the station, asks about her father, visits his grave in sorrow, and gives money to the priest.

The Tales of Belkin are in some cases interesting for the insights they provide into Pushkin's intimate thoughts. *The Shot,* for example, shows without doubt that Pushkin was, at the time of writing, taken with the problem of the value of life, insignificant perhaps at one moment, at another immeasurably enhanced by the love of a woman.[14] *The Tales* are interesting, too, for the light they cast on Pushkin's views on Russian prose and his quest for extreme simplicity. They are of significance, although this has been exaggerated, for the development of Russian prose. But today's reader does best to take them for what they are— modest anecdotes skillfully told.

Pushkin's *The Queen of Spades* (1834) is something rather different, though its significance should not be overemphasized, either. Pushkin, as we know, loved to gamble. Pushkin was also a pioneer in describing the peculiar madness induced by Saint Petersburg, and was familiar with the works of E. T. A. Hoffmann. Out of all this arose *The Queen of Spades.* Critics have sometimes discovered in this story a profundity of thought that is not really there. Like *The Tales of Belkin* it is really an anecdote, a good yarn. The characterization, it is true, is somewhat more detailed, and the mood is different. Its syntax shows a tendency to be less austere, which only shows that Pushkin's Voltairean prose simplicity could not be expected, in the long run, to handle the psychological complexities characteristic of nineteenth-century prose. *The*

Queen of Spades shows where Pushkin himself as a prose writer would have had to go, that he could not have produced another cycle of *The Tales of Belkin.*

The Queen of Spades opens with a scene of Russian officers gambling. Hermann, the part-German hero, invariably watches without participating in the play. "Gambling is of great interest to me," he says, "but I am not in a position to sacrifice what is necessary to me in the hope of acquiring a surplus." Tomsky—one of the gambling Russian officers—opines that Hermann is a good German: "He is calculating, that's all there is to it." Tomsky then tells of his grandmother, who had suffered catastrophic gambling losses in Paris but had recouped them by eliciting from a French nobleman a three-card formula that it seems, is *bound* to win but can never be repeated. Hermann is bewitched by the thought of a three-card sequence that affords the possibility of a once-in-a- lifetime coup.

The old Countess, Tomsky's grandmother, is still alive. In order to obtain her gambling secret, the ruthless Hermann is willing to woo her companion and ward, Lizaveta Ivanovna. By notes and other ploys he succeeds in this. After a ball that the Countess will be attending, Hermann and the ensnared Liza agree that he will install himself secretly in Liza's room and await her return. But no. After a long wait Hermann goes not to Liza's room, but conceals himself near the Countess's room after she returns from the ball. When the Countess is at last alone, Hermann confronts her. Will she not give up a secret that is useless to her, that would give him everything he could ever have wished? The old lady is frightened; when Hermann persists, she panics and dies. Hermann, having lost the chance of discovering the three-card formula, turns to Liza and explains his duplicity. She guides him out of the house.

Hermann is present at the funeral of the old Countess. As he approaches the coffin, in accordance with Orthodox tradition, he feels that the old Countess screws up one eye at him, and he faints. Later that night the Countess comes to him: "I have come against my own will," she says, "but I have to fulfill your wish. The three, the seven, and the ace, one after the other, will win for you—but on these conditions, that you never play more than one card in one day, and that you never gamble again. I forgive you my death on condition that you marry my ward, Lizaveta Ivanovna."

The three, the seven, and the ace. Hermann is frightened but resolute. He goes to the most exclusive gambling house in Saint Petersburg and is introduced to its owner, the distinguished Chekalinsky. Hermann asks to be allowed to play. When he announces the stake— 47,000 rubles, his entire savings—excitement runs high. The three wins, and Hermann leaves. On the following night he returns; he bets 94,000 rubles, and the seven wins. On the third night his arrival is eagerly awaited by one and all. People abandon their own gambling and cluster round as Hermann approaches the table. Chekalinsky is pale, but summons up his habitual smile. The cards are played. "'The ace wins,' said Hermann, turning up his card. 'Your queen loses,' said Chekalinsky gently. Hermann trembled: in very fact he had not the ace, but the queen of spades. He could not believe his eyes, could not understand how he had pulled the wrong card. At this moment he thought he saw the queen of spades screw up her eyes and smile at him ironically. He was struck by a definite similarity. 'The old woman,' he cried out in horror."

Hermann goes mad and spends the rest of his days repeating endlessly: "Three, seven, ace! Three, seven, queen!" Liza is happily married. Tomsky is promoted and marries. *The Queen of Spades* is an excellent, eerie, suspenseful, well-told story.

The Captain's Daughter (completed in 1836) is a historical novel, a genre very much in fashion at that time. Indeed, *The Moor of Peter the Great,* mentioned above, testifies to Pushkin's earlier interest in this genre rendered popular by Walter Scott. Pushkin's novel is, in comparison with Scott's, told simply, without Scott's lengthy descriptions of person and place. The historical event on which Pushkin's novel is based is the uprising against Catherine II's regime headed by Pugachev (1773). The hero is a young officer loyal to Catherine. A multitude of events, in which Pugachev is sympathetically depicted, brings about various circumstances in which the young hero, Grinev, is now united with, now separated from his love, Maria Ivanovna, until eventually— owing to his meetings with Pugachev—he is arrested on a charge of treason. A meeting between Maria Ivanovna and Catherine II results in Grinev's vindication, and everything ends happily, in the true tradition of the sentimental romantic novel. *The Captain's Daughter* is excellent reading.

It would be impossible to attempt a full critical appraisal of Pushkin's prose work here. But this much is certain: not one of his prose works fails to hold the reader's attention. Pushkin as a prose writer is an excellent yarn spinner. And this, I believe, should serve as a starting point in any evaluation of his prose. The reader interested in arriving at critical insight into the artistic merits of the prose works would do well to devote less attention to the different facets of Belkin's personality, whom Pushkin is parodying or when, symbolic meanings, or other esoteric matters—all of which have a place, but a secondary one—and focus instead on things closer to the surface, primarily the narrative sequence—as, I believe, Pushkin himself did.[15]

Chapter Eight

Lyric Poetry, 1820–1836

The term *lyric* is sometimes used in Russian criticism to denote any poem in the shorter genres—from the epigram to the elegy, from the personal theme to the patriotic or civic—anything, in effect, that can be listed under *stikhotvoreniya,* or short poems, as opposed to the longer *poemy.* There is also the more specific meaning of the word which envisages a lyric as a short poem in which the personal feelings of the author stand in the foreground; objective reality may well serve as a basis for such a poem, but it is the subjective feelings of the poet that receive the primary emphasis.

This chapter focuses on Pushkin's work in the lyric mode, understood in the narrower sense—very selectively, alas, for space does not allow a broad review. Pushkin's range of interests and his development as a lyric poet can be roughly broken down into the following periods:

1. *1813–1820.* This early period begins with Pushkin's juvenile experiments in the ready-to-hand classical and sentimentalist genres, particularly those favored by the Arzamas group. In 1816–17 his elegies sound a hitherto absent note of despondency produced by unhappiness in love. In 1817–20 there is some change in his love poetry, which would seem to reflect the greater first-hand experience of his Saint Petersburg years. The most important new feature of these three years consists in the writing of liberal verses betokening his opposition to the regime.

2. *1820–1826.* 1820 marks Pushkin's first encounter with Byron. Byronism, true, influences him more in the narrative poem than in the lyric, where nevertheless he gives vent to a Byronic pessimism involving a sense of betrayal by friends, alienation from society, unhappiness in love, and despair over the future. At the same time, under the influence of André Chénier (1762–1794), some of Pushkin's lyrics acquire a classically plastic quality not in evidence before. These years, especially around 1823, are marked by a newfound skepticism with regard to liberalism. His abundant love poetry is now "less literary," and more closely reflects actual situations and emotions.

130

3. *1827–1831.* The poetry of these years, which includes some of Pushkin's finest love poems, is marked by a growing awareness of the poet's isolated position in society, a profound disquiet over life's aimlessness, and a preoccupation with the past and the passing of youth. A new preoccupation, occasionally glimpsed before but clearly discernible from 1828 on, involves death, in two related ways: (1) the ousting of one generation by another, and (2) killing as something taken for granted, unmotivated, mechanical. Pushkin's concern for the fate of the Decembrists also emerges in the poetry of these years, as do his patriotic feelings prompted by the Polish uprising of 1831.

4. *1831–1836.* In Pushkin's last years there is a marked decrease in lyric output in general, particularly lyrics devoted to intimate personal emotions; a tendency to "objectify" personal emotions is apparent, as is an increased interest in formal experimentation devoted to nonsubjective themes and aimed at an extreme simplicity in style.

It cannot be overemphasized that this schema provides only the roughest of guides to thematic and stylistic development, not a series of watertight compartments.[1]

1820–1826

We will start with 1820 and Byron. In chapter 3 we have already traced Byron's influence in connection with the southern poems, where this influence is most significant. But the lyrics often parallel the themes and moods of Pushkin's longer works. Indeed, Byronism first found expression in a lyric poem (1820) that in conception is indebted in some degree to Childe Harold's farewell to his native land (canto I), which Pushkin wrote while sailing the Black Sea from Feodosia to Gurzuf. The following excerpt displays many of Byronism's essential components:

> Fly on, swift bark, and carry me to distant lands
> At the dread bidding of the e'er treacherous seas.
>   Yet not, not to the gloomy shores
>   That hem with mist my native land,
>   The land where first fierce passion's fire
>   Awoke, inflamed my youthful heart,
>   And where on me the tender muses secret smiled,
>   Where, battered by life's early storms,
>   My youth decayed, my youth was lost,

Where light-winged joy and happiness deceived, betrayed,
Marked, doomed to suffering my heart, benumbed and cold.
  I go to seek new sights and sounds;
  From you I flee, my native land. . . .

In one 1821 lyric Pushkin laments, "I've lived to bury my desires, /
I've ceased to love my dreams. . . ." And in "The Demon" (Demon,
1823) he describes the corrosive Byronic skepticism that leads to nega-
tion of all positive values in life:

    He looked with mockery on life—
    And for no thing in all the world
    One word of blessing would he speak.

The considerable number of Pushkin's poems written to different
women during the first half of the 1820s show a wide range of feeling:
grief in parting; jealousy; sorrow at the imminent death of a woman;
the poet's reluctance to divulge the story of his mad passions and suf-
ferings to an innocent and uncomplicated woman who has, for the
moment, made him happy.
  The link between love and inspiration was something of a cliché in
the age of sentimentalism and romanticism. This is the theme of his
famous lyric to Anna Petrovna Kern, with whom Pushkin had been
strongly impressed during a brief meeting in 1819 in Saint Petersburg.
In 1825, while Pushkin was in exile in Mikhaylovskoe, Anna Petrovna
visited her relatives on the neighboring estate of Trigorskoe. The following poem was the fruit of the second meeting:

    The wondrous moment I recall
    When you appeared before my view;
    You came, a dream ephemeral,
    The spirit of pure beauty, you.

    Through hopeless sorrows, somber, drear,
    Through life's vain follies, whirls, alarms,
    For long your gentle voice I'd hear,
    And call to mind your tender charms.

    Life's gusting storms—the years passed by—
    Dispersed my dreams, and I forgot,
    Forgot your gentle voice and I
    Your face's heavenly charms forgot.

> Remote, in gloomy isolation,
> My days dragged by, the months, the years—
> Without a god or inspiration,
> With neither love nor life nor tears.
>
> My soul awoke as at a call,
> Before me you appeared anew!
> You came, a dream ephemeral,
> The spirit of pure beauty, you.
>
> And my heart beats in wild elation,
> My spirit waked takes wing above;
> Reborn are god and inspiration.
> Reborn are life and tears and love.

But Pushkin's lyrics during the early years of the 1820s were not confined either to the theme of love or the depiction of ennui and disillusionment. Pushkin is still, for a while, the voice of Russian liberalism. In a verse epistle of 1821 to his fellow poet Nikolay Gnedich, Pushkin compares his situation to that of the exiled Ovid, though, unlike the latter, "I to Octavius, in blind hope, / Pour forth no prayers of flattery." In his most famous political poem of the period, "The Dagger" (Kinzhal, 1821), Pushkin views this weapon as a just instrument of retribution against tyranny and injustice. "The Dagger" is indeed more outspoken, belligerent, and vengeful than the "Ode to Freedom" of 1817. However, in this sense it is not entirely typical of his political verse written in the south and at Mikhaylovskoe. Between 1820 and 1825 we may discern two important changes in Pushkin's political verse. First, the narrowly political themes of 1817–20 are treated more broadly. Except in "The Dagger," the poet is no longer content to inveigh against tyranny, injustice, and serfdom as though the setting right of these abuses would solve all life's problems. Rather he now views these abuses in the wider context of more general problems such as the processes of historical change, the meaning of life, and the destiny of man. At the same time, these broader questions are interwoven with the poet's personal emotions and reflections, and there occurs a fusion between the political theme and the truly lyric element in Pushkin's poetry. And second, after about 1823 there is a new note of skepticism, concerning both the successful outcome of any revolutionary attempt and the genuine determination of the people to attain freedom.

The new mood was undoubtedly induced in large measure by the failures in those years of the revolutionary movements in Portugal, Spain, and Naples. Pushkin's misgivings may also have arisen to some extent as a result of his acquaintance in the south with various members of the Russian revolutionary secret societies. This disillusioning skepticism is expressed in an 1823 poem based on the parable of the sower: the seeds of freedom the poet has sown bring forth no fruit, his call falls on deaf ears, the enslaved peoples remain ingloriously unresponsive.

"To the Sea" (K moryu, 1824) exemplifies perfectly Pushkin's growing tendency to combine the problem of freedom—presented now on a broad, almost philosophical base—with the problems of his personal life. This lyric started out as a meditation on the sea and the poet's destiny, for the opening stanzas were written shortly before Pushkin's enforced departure from Odessa. The sea is seen—as in Byron's *Childe Harold* (IV, 179–84)—as a symbol of freedom and power, and the poet recounts his own failure to carry out the plans he had nursed during the Odessa period of escaping from Russia by sea. The thought of Byron's death caused Pushkin, who had meanwhile arrived in Mikhaylovskoe, to enlarge his original theme to embrace both Byron—identified with the sea, a symbol of freedom—and Napoleon.[2] Thus, in its final form, "To the Sea" is a lyric poem that focuses on the poet's subjective emotions, but which defines these emotions by reference to the sea and to the world arena from which two figures had recently passed who had in different ways dominated the age:

> Farewell, thou freedom's element!
> For the last time before my gaze
> Thy blue waves rise and surge and sink
> And sparkle, beautiful and proud. . . .
>
> Alas, I wished but never left
> The dull and tedious earth-locked shore
> To hail thee with enraptured joy
> And through thy troughs, atop thy crests
> To speed full-sail a poet's flight!
>
> And thou didst call . . . but I was chained;
> In vain my soul was torn and rent:
> Held back by passion's powerful spell,
> Alas, I stayed upon the shore. . . .

Oh why regret? And whither now
My carefree steps can I direct?
One point in all your vasty wastes
Would make an impress on my soul.

One sea-swept rock, proud glory's tomb. . . .
There memories of majesty
Waned and turned cold, were laid to sleep:
'Twas there Napoleon sank to rest.

There with his grief Napoleon lies.
And in his steps, like the storm's roar,
A second ruler of men's minds
Has sped away beyond our ken.

Has gone—and Freedom mourns his death—
Leaving the world his poet's wreath.
Surge waves, storm seas, and thunder gales:
He was thy bard, he sang of thee. . . .

The world's grown empty . . . Whither now,
Great ocean, could'st thou bear me? Where?
Man's fate is everywhere the same:
Where life seems blessed, there lies in wait
Man's petty sway or tyrant's tread.

Farewell, thou sea! I'll not forget
The solemn beauty of thy waves;
Long after this I still will hear
Their crashing roar at eventide.

Into the silent, lonely woods
I'll carry in my memory
Thy cliffs, thy headlands and thy bays,
Thy sunlight, shades and sound of waves.

"To the Sea" expressed a regretful conviction that with the passing of such gigantic spirits as Napoleon—his ambition and despotism notwithstanding—and Byron, the poet of freedom, the world had somehow become a smaller and emptier place. In the third from the last stanza, it also expresses skepticism as to the benefits likely to be obtained by replacing despotism with more liberal forms of government.

At the root of this skepticism is the poet's suspicion that no form of government can make men free and happy, and that the essence of freedom and happiness lies outside the sphere of government, in some spiritual independence that Pushkin himself never achieved.[3]

One problem that preoccupied Pushkin throughout his creative life was that of the role of the poet in society. Does the poet have a special mission? Can the criteria of utilitarianism be applied to his work? Does poetic art have purely aesthetic laws of its own, independent of any message to be propagated? What about art for art's sake? Is the poet answerable to himself alone for what he writes? And how does the poet fit into the outside world of society? Several of Pushkin's finest lyrics attempt to deal with one aspect or another of this broad problem. Over the years, as we shall see in the following pages, his answers to these questions were not entirely consistent, or, more precisely, there occurred shifts in emphasis occasioned by his own circumstances and moods. In "The Prophet" (Prorok, 1826), perhaps the best known of all his short poems, he views the poet's role as highly dynamic. Endowed through inspiration with an understanding of life's essence, the poet is charged to go forth like a biblical prophet and transform the heart of man:

> With fainting soul athirst for Grace,
> I wandered in a desert place,
> And at the crossing of the ways
> I saw the sixfold Seraph blaze;
> He touched mine eyes with fingers light
> As sleep that cometh in the night:
> And like a frighted eagle's eyes,
> They opened wide with prophecies.
> He touched mine ears, and they were drowned
> With tumult and a roaring sound:
> I heard convulsion in the sky,
> And flights of angel hosts on high,
> And beasts that move beneath the sea,
> And the sap creeping in the tree.
> And bending to my mouth he wrung
> From out of it my sinful tongue,
> And all its lies and idle rust,
> And 'twixt my lips a-perishing
> A subtle serpent's forked sting
> With right hand wet with blood he thrust.
> And with his sword my breast he cleft,

My quaking heart thereout he reft,
And in the yawning of my breast
A coal of living fire he pressed.
Then in the desert I lay dead,
And God called unto me and said:
"Arise, and let my voice be heard,
Charged with my will go forth and span
The land and sea, and let my Word
Lay waste with fire the heart of man.[4]

"The Prophet" was written in the late summer of 1826. At that time the sentencing of the Decembrists (five were hanged, and many exiled to Siberia) loomed large in the poet's mind. His very use of biblical style and imagery (see Isaiah 6) conforms to the Decembrist poetic tradition of depicting the Old Testament poet-prophet as scourging injustice and tyranny. This is not to impose on "The Prophet" a narrow political message, as some have sought to do. The poem lends itself rather to a broader, more general, almost philosophical interpretation, with roots in the distinction—already noted as a constantly recurring theme in Pushkin's work—between the poet in moments of inspiration and the poet reduced to mediocrity by the toils and snares of petty everyday preoccupations. The poet's superior wisdom and loftier view are granted him by virtue of his inspiration. This concept seems to have something in common with the pantheism of Schelling, popular among Moscow intellectuals at that time. It is true that "The Prophet" incorporates a basically romantic notion of the poet's role, but Schelling's ideas on life and art were essentially alien to Pushkin's earthy outlook. Just as it is a mistake to see "The Prophet" in narrowly political terms, so too it would be wrong to read into this poem either Schellingian "otherworldiness" or any specifically religious appeal. The poet's inspiration is the keynote of the poem. With all this, "The Prophet" remains a challenge to the poet to maintain the integrity of his vision and to speak out clearly on the side of truth and justice.[5]

1827–1830

The failure of the Decembrist uprising had important consequences for Pushkin's political thought. As we have already noted, a nascent political skepticism was apparent some time before December 1825, both in the short, bitter poem in which Pushkin likens himself to the sower of the New Testament parable, and in "To the Sea." After 14

December it was obvious to Pushkin and to others that the liberal cause
had been defeated and that Nicholas intended to rule with a firm hand.
However, the poet's reaction was not one of simple resignation. His
interest in Russian history, exemplified in his work on *Boris Godunov,*
which was completed about a month before the Decembrist debacle,
had been growing. He was beginning to ask himself—as did so many
Russian minds in the nineteenth century—whether Russia necessarily
had to follow the same path of historical development as other coun-
tries, particularly West European ones, or whether peculiarly Russian
conditions might not demand peculiarly Russian solutions.

Pushkin was acquainted with the views of the Russian writer and
historian Nikolay Karamzin, who justified his conservatism by the in-
disputable fact that progress and enlightenment had come to Russia not
through the efforts of society or the people, but as a result of deliberate
measures undertaken by her autocratic rulers, especially Peter the
Great. When we add to this general line of speculation the gratitude
Pushkin felt toward Nicholas for his reprieve from exile, we can understand how Pushkin might come to hope—and he was not alone in
this—that rational reforms would be forthcoming despite the brutal
suppression of the Decembrist revolt. But these reforms would be introduced from above, as indeed the czar appears to have made clear in
the interview of 8 September in expressing to Pushkin his concern for
the welfare of the Russian people. It is understandable also that Pushkin
might draw a parallel between Nicholas I and Peter the Great. "Stanzas" (Stansy), written in December 1826 at the outset of Nicholas's
reign and shortly after the poet's reprieve, conveys Pushkin's initial
optimism:

> In hope of happy days, renown,
> With confidence I gaze ahead:
> The start of Peter's glorious reign
> Was marred by risings crushed with blood.
>
> But he with truth won minds and hearts,
> With learning tamed the savage breast,
> Let Dolgoruky speak his mind,
> Saw not rebellion in his words.
>
> Boldly, with autocratic hand,
> He sowed the seeds of knowledge far
> And wide throughout his native land:
> Russia's proud destiny he knew.

Now scholar and now man of war,
Now carpenter, now mariner,
His mind and hand encompassed all;
A sovereign, he asked no rest.

His the proud line from which you stem;
Be proud, and follow in his steps:
Like him, work tirelessly, be firm,
Nor harbor rancor for what's past.

These noble sentiments bear testimony to Pushkin's delusions as to the amount of influence a poet's voice might be expected to have upon a czar. The poem is also an appeal for clemency for the exiled Decembrists. Moreover, as we have noted, the poet's optimism was shared by others at the time. Yet this poem marks the beginning of a problem which was to plague Pushkin increasingly; it was widely regarded, even by some of the poet's friends, as a betrayal of his former convictions and an attempt to flatter the czar. His desire to rebut charges of sycophancy prompted Pushkin to write in 1828 a thirty-two-line poem, "To My Friends" (Druzyam), which begins:

No flatterer I when to the czar
I freely write a poem of praise:
I speak sincerely, unrestrained,
I speak the language of the heart.

Pushkin goes on to say that he feels a genuine affection for his czar, who has returned him from exile and "liberated my thoughts." The real flatterers are those who would counsel the czar to repress a natural instinct for mercy, to despise the people, and to view enlightenment as the seed of depravity and rebellion. He concludes:

Woe to the land where round the throne
Only the slaves and flatterers stand,
And where the poet, heaven's elect,
Stays silent, with his eyes cast down.

"To My Friends" was submitted to Nicholas I, who caused to be conveyed to Pushkin his satisfaction, together with his wish that the poem not be published. "To My Friends" did not then mend Pushkin's affair. After 1828 (when "Stanzas" was published) Pushkin's position was one of isolation; surviving liberals rebuked him, and he never gained the trust of official Saint Petersburg.[6] And in 1828 his malaise was significantly aggravated by anxiety over the *Gavriiliada* affair. This found expression in "Foreboding" (Predchuvstvie):

> Once again above my head
> The calm sky fills with clouds of bane
> And envious fate with evil tread
> Stalks my footsteps once again.
> Can I still my fate deride?
> Shall I still to fate oppose
> The staunchness of my youthful pride
> Unbowed before her sternest blows?
>
> Bruised, battered by Life's cruel wind,
> The storm, indifferent, I await;
> Perhaps, saved even now, I'll find
> Some port of refuge from my fate.
> But parting's dread hour—I feel 'tis true—
> Looms near, forbidding, merciless,
> For the last time I haste to you,
> And your hand, my angel, press.
>
> Serene and gentle at the last.
> Angel, bid a quiet farewell;
> Let eyes uplifted or downcast
> Tenderly your sorrow tell.
> And your memory inside
> For me the heart's lone flight will wage,
> Replace the hope, the strength, the pride,
> The daring of my youthful age.

The woman from whom Pushkin seeks courage in this poem is A. A. Olenina. At the time Pushkin was courting her with a view to marriage, but she rejected him.

As we know, it was Natalya Goncharova to whom Pushkin became engaged and eventually married. His attitude toward marriage and his fiancée was psychologically extremely complicated. On the one hand there was the hope of genuine happiness and spiritual rejuvenation, as well as, on a less ambitious level, the desire to organize his life on a firmer and more conventional footing. On the other hand, he had grave misgivings as to whether happiness could ever be his. He cast at times reluctant, at times nostalgic backward glances at his past and the women he had once known and loved, still loved perhaps; there was a sorrowful feeling that his youth now lay behind him. This stocktaking and consciousness of an imminent change in his way of life gave rise to some of his most moving lyrics. "Remembrance" (Vospominanie), for example, was written in 1828:

> When the loud day for men who sow and reap
>   Grows still, and on the silence of the town
> The unsubstantial veils of night and sleep,
>   The meed of the day's labor, settle down,
> Then for me in the stillness of the night
>   The wasting, watchful hours drag on their course,
> And in the idle darkness comes the bite
>   Of all the burning serpents of remorse;
> Dreams seethe; and fretful infelicities
>   Are swarming in my over-burdened soul,
> And Memory before my wakeful eyes
>   With noiseless hand unwinds her lengthy scroll.
> Then, as with loathing I peruse the years,
>   I tremble, and I curse my natal day,
> Wail bitterly, and bitterly shed tears,
>   But cannot wash the woeful script away.[7]

The pangs of remorse revealed in this poem were (as the unpublished continuation indicates) connected in the poet's mind with memories of past idleness and dissipation, of false friends, and of two women, now both dead, the remembrance of whom inspires in him feelings of guilt, though it is not clear why.

No less oriented to memories of the past—increasingly at this time a principal Pushkinian preoccupation—is his famous short poem of 1829, which reads like an act of painful renunciation:

> Ya vas lyubil; lyubov' eshche, byt' mozhet,
> V dushe moyey ugasla ne sovsem;
> No pust' ona vas bol'she ne trevozhit;
> Ya ne khochu pechalit' vas nichem.
> Ya vas lyubil bezmolvno, beznadezhno,
> To robost'yu, to revnost'yu tomim;
> Ya vas lyubil tak iskrenno, tak nezhno,
> Kak day vam Bog lyubimoy byt' drugim.
>
> I loved you once: love even now, may be,
> Love's embers still within my heart remain;
> But trouble not; no, think no more of me;

I would not cause you sorrow, bring you pain.
I loved in silence, without hope, design;
Now shy, now jealous, torn by deep distress;
So tender and sincere a love was mine:
God grant some other love you no whit less.

Readers, especially of the original Russian, will be struck by the use
of anaphora (in this poem, lines starting with the first-person pronoun
and the verb) and by the way in which the poet uses symmetrically
arranged, grammatically similar pairs of words to reinforce his message (*bezmolvno/beznadezhno*— silently/hopelessly; *robust'yu/revnost'yu*—
shyness/jealousy; *iskrenno/nezhno*—sincerely/tenderly).[8]

    This latter device is put to use in another famous short poem, writ-
ten in the same year (1829), and equally oriented toward the remembrance of things past:

    Na kholmakh Gruzii lezhit nochnaya mgla;
        Shumit Aragva predo mnoyu.
    Mne grustno i legko; pechal moya svetla;
        Pechal moya polna toboyu,
    Toboy, odnoy toboy . . . Unynya moego
        Nichto ne muchit, ne trevozhit,
    I serdtse vnov gorit i lyubit—ottogo,
        Chto ne lyubit ono ne mozhet.

    On the Georgian hills the night mist lies;
        Before me the Aragva river roars.
    I am both sad and light at heart; my sorrow is unclouded;
        My sorrow is full of you,
    Of you, of you alone . . . My despondency
        Is untormented and untroubled,
    And once again my heart burns and loves—because
        It cannot not love.

Here, along with the complementary pairs (*untormented* and *untroubled*
work semantically in the same direction, as do *burns* and *loves*) we have
the oxymoronic *sad* and *light at heart* (*grustno i legko*); the function is
nonetheless one of mutual reinforcement. It will be noted that both
these two last short poems build smoothly up to a climax that can be
anticipated by the reader, and is then resolved in a last-line twist, or
pointe.[9]

Not only were memories at this time an important preoccupation for Pushkin: he was also beset by a sense of aimlessness and frustration. And there were moments when the thought of death lay obsessively upon him. One fairly frequent theme throughout Pushkin's life was that of the younger generation forcing aside and replacing the older generation. This thought emerges clearly in stanzas 3 and 4 of the following 1829 poem—deservedly one of Pushkin's most famous on the subject of death:

Whene'er I walk on noisy streets,
Or watch the crowd that throngs the church,
Or sit and feast with reckless youth,
Then to my mind come brooding thoughts.

I think: the years will swiftly pass
And, many though we now may be,
The grave's eternal vaults await,
And someone's hour is now at hand.

I see, perchance, a lonely oak,
I think: this forest patriarch will
Outlast my petty span as he
Outlasted those who went before.

A dear, sweet infant I caress,
At once I think: farewell! farewell!
To you my place on earth I yield:
For you shall bloom, while I decay.

To every day and hour I bid
Farewell and speed them on their way,
Wondering which day shall prove to be
The anniversary of my death.

And where will fate send death to me?
In battle, travel, on the sea?
Or will a neighboring vale receive
Me when I turn to earth's cold dust?

And though the unfeeling body knows
Not where it's laid, where it decays,
Still I would rather take my rest
Near places which I once held dear.

And at the entrance of the grave
May youthful life laugh, romp and play,
And may unheeding nature there
With everlasting beauty shine.

Pushkin's lyric poetry reaches a climax of nostalgic retrospection in the highly productive autumn of 1830, when a cholera epidemic confines him to the Boldino estate. As marriage draws ever closer, the poet musters memories of past loves, and bids them and his bachelor days farewell. Ekaterina Vorontsova, wife of the governor-general in Odessa, was certainly one woman who left a lasting impression on Pushkin. With her in mind he writes his "Farewell" (Proshchanie):

For the last time I dare embrace
In thought your image dear to me,
To have my heart relive its dream
And with despondent, shy desire
To recollect once more your love.

The changing years pass swiftly by,
Bring change to all, bring change to us,
And for your poet you are now
Cloaked in sepulchral shade, while he—
For you—has vanished from the scene.

And yet accept, my distant friend,
A farewell greeting of my heart,
Just as some widowed wife might do,
Or friend embracing silent friend
Before the prison door is closed.

Pushkin's "Elegy" (Elegiya) written one month earlier, on 8 September, professes a desire to live in order to think and suffer, but the mood is somber, the fragile pleasures and fleeting moments of inspiration he anticipates are outweighed by ominous forebodings, even the love he still hopes for will be flawed with the sadness of decline:

The extinguished merriment of madcap years
Weighs on me like a hangover's dull ache.
But—as with wine—the sadness of past days
With age its strength increases in the soul.
My path is dark. The future's troubled sea
Holds little for me, mostly sorrow, toil.

> But no, my friends, I do not wish to die;
> I wish to live that I may think and suffer;
> And I know too that pleasures will be mine
> Amid my troubles and my tribulation:
> At times again the Muses will delight,
> Creation's work will cause my tears to flow;
> Perhaps once more my waning star will shine
> Beneath the fleeting, farewell smile of Love.

One outgrowth of the increasingly tragic view of life expressed in Pushkin's lyrics at this time was a more devotional frame of mind. To be sure, Pushkin was still capable of the irreverence of his *Gavriiliada* days, but a newfound respect for purity and sanctity is more characteristic of the period around 1830. This is not, in the narrow sense, a religious feeling. It is partly aesthetic, as always with Pushkin, but it is also partly ethical in its aspiration toward something pure and unchanging. A famous poem of 1829 describes a poor knight who, after seeing an image of the Virgin Mary, no longer looks at women or speaks to them, but spends entire nights weeping before the Virgin's image. Upon returning from Palestine, where he has fought bravely as a Crusader, the knight retreats to his secluded castle: "Still adoring, grieving ever, / And unshriven there he died." The Devil claims his soul since the knight had neither prayed to God nor observed the fasts, and had adored the Mother of Christ in an unseemly way, but the Virgin intercedes and admits "her paladin" to heaven. Among other stimuli contributing to the makeup of this poem there is undoubtedly an erotic element.

This same sublimated eroticism is clearly evident in Pushkin's "Madonna" (1830). This work was inspired by a painting of the Madonna and Child, as we know from a letter Pushkin wrote to his fiancée on 30 July, and the madonna of the poem is linked with Natalya Goncharova in the poet's mind.

1831–1836

The poet's marriage in February 1831 coincided with an abrupt change in his lyric output. Compared with the highly productive 1827–30 period, 1831 was a lean year; there are only five lyrics with serious pretensions, of which three are devoted to patriotic themes, reflecting both Pushkin's support for Russia during the Polish uprising and his temporarily improved relationship with Nicholas I. In the years

remaining (1832–36) Pushkin was never again to achieve that high
level of productivity—nor in his love lyrics that intensity of feeling—
that characterizes the end of his bachelor period. Undoubtedly the social
round interfered with his work, and almost certainly there were poems
of a highly intimate nature that have not survived. Then too, Pushkin
was in his last years directing his efforts more and more to prose. But
it is also reasonable to assume that Pushkin's pleasures and anxieties as
a married man did not lend themselves very well to lyric expression.
An opposition as simple as that between happiness and unhappiness is
not involved here—Pushkin was never very happy for very long. Nor
should it be thought that unhappiness is the essential stuff of good
poetry. It is, rather, that the problems that beset Pushkin in 1827–30,
though very much his own, were also universal problems that inevitably
concern mature men. And it is this that makes this period, both in
quality and quantity, a high-water mark in his career as a lyric poet.
After Pushkin's marriage, these problems were either less often in his
thoughts, or else he felt inhibitions about writing about them. One
interesting illustration of the difficulties that can beset a married lyric
poet is a small poem, probably inspired by Pushkin's wife. It was published posthumously and is of uncertain date, but was probably written
early in his marriage:

> Abandon's pleasures are not dear to me,
> Frenzy, voluptuous rapture, ecstasy,
> The young Bacchante who with groans and cries
> Writhes in my grasp and with hot ardor tries
> Her burning touch, her biting lips to lend
> To haste the shudd'ring instant of the end.
>
> How far more sweet the meekness of your kiss;
> With you I know O what tormented bliss,
> When yielding to long prayers, you tenderly
> And without rapture give yourself to me.
> Modestly cold, to my elation's cry
> Heedless of all, you scarcely make reply.
> Then passion wakes, burns, blazes hotter, till—
> You share at last my flame—against your will.

Whenever Pushkin did permit himself to vent his personal feelings
during his last years, he revealed with appalling starkness the tragic

impasse to which his married and social life had brought him. In one poem, written in 1833 or later, Pushkin—the epitome of intellectual balance and restraint—toys with the temptation of madness:

> God grant that I not lose my mind.
> Better the beggar's staff and pouch;
>   Or better hunger, toil.
> I do not mean that reason I
> Now hold so dear; nor that with it
>   I'd not be glad to part.
>
> If only they would leave me free,
> How swiftly, gaily would I flee
>   Into the darkling woods!
> I'd sing, delirious, possessed,
> And lose myself enraptured in
>   Chaotic, wondrous dreams.
>
> And I would harken to the waves,
> And I would gaze, in happiness,
>   Up in the empty skies;
> And I would be so strong and free
> Like to a whirlwind cutting swaths
>   Through fields and forest trees.
>
> But here's the rub: if you go mad,
> Then men will fear you like the plague,
>   And, fearing, lock you up,
> And they'll attach you with a chain,
> And come and through the cage's bars
>   Torment you like some beast.
>
> And so by night I would not hear,
> Not hear the nightingale's clear voice,
>   The rustling of the trees—
> I'd hear my comrades' shouts and cries,
> The cursing of the nighttime guards,
>   And shrieks and sounds of chains.

An unpublished excerpt, written probably in June 1834, reflects the poet's extreme weariness with the life of the capital and his longing to retire to the country. It is also clearly an appeal to his wife:

'Tis time, my friend, 'tis time! the heart has need of peace—
Days follow swiftly days, and each hour bears away
Some fraction of our being—while we all unawares,
Imagining we live, in life we are in death.

Happiness none knows—but calm, and freedom: these can be.
An enviable lot has long since been my dream,
Long since, a weary slave, I've contemplated flight
To some far-off abode of work and simple joys.

The manuscript contains Pushkin's plan for this unrevised and
apparently unfinished excerpt: "Youth has no need of an *at home* [in
English], mature age feels horror at *its own* isolation. Happy the man
who finds a woman to share his life—he should make for *home*. Oh,
shall I soon transfer my Penates to the country—fields, garden, pea-
sants, books; poetic labors—family, love, etc.—religion, death"
(III(2), 941).

But for Pushkin there was to be no escape. A visit to Mikhaylovskoe
in September of 1835 did not bring the relief he hoped for. In a somber
poem Pushkin laments that his old nurse Arina Rodionovna is now
dead. He notes that young pines are beginning to grow up near the
three tall pines he so often rode by in the past. He himself will not live
to see the young ones fully grown, but he hopes that his grandchild
may see them and remember him.[10]

Beset by marital problems, at odds with a society in which he was
cutting a sad figure, and suffering from a sense that he was regarded as
a writer who had outlived his day, the poet is plagued by a foreboding
of imminent doom through much of 1836. A poem written for the
lycée anniversary of 1836 begins:

There was a time: 'twas then our youthful feast
Shone, noisy, gay and garlanded with rose,
The clink of glasses mingled with our songs. . . .
This is no longer so: our rakish feast,
Like us, has with the years now run its course,
It has grown tamer, quieter and more staid,
The toasts and clinking glasses ring less loud,
Less playfully the conversation flows,
Some seats are empty, sadder now we sit,
More rarely 'mid the songs is laughter heard,
More often now we sigh, and silence keep. . . .

One of Pushkin's last poems, dated 21 August 1836—so to speak his final will and testament—is his contribution to a long-standing literary tradition that includes in Russia Derzhavin and Lomonosov, and extends back to Horace's *Exegi monumentum,* "I've raised a monument. . . ." It is fitting that it be the last poem treated in this chapter. But I will first return to a poem I deliberately skirted earlier in order to treat it in isolation as an example of an interesting viewpoint touched upon at the beginning of this chapter—the view of unmotivated killing and destruction as an integral part of life. Above, we said this Pushkin attitude surfaced in the years 1827–31, although in fact it may be glimpsed even earlier, in "Scene from Faust" (1825). The poem I here have in mind, "Anchar" (The Vpas Tree), was written in 1828:

> In the scrub, ungiving desert,
> On heat-scorched soil,
> The upas tree, like a menacing sentinel,
> Stands alone—one only in all the universe.
>
> The nature of the thirsting steppes
> Produced it on the day of wrath,
> And fed with poison
> Its dead leaves and roots.
>
> Poison drips through its bark,
> Melting from the noonday heat,
> And at evening congeals,
> A thick, transparent resin.
>
> No bird flies to the tree,
> Nor does the tiger go there; only the black whirlwind
> Hurls itself on the tree of death,
> And hastes away—putrefactive.
>
> And if a wandering cloud should water
> Its dense foliage,
> Then from its branches the rain,
> Filled with poison, runs down into the burning sand.
>
> But with imperious gaze
> One man sent his fellow man to the upas tree,
> And obediently he dashed on his way
> And by morning returned with the poison.

> He brought the death-dealing resin
> And a branch with the withered leaves,
> And the sweat on his pale brow
> Flowed down in cold streams;
>
> He brought the poison—grew weak, lay down
> On the hut's bast-covered floor;
> And the poor slave died at the feet
> Of the invincible ruler.
>
> And with that poison the prince
> Anointed his obedient arrows,
> And with these sent destruction abroad
> On his neighbors in foreign lands.

This is a stark and unforgiving poem. There is not just one act of destruction, but a sequence of destructive acts: the very planting of the poison tree in the day of wrath must be reckoned a first destructive step; then, in obedience to orders, the fetching of the poison, which causes the slave's death; finally, the apparently indiscriminate spreading abroad of destruction among the neighbors—neighbors, be it noted, are simply assumed to be natural targets. The poem divides into two parts: in the first five stanzas, dominated by verbs of imperfective aspect, the scene is laid, the tree planted, and its effects described on bird, beast, whirlwind, and rain. Then, with the electrifying line "*No cheloveka chelovek*" (literally, "But man [subject] man [object]"), man comes upon the scene, and—with the perfectives now predominating—a rapidly unfolding sequence of destructive acts is launched. Inevitably the Rousseauesque idea comes to mind that man alone is destructive and out of harmony with nature. That thought should be retained, for it is after all the line "*No cheloveka chelovek*" that marks the great transition in the poem. But Rousseau is not the entire answer. Man is clearly the most effective destroyer and major culprit, but the upas tree was planted and imbued with poison by Nature. Nature herself produces and sustains the mechanism that sets in play the principle of sequential destruction.[11]

More of this somber outlook can be found in "Delibash" (1829), describing the mindless and simultaneous killing of each other by a Cossack and a mountain tribesman—though war here does provide a motive. One of Pushkin's greatest short poems is "Stambul" (Istanbul, 1830). To the principle of destruction is here added the almost Job-like irony of virtue being rewarded by death while depravity triumphs. The same principle is abundantly attested in the 1834 collection "Songs of the Western Slavs."

While some of Pushkin's poetry, including his lyric verse, may owe its existence to the timeliness of his appearance on the Russian literary stage, which enabled him to state time-honored poetic truths before anyone else, this can in no way apply to poems like "The Upas Tree" or "Stambul." Pushkin's preoccupation with destruction as a part of creation is entirely his own, an important vein in his individual *Weltanschauung*.

We return, as promised, to Pushkin's Horatian farewell poem.

> I've raised a monument no human hands could build;
> The path that leads to it can ne'er be overgrown,
> Its head, unbowed, untamed, stands higher from the ground
>   Than Alexander's column stands.
>
> Not all of me shall die: in verses shall my soul
> Outlive my mortal dust and shall escape decay—
> And I shall be renowned so long as on this earth
>   One single poet is alive.
>
> My hallowed fame shall spread through Russia's mighty land,
> And each and every tribe shall venerate my name:
> The proud Slav and the Finn, the still untamed Tungus,
>   The Kalmuk, dweller of the steppe.
>
> Long after this my name shall warm the people's heart,
> Because my lyre has sung of feelings good and kind,
> And in my cruel age I sang blessed freedom's praise
>   And for the fallen mercy begged.
>
> Be thou obedient, Muse, to the Command of God!
> Not fearing hurt nor wrong, seeking no laurel crown,
> Remain indifferent to calumny and praise,
>   And do not quarrel with the fool.

Pushkin proved right in predicting his own lasting fame. He was right, too, in the sense of timing that prompted him to write this poem—concealing beneath its traditional surface a mass of suffering— six months before his death. [12]

What, in conclusion, can be said of the best of Pushkin's lyric poetry? The sounds in translation elude us. Those denied the privilege of reading Pushkin in the original must take on faith that the sound patterns in his lyrics, though seldom obtrusive, are not only beautiful but also functional in that they harmonize with and contribute to the sense. The same must also be said, specifically, of the rhymes, which play an important part in most of the lyrics, not merely as embellishments or line-markers, but also as structural factors that shape the syntax and point up the thought to which they are subordinated.

The themes and thoughts of Pushkin's lyrics speak largely for themselves. But some further understanding of his remarkable achievement as a lyric poet may be gained by comparing the best poems of his mature years with his youthful work. When, for example, in his 1816–17 elegies Pushkin speaks of unrequited love, of sorrow, and of death, though he is certainly sincere, one is aware that these are moods that sometimes beset the very young, moods that respond to the treatment of experience and adjustment, moods that also reflect a literary era. But when in his mature writing he speaks of such things, he speaks with his own voice, with a freshness, directness, and immediacy that give the impression that such emotions have never before been treated in literature. He speaks for himself in such a way that the natural words he uses seem to emanate directly from the specific experiences of one man, experiences and impressions that could be precisely conveyed in those words alone. At the same time the balance, sense of proportion, and self-restraint impart to his writings a universal quality. For Pushkin's writings are characterized—in form as well as content—by that self-restraint in dealing with deeply felt emotion that life demands of all men. Furthermore, this very self-restraint renders intelligible and doubly poignant to others the tribulations that motivated Pushkin in writing of himself. And he wrote of things that are the common lot of grown men everywhere, of the limitations life imposes on each and all, limitations that impart to life a tragic element that cannot be overlooked.

Chapter Nine

Conclusion

The final questions remain—for Pushkin as for any other writer—What does his achievement amount to? What is the peculiar nature of his appeal? Can we identify specific qualities that make up a whole and would justify our speaking of a specifically Pushkinian poetic world?

First, in terms of achievement, it should be said that Pushkin had the good fortune to come on the Russian scene when the tide was at the flood. The Russian language had been honed until it stood ready to serve as the instrument of his voice. His predecessors (Derzhavin, Zhukovsky, and Batyushkov) had laid the foundations of a literary tradition of extremely high quality and had brought Russian literature into the mainstream of western European literatures. For Pushkin everything lay ready, yet everything was still to do. Pushkin must—not always, but often—have felt a pulsating sense of adventure difficult for those moderns to understand who are subject to "the anxiety of influence." Pushkin's timeliness becomes doubly apparent if we for one moment picture him as sharing the groundbreaking labors of a Vasily Trediakovsky or Mikhail Lomonosov, or for that matter as the contemporary of a Nikolay Chernyshevsky. We might as well picture Shakespeare as pre-Chaucerian or as the contemporary of Alexander Pope!

Because Russia was a recent arrival on the European scene and because the age was one of rapid change, Pushkin was exposed to the influences of more than one literary school and encouraged to try his hand at several genres. This—in two different but related ways—gives his *oeuvre* a considerable breadth. When he started to write, classicism and sentimentalism held the field. From the French, primarily, but also from Batyushkov, Pushkin learned good taste, restraint, appropriateness, precision, and balance. These qualities would remain with him and stand him in good stead throughout his subsequent career. At this early stage he tried his hand at all the humorously light and melancholically elegiac minor genres then in vogue. He also wrote his first truly important work, the six-canto comic epic *Ruslan and Lyudmila,* a masterpiece in its way. With this work completed in 1820, Pushkin was immediately confronted by a new wave, romanticism in the person of

Byron. He quickly moved from the position of follower to that of pioneer. While classicism and sentimentalism had established themselves
in Russian literature before Pushkin's birth, romanticism in its Byronic
form was a new phenomenon.

Just as there are essentially two Byrons—the Byron of *Childe Harold*
and the "eastern tales," on the one hand, and on the other, the Byron
of *Beppo* and *Don Juan*—so in Pushkin we may distinguish two overlap-
ping stages of Byronism, manifested first in his southern poems, and
then in his "novel in verse" *Eugene Onegin,* his greatest work, finally
completed in 1831. A third stage may be detected, if you will, in the
basically unsatisfactory *Little House in Kolomna* (1830). Meanwhile,
Pushkin was in the forefront of developments in his bid to switch Russian theater from the "courtly" French drama of Racine (six-foot iambic
rhymed couplets) to the more earthy, popular manner of Shakespeare
(predominantly unrhymed five-foot iambs with prose scenes interspersed). We mean, of course, *Boris Godunov* (1825). Also new in Russian drama were Pushkin's little tragedies, modeled on Barry Cornwall's
"dramatic scenes."

A word is in order on the staging of Pushkin's plays. The very
shortness of the little tragedies (with the possible exception of *The Stone
Guest*) militates against their successful staging. I am therefore all the
more pleased to report that I saw three of the four (*The Stone Guest,
Mozart and Salieri,* and *The Covetous Knight*) performed together in one
evening in Leningrad, and with complete success (it is, incidentally,
amazing how long it can take the Baron to recite his 118-line monologue if he must go slowly around the stage with a taper in his hand,
lighting a candle on each and every one of his treasured chests). As for
Boris Godunov, scholars and public alike are agreed that it does not stage
well. Yet, also in Leningrad, I witnessed a performance of all roles, both
male and female, by a single actor, who for stage props made use of one
unappealing Soviet chair. This manner of staging *Boris Godunov* was
not, presumably, what Pushkin had in mind, but I assure the reader
that it was altogether convincing and deeply moving. My lyric digression now at an end, the point I wish to make is that a play need not be
judged aesthetically by its ease in staging. Although plays are assumed
to be written for staging—and this consideration affects their shape—it
does not determine their merits. Many genuine admirers of ancient
Greek tragedies have never seen some of them on stage. How many
people have seen Sophocles' *Philoctetes* on stage? Yet it is one of the
dramatic masterpieces of all time.

Finally, Pushkin left his mark also on the relatively unexplored domain of Russian prose.

There is an irony to this impressive achievement. The Byronic poem was short-lived. *Eugene Onegin* produced imitations and parodies, but was never matched. *Boris Godunov* could not serve as a springboard for a popular theater tradition. And in prose it was Gogol and Lermontov with their greater complexity who set the tone. Pushkin was both an alpha and an omega. But throughout the years Russian writers have constantly returned to him for sustenance. Tolstoy, for instance, is deeply indebted to Pushkin for the tightly constructed early chapters of *Anna Karenina,* before the work unraveled at the hands of Levin and Kitty. Yes, the debt is there—from Ivan Turgenev to Anna Akhmatova to Alexander Tvardovsky. And if we see Pushkin as belonging in part to the past, then we can say no less of Shakespeare, of Dante, even of Goethe. The scope of Pushkin's achievement is truly immense.

We have noted Pushkin's passage from classicism and sentimentalism to romanticism. In assessing his overall contribution to Russian letters, we must inevitably—inevitably because Russian scholars themselves have dwelt on it so extensively—ask whether Pushkin actually broke through to that "higher" plateau of realism. Was Pushkin a realist? First, let us make clear that whether he was or was not has nothing to do with his artistic merits on the scales of eternity. Nevertheless, since Russian and Soviet critics are so teleologically oriented, we must answer the question. L. N. Brodsky, we noted above, claimed that *Eugene Onegin* was "the first Russian realist novel."[1] But this is a patently exaggerated claim. On the other hand, Pushkin cannot simply be labeled a romantic. Pushkin's mature work drew its sustenance from a variety of sources, but he is a romantic in the sense that romanticism served as an emotional point of departure for many of his finest creations. Despite that, we must insist that much of Pushkin's achievement lies in what he did with romanticism's attitudes, moods, and problems. What he did, of course, was to subject the romantic outlook to the severe scrutiny of his realist eye. But we distinguish between realism and "realism." The strongly realist element in Pushkin's mental outlook was, as much as anything, a result of the formative influences of French classicism and also a part of the poet's innate personality. We are apt to forget that there is an indubitable link between the down-to-earth realism of classicism and the realism of the nineteenth century, to say nothing of the fact that romanticism too carried seeds that bore fruit on the soil of realism. The poetic world of Pushkin's most outstanding

serious writings reflects a tension between romantic emotional attitudes
and an intellect constantly brought into play to assay, to moderate, and
to translate those attitudes.

What then can we say of Pushkin's poetic world? Wherein are we to
seek a fundamental unifying theme, a consistent *Weltanschauung?*
Pushkin's poetic world is striking by its pluralism and multiformity.
One strong vein in his work is that of humor, evidenced in many of his
short poems and verse epistles to friends. It is displayed at its best in
such works as *Ruslan and Lyudmila, Gavriiliada, Count Nulin,* and certain portions of *Eugene Onegin.* This trait has its literary inception in the
eighteenth century (Voltaire first and foremost) and parallels in its development the early nineteenth-century humor of Byron's *Beppo* and *Don
Juan.* We have here a Pushkin who can be witty, ironic, irreverent,
zestful, gay, and sometimes bawdy. We have also—and this is, alas,
all too often forgotten—Pushkin at his very best. It is sad when some
content-hungry, development-obsessed critics pluck profundity from
certain Pushkin poems while dismissing as delightful trivia such masterpieces as *Ruslan and Lyudmila* and *Count Nulin.* Or worse still, find
in these two works profundity. Their emotional range is limited, for
such was the author's intent. But in their own way they approach perfection as nearly as anything Pushkin ever wrote. As Byron once put it
in his defense of Pope, "The poet who *executes* best is the highest,
whatever his department"; and again, "A good poet can imbue a pack
of cards with more poetry than inhabits the forests of America."
Pushkin's humorous poetry must rank very high in any assessment of
his achievement and must be taken into account in any attempt at
defining his poetic world.

At the opposite pole is the Pushkin of the southern poems—humor-
less, disillusioned, nostalgic, antisocial, acquainted with love's torments and with despair. There is also the Pushkin of 1829 and 1830,
preoccupied with the thought of death. There is the weary, persecuted
Pushkin of *The Bronze Horseman* and some of the later lyrics. And there
are other facets to Pushkin's genius: his patriotism, his intense interest
in the processes of Russia's historical evolution, his liberalism, his conservatism, his delight in formal perfection displayed, for example, in
his graceful fairy tales in verse. And finally (though not chronologically)
there is *Eugene Onegin,* which weaves together so many strands of
Pushkin's thoughts, feelings, and moods, and which, more fully than
any other work, reflects the diversity of his poetic world. With all due
respect to other opinions, *Eugene Onegin* is not only his most popular,
but also his greatest achievement.

In his perceptive booklet *The Hedgehog and the Fox,* Isaiah Berlin categorizes writers as "hedgehogs . . . who relate everything to a single central vision, one system less or more coherent or articulate, in terms of which they understand, think and feel," or as "foxes . . . who pursue many ends, often unrelated and even contradictory . . . seizing upon the essence of a vast variety of experiences and objects for what they are in themselves."[2] Pushkin, as Berlin points out, clearly belongs to the foxes. But even the most wide-ranging of foxes will inevitably seize upon experiences that for some overt or covert reason are of particular interest to *him.* This process of selection and treatment, conscious or unconscious, can yield insights into the writer's perhaps unformulated view of life. Pushkin is no exception. He did not simply choose to write about Don Juan out of caprice; his choice of the Don Juan theme and his manner of handling it were dictated from within. In fact, here and elsewhere he injected into allegedly "objective" third-person situations his own most intimate thoughts and feelings. It is, therefore, in the recurrence of certain themes, preoccupations, notes, and moods in Pushkin's writings that we seek a unified, though not specified, view of life, a point of reference for Pushkin's poetic inspiration, and some insight into the nature of the appeal his poetry exerts.

Pushkin's "foxlike" diversity, or—in Berlin's words—his "protean genius," would seem an obstacle to any attempt at establishing unity. Yet it is precisely here that a start must be made. For the absence of a "central vision" is no less significant than its presence. The central vision of a Dante or a Dostoevski posits the existence of some point of anchorage in the shifting sea of life, some stable point to which life's vagaries can be related. The very lack of this in Pushkin accounts for a great deal. Pushkin's was a pragmatic mind, concerned primarily with the immediacy of life on earth. At the same time Pushkin was intensely aware of death, to which, indeed, at times he seemed irresistibly drawn. Pushkin's feeling for death provides a key to many of his feelings for life's experiences. Lacking a central vision—and in particular a Christian central vision—he could not view death as a prelude to some continued existence hereafter; for him death simply rang down the curtain on the final act of life here below. This almost pagan view of death's finality imbues with added poignancy what he wrote about our earthly existence—which is in fact his sole concern. Life's unrelenting ebb, the irretrievable passage of time, the unpredictability of fate—the vulnerability of man's destiny, metaphysical despair—these preoccupations and moods go hand in hand with the more dynamic sides of Pushkin's passionate nature: his zest for life, his wit and humor, his pursuit of love, his intense feeling for beauty in many forms. There is in much of Pushkin's work an exuberant, uncomplicated, almost sunlit quality. But in the final analysis his view of the world is bleak and tragic.

It is, I believe, on this ontological foundation that Pushkin's poetic achievement rests. But this is not his achievement. His achievement lies in the individual poems, concrete images, and specific words he composed. Critics often enough hail Pushkin as a brilliant and profound thinker. This approach is misleading and inaccurate. There is nothing radically original in the view of life embedded in Pushkin's poetry. The originality lies in the poems themselves. Pushkin may justifiably be considered preeminent as a thinker only in the sense that *content* and *form* are indissoluble, and that therefore Pushkin's *thought* was his *poetry*, for, as T. S. Eliot reminds us, "the meaning of a poem exists in the words of the poem, and in those words only."[3] Moreover, the "words" of which Eliot speaks are, in Pushkin's case, Russian words. Their sounds, meanings, associations, and sequences can never be rendered perfectly in any language other than Russian. This is what distinguishes them from the words of the abstract thinker, the technological expert, or the pamphleteer. Herein lies their extra dimension. They defy not only paraphrase, but even, at the last, stylistic analysis. A poem's meter, rhythm, alliterations, assonances, and other qualities can be discussed. Finally, however, it cannot be explained why a sensitive reader like Maurice Baring was so deeply moved by the simple enough line from *The Covetous Knight*: "*I more, gde bezhali korabli*" (And the sea where ships were scudding free).[4] There are many such lines in Pushkin's writings—some charged with thought, others completely unpretentious in this respect. I take the liberty of citing four lines from *Ruslan and Lyudmila* which have always impressed me both by their complete lack of profundity and by their perfection:

> Ya kazhdy den vosstav ot sna
> Blagodaryu serdechno Boga
> Za to, chto v nashi vremena
> Volshebnikov uzh ne tak mnogo.

> Each single day when I awake,
> I give my heartfelt thanks to God
> For having so arranged it that
> We've fewer wizards in our age.

Let us not, however, forget that there is the other side of the same coin, that the same Pushkin who wrote the "nonsense" lines just quoted could also write:

> *No cheloveka chelovek*
> Poslal. . . .
>
> But man man
> Sent. . . . —"Anchar" (The Upas Tree)

Or finally:

> *Tak bezrashchetny duraley,*
> Votshche reshas na zloe delo,
> Zarezav nishchego v lesu,
> Branit obodrannoe telo
>
> Thus the heedless fool,
> For no reason deciding to commit a crime,
> Having knifed a beggar in the woods,
> Curses the ill-clad corpse—"Stsena iz Fausta" (Scene from Faust)

For Pushkin as for other poets, it is meaningful to speak of his poetic world in terms of his psychology, his ideas, the outlook on life that emerges from his writings. But we remember that his achievement and his appeal are to be found in the manner in which he gave concrete expression to this poetic world.

Notes

Chapter One

1. O. S. Pavlishcheva, "Vospominaniya o detstve A. S. Pushkina," [Reminiscences of Pushkin's Childhood], *Pushkin v vospominaniyakh sovremennikov* [Pushkin in the Reminiscences of His Contemporaries] (Leningrad, 1950), 25–28.
2. Quoted from A. Tyrkova-Vilyams, *Zhizn' Pushkina* [Pushkin's Life] (Paris, 1929), I, 46.
3. I. I. Pushchin, "Zapiski o Pushkine" [Notes on Pushkin], *Pushkin v vospominaniyakh sovremennikov* [Pushkin in the Reminiscences of His Contemporaries], 68–70.
4. Quoted from Ernest J. Simmons, *Pushkin* (Cambridge, Mass., 1937), 100–1.
5. Tyrkova-Vilyams, II, 125–26.
6. V. Veresaev, *Pushkin v zhizni* [Pushkin in Life] (Moscow, 1936), I, 313–19.
7. Simmons, 290–91.
8. See Anna Akhmatova, "Pushkin v 1828 godu," [Pushkin in 1828], *O Pushkine* [On Pushkin] (Leningrad, 1977), 207–22.
9. A. S. Pushkin, *Polnoe sobranie sochineniy* [Complete Works], 21 vols. (Moscow-Leningrad: Akademiya nauk SSSR [Soviet Academy of Sciences], 1937–59), XII, 314–17. Hereafter cited in notes as *Ak. nauk.*, with volume and page numbers; in the text with volume and page numbers only.
10. Simmons, 366–70.
11. Henri Troyat, *Pushkin* (New York, 1970), 531–35.
12. Akhmatova, 111. Akhmatova's treatment of the whole Pushkin tragedy is an extreme example of the sort of paranoia it creates in some Russian minds.
13. See, especially, S. L. Abramovich, *Pushkin v 1836 godu* [Pushkin in 1836] (Leningrad, 1984). But, regrettably, see also Kuleshov, who, while handing a number of accolades to Abramovich, attempts to undermine her good work by reviving the specter of Nicholas I's evil intentions: V. Kuleshov, *Zhizn i tvorchestvo A. S. Pushkina* [Pushkin's Life and Work] (Moscow, 1987), 374–414.

Chapter Two

1. Thirty-eight introductory lines in the first canto were written later, around 1824.

2. Pushkin was also indebted to the Russian tradition. Noteworthy are two eighteenth-century comic-epic predecessors, V. I. Maykov, author of *Elisey*, and I. P. Bogdanovich, author of *Dushenka*, the latter himself strongly influenced by La Fontaine. Further, a wealth of Russian sources for Pushkin's poem have been indicated: see V. V. Sipovsky, *"Ruslan i Lyudmila* (K literaturnoy istorii poemy)" [*Ruslan and Lyudmila*: On the Literary History of a Poem], *Pushkin i ego sovremenniki* [Pushkin and His Contemporaries], IV, 59–84. However, not only will the comparison with Ariosto and Voltaire be more meaningful to the Western reader, but—it is safe to add—this comparison was in 1817–20 more meaningful for Pushkin himself. Voltaire in particular was greatly admired by Pushkin, and in two previous uncompleted attempts to write comic epic, "The Monk" (1813) and "Bova" (1814), Pushkin had specifically paid tribute to him.

3. For a discussion of these Arzamas attempts at the epic, see A. L. Slonimsky, "Pervaya poema Pushkina" [Pushkin's First Narrative Poem], *Pushkin: Vremennik pushkinskoy, komissii* [Pushkin: Chronicle of the Pushkin Commission] (Moscow-Leningrad, 1937), III, 183–202.

4. The probable relationship between Zhukovsky's projected *Vladimir* and *Ruslan and Lyudmila* is discussed by L. N. Nazarova, "K istorii sozdaniya poemy Pushkina *Ruslan i Lyudmila*," [On the History of the Creation of Pushkin's Poem *Ruslan and Lyudmila*], *Pushkin: Issledovaniya i materialy* [Pushkin: Research and Materials] (Moscow-Leningrad, 1956), I, 216–21; also B. Tomashevsky, *Pushkin* (Moscow-Leningrad, 1956), I, 299–302; hereafter cited in text.

5. Tomashevsky (I, 456ff.) is inclined to place unnecessary emphasis on the contemporary quality of *Ruslan and Lyudmila*, which he quite correctly links with the narrator's digressions and a certain lyricism in Pushkin's poem. Tomashevsky's insistence appears to be motivated by the desire to set Pushkin off clearly from Ariosto and Voltaire. But Ariosto and Voltaire were in their own day and way equally "contemporary," and though Voltaire's anticlerical satire is entirely absent from *Ruslan and Lyudmila*, the link between Pushkin's poem and *La Pucelle* is substantial.

6. Pushkin eventually removed from his poem some of the erotic details that appeared at this point in the first edition. For an even more outspoken description of a roughly similar situation, see *Orlando Furioso*, VIII, stanzas 49 and 50, with which Pushkin was familiar. In two other places, changes made by Pushkin were also dictated by modesty.

7. Situations in which a man finds himself obliged to make love to an old crone occur also in Chaucer, Dryden, and in Voltaire's "Ce qui plait aux dames." However, with these three poets the old crone turns out to be a beautiful maiden in disguise, and everything ends well. Pushkin has, so to speak, reversed this situation in a delightfully telling way; particularly effective is Finn's oversight with regard to the passing of time.

8. See "Oproverzhenie na kritiki" [Rebuttal to Criticisms], *Ak. nauk.*, XI, 144.

9. This is not the place to go into the extremely complicated and often disputed critical question as to the nature of the poetic world created in *Orlando Furioso*. We can, however, say in very general terms that Pushkin's lightness of touch in *Ruslan and Lyudmila* conveys an impression similar to that created in certain episodes of *Orlando Furioso*.

Chapter Three

1. The outstanding work on the Byron-Pushkin literary relationship during Pushkin's southern exile is that of V. M. Zhirmunsky, *Bayron i Pushkin* [Byron and Pushkin] (Leningrad, 1924).

2. See letter to V. P. Gorchakov of October–November 1822, *Ak. nauk.*, XIII, 52; and "Oproverzhenie na kritiki" [Rebuttal to Criticisms], *Ak. nauk.*, XI, 145.

3. From a letter to A. I. Turgenev, 10 December 1822; see *Ostafevsky arkhiv knyazey Vyazemskikh* [Ostafevo Archive of the Princes Vyazemsky]; here quoted from Tomashevsky, II, 430.

Chapter Four

1. This is in the final version, which was not only worked over by Pushkin, who excluded two scenes, but also suffered some change at the hands of the censor.

2. It is true that Pushkin was reading Shakespeare in the spring of 1824 in Odessa, as is clear from a letter written in April or the first half of May 1824 (*Ak. nauk.*, XIII, 92). However, this does not alter the fact that the influence of *Beppo* and *Don Juan* preceded that of Shakespeare. The point that Byron's later works were instrumental in "emancipating" Pushkin from his "southern Byronism" is well made by V. Zhirmunsky, "Pushkin i zapadnye literatury" [Pushkin and Western Literatures], *Pushkin-Vremennik pushkinskoy komissii* [Pushkin: Chronicle of the Pushkin Commission] (Moscow-Leningrad, 1937), III, 77.

3. See W. N. Vickery, "Parallelizm v literaturnom razvitii Bayrona i Pushkina" [Parallelism in the Literary Development of Byron and Pushkin], *American Contributions to the Fifth International Congress of Slavicists* (The Hague, 1963), 371–401.

4. V. Belinsky, *Polnoe sobranie sochineniy* [Complete Works] (Moscow, 1953–56), VII, 505.

5. V. P. Gorodetsky, "Dramaturgiya" [Playwriting] *Pushkin: Itogi i problemy izucheniya* [Pushkin: Research Results and Problems] (Moscow-Leningrad, 1966), 446.

6. Gorodetsky, 453.

7. Gorodetsky, 449.

8. See I. Vinogradov, "Put' Pushkina k realizmu" [Pushkin's Path to Realism] Literaturnoe nasledstvo [Literary Heritage], 1934, XVI–XVIII, 84.

9. I. V. Kireevsky, Polnoe sobranie sochineniy v dvukh tomakh [Complete Works in Two Volumes] (Moscow, 1911), II, 45.

10. Affinities between Boris and Pushkin's apathetic "southern" Byronic heroes, especially Aleko, are noted by D. Bernstein, "Boris Godunov," Literaturnoe nasledstvo [Literary Heritage], 1934, XVI–XVIII, 223.

11. The play originally ended with the crowd obediently echoing: "Long live Czar Dimitry Ivanovich!" This ending could not have been interpreted as a happy one, since only an instant earlier the crowd maintained a horrified silence on hearing the news of the death of Boris's widow and son. The present accepted ending—with the crowd again maintaining silence—reflects a change thought at one time to have been dictated by the censor, but now regarded as almost certainly Pushkin's own. The crowd's silence is seen as a stronger ending that indicates the people's moral condemnation of the killing of Boris's widow and son, it's potentially menacing attitude. See M. P. Alekseev, "Remarka Pushkina 'Narod bezmolvstvuet'" [Pushkin's Stage Direction 'The people are silent'], Russkaya literatura [Russian Literature], 1967, No. 2, 36–58.

12. An interesting comparison in the manner of handling Boris's death is provided by Musorgsky's opera Boris Godunov, in which the dying takes longer and the czar's sickness seems more closely connected with his feelings of guilt—all aided by the audience's inability to hear the words of the libretto.

13. See P. E. Shchegolev, "Iz razyskaniy v oblasti biografii i teksta Pushkina" [Investigating in the area of Pushkin's Biography and Text], Pushkin i ego sovremenniki [Pushkin and His Contemporaries] (Saint Petersburg, 1911), XIV, 176–81.

14. See B. Koplan, "Poltavsky boy Pushkina i ody Lomonosova" [Pushkin's Battle of Poltava and Lomonosov's Odes], Pushkin i ego sovremenniki [Pushkin and His Contemporaries] (Leningrad, 1930), XXXVIII–XXXIX, 113–21. See also A. N. Sokolov, "Poltava Pushkina i Petriady" [Pushkin's Poltava and the Petriades], Pushkin: Vremennik pushkinskoy komissii [Pushkin: Chronicle of the Pushkin Commission] (Moscow-Leningrad, 1939), IV–V, 57–90.

15. Lines 345–68 in the first canto (starting Kto pri zvezdax . . .) were in an early variant written in the trochaic meter, which was sometimes used in Russian for ballads. See Ak. nauk., V, 28–29 and 215–218.

16. See V. V. Vinogradov, Stil' Pushkina [Pushkin's Style], (Moscow, 1941), 237–39.

17. For contemporary criticisms and Pushkin's views see Pushkin: itogi i problemy izucheniya [Pushkin: Research Results and Problems] (Moscow-Leningrad, 1966), 25–27 and 385–88. See also Ak. nauk., XI, 158–60 and 164–65.

18. See D. D. Blagoy, *Sotsiologiya tvorchestva Pushkina* [Sociology of Pushkin's Art] (Moscow, 1931), 79–105, especially 99–105; hereafter cited in text.

19. Paul Debreczeny, "Narrative Voices in Pushkin's *Poltava,*" *Russian Literature,* XXIV (1988), 319–48.

Chapter Five

1. Often included among the "little tragedies" is "The Water-Nymph" (1832), which remained unfinished and is not dealt with in this book.

2. S. V. Shervinsky, *Ritm i smysl* [Rhythm and Meaning] (Moscow, 1961), 157–58.

3. L. Polivanov, quoted here from Shervinsky, 158.

4. Noted by V. Setschkareff, *Alexander Puschkin* (Wiesbaden, 1963), 152; hereafter cited in text.

5. See Shervinsky, 218.

6. See M. P. Alekseev, "*Mozart i Salieri,*" in *Polnoe sobranie sochineniy* [Complete Works], *Dramaticheskie proizvedeniya* [Dramatic Writings] (Leningrad, 1935), VII, 524.

7. The link between *The Covetous Knight* and *Mozart and Salieri* is pointed out by D. D. Blagoy, "Pushkin—master psikhologicheskogo analiza" [Pushkin as Master of Psychological Analysis], *Literatura i deystvitelnost* [Literature and Reality] (Moscow, 1959), 366–400.

8. For a fuller treatment of Pushkin's relation to his hero and of other ways in which his personal life influenced this work, see the extremely perceptive article by Anna Akhmatova, "*Kamenny gost'* Pushkina" [Pushkin's Stone Guest] *Pushkin: Issledovaniya i materialy* [Pushkin: Research and Materials] (Moscow-Leningrad, 1958), 185–95.

9. C. Courbet, "L'originalité du *Convive de Pierre* de Pouchkine," *Revue de Litterature Comparée* [Review of Comparative Literature] (Paris, 1955), XXIX, 48–71. See also Leo Weinstein, *The Metamorphoses of Don Juan* (Stanford, 1959), 92–93.

10. H. Kucera, "Pushkin and Don Juan," *For Roman Jakobson,* ed. Morris Hallé, Horace G. Lunt, Hugh McLean, and Cornelis van Schoonefeld (The Hague, 1956), 273–84.

11. O. Mandel, *The Theatre of Don Juan* (Lincoln, Neb., 1963), 449.

Chapter Six

1. Part of Onegin's letter to Tatyana in chapter VIII was written in October 1831.

2. For a complete critical discussion of the "tenth" chapter, see Tomashevsky, "Desyataya glava 'Evgeniya Onegina,' (Istoriya razgadki)" [The Tenth Chapter of Eugene Onegin: History of a Solution], *Pushkin,* II, 200–44.

3. Pushkin seems to have toyed with the idea of continuing his poem as late as 1835: see, for example, V. Nabokov, *Eugene Onegin* (New York, 1964), III, 376ff; hereafter cited in text.

4. The final version, as approved by the poet, is that of 1837; this edition does not, however, for reasons of censorship, include a number of passages normally considered part of *Eugene Onegin,* which do appear in the Academy of Sciences edition (VI, 1937). The differences are, for our purposes, negligible.

5. R. D. Waller, quoted by E. Boyd, *Byron's Don Juan* (New Brunswick, N.J., 1945), 51; hereafter cited in text. The final rhymed couplet can, of course, be found elsewhere, for example, in Shakespeare's sonnets, where it performs a similar function.

6. This viewpoint is so firmly established that it is impossible to associate it with one particular critic. In the introduction to his *Evgeny Onegin: Roman v stikhakh* [Eugene Onegin: A Novel in Verse] (Moscow, 1957), N. L. Brodsky declares (p. 7) that "Belinsky saw in *Eugene Onegin* first and foremost a realist novel." Brodsky then proceeds (pp. 7–8) to the effect that with his *Eugene Onegin* Pushkin "wrote the first Russian realist novel." Brodsky also enlists (p. 10) in support of the realist cause D. D. Blagoy, who "correctly reminds us that *Eugene Onegin* was the first genuinely great realist work in all of nineteenth-century world literature, since it preceded in time the generally recognized models of European classical realism, the novels of Balzac and Stendhal, which appeared at the beginning of the thirties, at a time therefore when Pushkin had already completed all of *Eugene Onegin.*" The tendency of Brodsky and like-minded critics is, further, to equate realism with social protest. This in turn leads to a quite disproportionate stressing of Pushkin's allegedly negative attitude toward his own class. The ridiculous lengths to which this approach has been pushed can be clearly seen in L. Grossman's treatment of the subject. In his *Pushkin* (Moscow, 1960), 387, Grossman suggests that the peasant masses emerge as more noble than their masters and, as an illustration, quotes some rather sentimental phrases uttered by the authoritative Belinsky on the subject of Tatyana's nurse; but it is clear to any unbiased reader not only that Tatyana's nurse is obtuse and senile but that her role in *Eugene Onegin,* notwithstanding its symbolic significance, is a very small one.

7. See L. N. Stilman, "Problemy literaturnykh zhanrov i traditsiy v 'Evgenii Onegine' Pushkina" [Problems of Literary Genres & Traditions in Pushkin's *Eugene Onegin*] *American Contributions to the Fourth International Congress of Slavicists* (s'Gravenhage, 1958), 321–67; and A. A. Akhmatova, "'Adolf Benzhamena Konstana v tvorchestve Pushkina" [Constant's Adolphe in Pushkin's Art], *Pushkin-Vremennik pushkinskoy komissii* [Pushkin: Chronicle of the Pushkin Commission] (Moscow-Leningrad, 1936), I, 91–114.

8. Boyd, 34.

9. Henry Fielding's oft-quoted statement that "a comic romance is a

comic epic poem in prose" (Preface to *Joseph Andrews*) is more revealing in connection with *Don Juan* than *Eugene Onegin*; however, it does have application in the present context, if only for the attention it draws to the tendency of different genres to coalesce.

10. Individual portions of *Eugene Onegin* can, it has been pointed out, be identified as germane to the idyll, ode, satire, parody, epigram, or even drama: see Vsevolod Setschkareff, *Alexander Pushkin: Sein Leben und sein Werk* [Alexander Pushkin: His Life and Work] (Wiesbaden, 1963), 125. As Setschkareff points out (p. 124), while Pushkin's work has affinities mainly with the eighteenth-century sentimental novel and the modern psychological novel (for example *Adolphe*), Byron's is more closely linked with the picaresque novel and the burlesque epic of the Renaissance. Actually, the strands of tradition are so intertwined in both works that even the distinctions made by Setschkareff can legitimately be further modified. Thus while Pushkin's narrative technique owes some debt to Fielding and Sterne, the Haidée episode in *Don Juan* reflects the influence of Rousseau.

11. The description of Tatyana's falling in love at a physically and emotionally predetermined moment in her life parallels closely and is clearly indebted to Karamzin's 1792 story, *Natalya boyarskaya doch'* [Natalya the Boyar's Daughter].

12. D. Cizevsky, *Evgenij Onegin: A Novel in Verse* (Cambridge, 1953), xxviii; hereafter cited in text.

13. See L. N. Stilman, "Problemy literaturnykh zhanrov i traditsiy v 'Evgenii Onegine' Pushkina" [Problems of Literary Genres and Traditions in Pushkin's *Eugene Onegin*], *American Contributions to the Fourth International Congress of Slavicists* (s'Gravenhage, 1958), 351–52.

14. For a discussion of symmetry in *Eugene Onegin*, see V. Nabokov, I, 15–20, and the analysis of the work's structure in the following pages.

15. My interpretation here is, I believe, basically in accord with that of D. S. Mirsky (who, by the way, has pointed out that Tatyana's conduct in the final chapter was partly determined by Pushkin's desire to provide his future wife with a model of correct and loyal behavior). In *A History of Russian Literature* (New York, 1958), 92, Mirsky writes: "The greatness of Pushkin in the creation of Tatiana is that he avoided the almost unavoidable pit of making a prig or a puritan out of the virtuous wife who coldly rejects the man she loves. Tatiana is redeemed in her virtue by the sadness she will never conquer, by her resigned and calm resolve never to enter her only possible paradise, but to live with never a possibility of happiness."

16. See R. F. Gustafson, "The Metaphor of the Revolving Seasons in *Evgenij Onegin*," *Slavic and East European Journal*, VI (1962), 6–20.

17. E. Lo Gatto, *Pushkin: Storia di un poeta e del suo eroe* [Pushkin: History of a Poet and His Hero] (Milan, 1959), 38; hereafter cited in text.

18. In this respect Pushkin's work differs markedly from Tchaikovsky's

opera: in the story of the opera it is the actions of the main characters which
are all-important.

Chapter Seven

1. D. S. Mirsky, *Pushkin* (New York, 1963), 207.
2. George Gibian, *"Measure for Measure* and Pushkin's *Angelo,"* *PMLA,*
LXVI (1951), 426–31.
3. See Walter N. Vickery, "Pushkin's *Andzelo*: A Problem Piece,"
Mnemozina (Munich, 1974), 325–39.
4. Also basically completed was the earlier (1830) *The Tale of the Priest
and His Worker Balda.* Censorship considerations prevented Pushkin from putting it in final form. A mutilated version was published in 1840 by Zhukovsky, who replaced the priest with a merchant. In later editions the priest
was reinserted. It is of considerable interest to the student of versification,
since its lines lack regularity both in the number of syllables and the number
and positioning of the stresses; its only technical regulating principle is rhyme.
5. See further M. K. Azadovsky, "Istochniki skazok Pushkina" [Sources
of Pushkin's Fairy Tales], *Pushkin: Vremennik pushkinskoy komissii* [Pushkin:
Chronicle of the Pushkin Commission] (Moscow-Leningrad, 1936), I, 134–63;
also S. A. Bugoslavsky, "Russkie narodnye pesni v zapisi Pushkina" [Russian
Folksongs in Pushkin's Transcription], *Pushkin: Vremennik* [Pushkin: Chron-
icle] (Moscow-Leningrad, 1941), VI, 183–210.
6. See R. Jakobson in "The Kernel of Comparative Slavic Literature,"
Harvard Slavic Studies, I (1953), 16; L. V. Pumpyansky, "Medny vsadnik i
poeticheskaya traditsiya XVIII veka" [*The Bronze Horseman* and the Eighteenth-
Century Poetic Tradition], *Pushkin: Vremennik pushkinskoy komissii* [Pushkin:
Chronicle of the Pushkin Commission] (Moscow-Leningrad, 1939), IV–V,
91–124; W. N. Vickery, "'Mednyj vsadnik' and the Eighteenth-Century He-
roic-Ode," *Indiana Slavic Studies,* III (1963), 140–62; P. Call, "Pushkin's
Bronze Horseman: A Poem of Motion," *Slavic and East European Journal,* XI (2)
(1967), 137–44.
7. The best-documented and most illuminating study of this poem is
by W. Lednicki, *Pushkin's Bronze Horseman* (Berkeley and Los Angeles, 1955);
hereafter cited in text.
8. A. Bely, *Ritm kak dialektika i* "Medny vsadnik" [Meter as Dialectic
and *The Bronze Horseman*] (Moscow, 1929), 266–79. Unfortunately, Bely goes
too far in subscribing to the rather widely held view that Nicholas I rather than
d'Anthès constituted the real threat to Pushkin's marriage. As I have stated in
this book and elsewhere, I consider this improbable. It is in any case unnecessary to Bely's perfectly convincing thesis. We know that Pushkin resented the
czar's flirting with his wife. And there may perfectly well have been some
analogy in Pushkin's mind between the czar's flirtatiousness and Peter's "rob-
bing" Evgeny of his Parasha. But the main point is that Nicholas, in Pushkin's

mind, intruded into Pushkin's life by forcing him to live in Saint Petersburg and to lead a life that was frustrating, degrading, and confining. Pushkin felt himself to be Nicholas's prisoner. Nicholas seemed omnipresent, just as the will of Peter the Great was omnipresent in the life of Evgeny.

9. *O literature* [On Literature] (Moscow, 1962), 23.

10. *O literature* [On Literature], 67, 173.

11. Actually, he started writing his autobiographical memoirs as early as 1821. However, he burned most of this material after the catastrophe of 14 December 1825. Only relatively recently have attempts been made to "reconstruct" this early autobiographical undertaking, which is known to have occupied a great deal of Pushkin's time during 1824 in Mikhaylovskoe. See I. Feinberg, *Nezavershennye raboty Pushkina* [Pushkin's Unfinished Works] (Moscow, 1955).

12. See B. O. Unbegaun, *Tales of the Late Ivan Petrovich Belkin* (Oxford, 1947).

13. For a more detailed study of parody in *The Tales of Belkin* see V. Setschkareff, *Alexander Puschkin* (Wiesbaden, 1963), 165–72.

14. *The Shot* can reasonably be compared with *Mozart and Salieri* and also with *The Stone Guest,* both written during the same Fall, 1830, period at Boldino. The comparison suggests itself for two reasons: (1) the problem of envy of another person who appears to have or acquire things without effort; (2) the question of when life is easy to sacrifice, and when not, in particular the added meaning that may be given to life by love or marriage. See A. A. Akhmatova, "'Kamenny gost' Pushkina" [Pushkin's *Stone Guest*], *Pushkin: Issledovaniya i materialy* [Pushkin: Research and Materials] (Moscow-Leningrad, 1958), II, 185–95.

15. A very welcome turn in the direction of this emphasis on narrative is seen in Yu. K. Shcheglov, "Syuzhetnoe iskusstvo Pushkina v proze" [Pushkin's Skill in Plotting Prose Works], *International Journal of Slavic Linguistics and Poetics,* 1988, XXXVII, 115–52.

Chapter Eight

1. See also B. P. Gorodetsky, *Lirika Pushkina* [Pushkin's Lyric Poetry] (Moscow-Leningrad, 1962), 29, and Gorodetsky, "Lirika" [Lyric Poetry], *Pushkin: itogi i problemy izucheniya* [Pushkin: Research Results and Problems] (Moscow-Leningrad, 1966), 408–13.

2. For details concerning the composition of this poem see N. Izmaylov, "Strofy o Napoleone i Bayrone v stikhotvorenii 'K moryu'" [Strophes on Napoleon and Bryon in "To the Sea"], *Pushkin: Vremennik pushkinskoy komissii* (Moscow-Leningrad, 1941), VI, 21–29; and also N. L. Stepanov, *Lirika Pushkina* [Pushkin's Lyric Poetry] (Moscow, 1959), 310–26.

3. "From Pindemonte" (1836) expresses more plainly the poet's misgivings as to the relationship between different forms of government and the

true nature of human freedom and happiness. Incidentally, "From Pinde-monte," contrary to the assertions of many scholars, truly is from Pindemonte, also Musset, and—probably unknown to Pushkin—from Goldsmith's "Trav-eller." See W. N. Vickery, "Lexical Similarities and Thematic Affinities: Three Pushkin Lyrics," *International Journal of Slavic Linguistics & Poetics,* XXVIII, 137–47.

4. Translated by Maurice Baring, *Have You Anything to Declare?* (London, 1936), 246.

5. The views here expressed on the ideas informing "The Prophet" are, in large measure, a condensation of N. L. Stepanov's evaluation in his *Lirika Pushkina* [Pushkin's Lyric Poetry], 347–63.

6. For Pushkin's wretched 1828 situation see A. A. Akhmatova, "Pushkin v 1828 godu" [Pushkin in 1828], *O Pushkine* [On Pushkin], 207–22.

7. Translated by Maurice Baring, *Have You Anything To Declare?,* 244.

8. The woman to whom these eight lines were addressed remained un-known for many years, and her identity has still not been established with complete certainty. However, convincing evidence points to Karolina Soban-skaya, whom Pushkin first met in Kiev or Odessa in 1821 (while on leave from Kishinev) and with whom he again became embroiled in Saint Petersburg after his return from exile. See M. A. Tsyavlovsky, *Rukoyu Pushkina* [In Pushkin's Hand] (Moscow-Leningrad, 1935), 179–208. At the same time, it seems probable that Pushkin copied this same poem into the album of A. A. Olenina, who in 1828 rejected his marriage proposal; see T. G. Tsiavlovskaya, "Dnevnik Oleninoy" [Olenina's Diary], *Pushkin: Issledovaniya i materialy* [Pushkin: Research and Materials] (Moscow-Leningrad, 1958), II, 289–92. For literary precedents—Dante and Sainte-Beuve—see W. N. Vickery, "Ja vas ljubil . . . : A Literary Source, *International Journal of Slavic Linguistics and Poetics,* XV (1972), 160–67.

9. "On the Georgian Hills" is almost certainly addressed to Maria Raevskaya, whom Pushkin first met in 1820 in the south and who is consid-ered by some to have been his great love.

10. "Vnov ya posetil. . . ."

11. See W. N. Vickery "'Abchar': Beyond Good and Evil," *Canadian-American Slavic Studies,* 10 (1976), no. 2, 175–88.

12. For an excellent study of this poem see M. P. Alekseev, *Stikhotvorenie Pushkina "Ya pamyatnik sebe vozdvig . . ."* [Pushkin's Poem "I've Raised a Mon-ument"] (Leningrad, 1967).

Chapter Nine

1. *Evgeny Onegin: roman A. S. Pushkina* [Eugene Onegin: A Novel by Pushkin] (Moscow, 1964) 10.

2. Isaiah Berlin, *The Hedgehog and the Fox* (New York, 1953), 1.
3. T. S. Eliot, *On Poetry and Poets* (London, 1957), 225.
4. "Introduction," *The Oxford Book of Russian Verse,* 2d ed. (Oxford, 1948), xliii.

Selected Bibliography

PRIMARY SOURCES

Polnoye sobranie sochineniy [Collected Works]. Moscow-Leningrad: Akademiya nauk, 1937–1959, 21 vols.
A. S. Pushkin: Polnoye sobranie sochineniy, ed. by B. V. Tomashevsky. Moscow: Akademiya nauk, 1962–1966, 10 vols.

English Translations

Alexander Pushkin: Collected Narrative and Lyrical Poetry, tr. by Waiter Arndt. Ann Arbor, Mich.: Ardis, 1984.
Boris Godunov, tr. by Philip L. Barbour. New York: Columbia University Press, 1953.
Complete Prose Fiction, tr. by Paul Debreczeny. Stanford, Calif.: Stanford University Press, 1983.
Complete Prose Tales of Alexandr Sergeyevitch Pushkin, tr. by G. R. Aitken. New York: Norton, 1966.
Eugene Onegin, tr. with notes by Vladimir Nabokov. New York: Bollinger Foundation, 1964 and 1975, 4 vols.
Eugene Onegin, tr. by Walter Arndt. New York: Dutton, 1963.
Poems, Prose and Plays of Alexander Pushkin, ed. by A. Yarmolinsky. New York: Modern Library, 1943.
Works of Alexander Pushkin, ed. by A. Yarmolinsky. New York: Random House, 1936.

SECONDARY SOURCES

Russian

Akhamatova, Anna. *O Pushkine* [On Pushkin]. Leningrad: Sovetsky pisatel [Soviet Writer], 1977. Articles on Pushkin's works are excellent; those on his last year are marred by paranoiac indignation.
Alekseev, M. P. *Pushkin: Sravnitelnoistoricheskie issledovaniya* [Pushkin: Comparative Historical Investigations]. Leningrad: Nauka [Science], 1984. A collection of well-documented and very informative articles, previously published.

172

Bitsilli, P. *Etudy o russkoy poezii* [Studies on Russian Poetry]. Prague: Plamya [Flame], 1926. An excellent presentation of the development of Russian verse, including, of course, a study of Pushkin's place.

Blagoy, D. D. *Sotsiologiya tvorchestva Pushkina* [Sociology of Pushkin's Art]. Moscow: Mir [Peace], 1931. Blagoy's most interesting and provocative writing on Pushkin, the social background, and its effect on him.

Chernyaev, N. I. *Kriticheskie stati i zametki o Pushkine* [Critical Articles and Notes on Pushkin]. Kharkov: Tip. "Yuzhnago kraya" [Southern Land Printing Press], 1900. This collection contains some interesting articles on individual works.

Cizevsky, D. *Evgenij Onegin: A Novel in Verse*. Cambridge: Harvard University Press, 1953.

Etkind, Efim. *Simmetricheskie kompozitsii u Pushkina* [Symmetrical Compositions in Pushkin]. Paris: Institut d'etudes slaves, 1988. Contains many stimulating insights.

Frank, S. L. *Etyudy o Pushkine* [Studies on Pushkin]. 3rd ed. Paris: YMCA-Press, 1987. Some interesting and rarely voiced views on Pushkin, especially as a political thinker.

Ginzburg, Lidiya. *O lirike*. Leningrad: 1964 and 1974. Along with Bitsilli's (see above), probably the best account of the development of Russian verse.

Gorodetsky, B. P., ed., and others. *Pushkin: Itogi i problemy izucheniya* [Pushkin: Research Results and Problems]. Leningrad: Nauka [Science], 1966. An excellent survey of Russian Pushkin scholarship through 1966.

Kuleshov, V. *Zhizn i tvorchestvo A. S. Pushkina* [Pushkin's Life and Work]. Moscow: Khudozhestvennaya literatura [Artistic Literature], 1987. Well documented.

Lerner, L. O. *Trudy i dni Pushkina* [Pushkin's Works and Days]. Saint Petersburg: Akademiya nauk [Academy of Sciences], 1910. An invaluable reference for Pushkin's day-to-day activities.

Shchegolev, P. E. *Duel i smert Pushkina* [Pushkin's Duel and Death]. Moscow-Leningrad: Gosizdat [State Publishing House], 1928. Shchegolev was a pioneer in adopting a scientific approach to Pushkin's biography. Excellent; the 1928 edition contains the most materials.

Sinyavsky, A. (Abram Terts). *Progulki s Pushkinym* [Strolls with Pushkin]. London: Collins and Overseas Publications Interchange, 1975. Controversial in its approach; offers valuable insights. Very readable.

Slovar' yazyka Pushkina [Dictionary of Pushkin's Language]. Moscow-Leningrad: Gosudarstvennoe izdatelstvo inostrannykh i natsionalrykh slovarey [State Publishing House for Foreign and National Dictionaries], 1956–61. 4 vols. This dictionary is an excellent tool for the use and location of lexical items.

Tomashevsky, B. *Pushkin*. Moscow-Leningrad: Akademiya nauk [Academy of Sciences], 1956–1961, 2 vols. The first volume is an authoritative and, on the whole, fair account of Pushkin's creative development up to his exile. Its continuation was prevented by the author's death. The second volume is a miscellany of posthumously published articles on various subjects relating to Pushkin.

Tsyavlovsky, M. A. *Letopis zhizni i tvorchestva A. S. Pushkina* [Chronology of Pushkin's Life and Work]. Moscow: Akademiya nauk [Academy of Sciences], 1951. A very useful chronicle of Pushkin's life, work, and background events, unfortunately extending only to 1826.

Tsyavlovsky, M. A. and others. *Rukoyu Pushkina* [In Pushkin's Hand]. Moscow-Leningrad: Academia, 1935. Contains interesting materials for the Pushkin specialist.

Tyrkova-Vilyams, A. *Zhizn'Pushkina* [Pushkin's Life]. Paris: Vozrozhdenie [Rebirth], 1929. A very competent and useful biography.

Veresaev, V. *Pushkin v zhizni* [Pushkin in Life]. Moscow: Sovetsky pisatel [Soviet Writer], 1936. A very informative collection of biographical materials.

Vinogradov, V. V. *Stil' Pushkina* [Pushkin's Style]. Moscow: OGIZ [Artistic Literature], 1941. Contains valuable insights, turgidly written.

Zhirmunsky, V. *Bayron i Pushkin: Iz istorii romanticheskoy poemy* [Byron and Pushkin: From the History of the Romantic Narrative Poem]. 1924. Reprint. The Hague and Paris: Mouton, 1970. Excellent.

Non-Russian

Bayley, John. *Pushkin: A Comparative Commentary*. Cambridge: Cambridge University Press, 1971. Contains interesting insights—some, however, designed more to *épater* than to advance understanding.

Clayton, J. Douglas. *Ice & Flame: Pushkin's Eugene Onegin*. Toronto: University of Toronto Press, 1985. Raises a number of relevant questions.

Debreczeny, Paul. *The Other Pushkin: A Study of Pushkin's Prose Fiction*. (Stanford, Calif.: Stanford University Press, 1983). Well documented from the Soviet standpoint.

Lednicki, Waclaw. *Pushkin's Bronze Horseman: The Story of a Masterpiece*. Berkeley and Los Angeles: University of California Press, 1955. The best account of *The Bronze Horseman*.

Lo Gatto, Ettore. *Pushkin: storia di un poeta e del suo eroe* [Pushkin: History of a Poet and His Hero]. Milan: Munsia, 1959. Contains very valuable insights.

Mirsky, D. S. *Pushkin*. 1926. Reprint. New York: Dutton, 1963. A critical biography. Unsatisfyingly brief in its treatment of many works and dogmatic in some of its views, Mirsky's work shows much perception in its insights into Pushkin's psychology and the aesthetic merits of his writing.

Nilsson, N. A., ed. *Russian Romanticism. Studies in the Poetic Codes*. Uppsala,

Sweden: Almquist and Wicksell, 1979. A collection of nine articles, five in English, four in Russian. Stimulating.

Setschkareff, V. *Alexander Puschkin*. Wiesbaden: Harrassowitz, 1963. A skillfully constructed critical biography. Covers a great deal of material, but briefly. Lacks notes.

Shaw, J. Thomas, ed. *The Letters of Alexander Pushkin*. Bloomington and Philadelphia: Indiana University Press and University of Pennsylvania Press, 1963. 3 vols. The only work available for those reading Pushkin's letters in English. Excellently annotated with a valuable biographical index.

―――, *Pushkin: A Concordance to the Poetry*. Columbus, Ohio: Slavica Publishers, 1985. 2 vols. The most valuable reference contribution made by Shaw.

―――, *Pushkin's Rhymes*. Madison: University of Wisconsin Press, 1974. An excellent reference.

Simmons, Ernest J. *Pushkin*. Cambridge, Mass.: Harvard University Press, 1937. A well-written, well-documented account of Pushkin's life. Its views of Pushkin's tragic end may be open to question. Makes little attempt to discuss his works.

Vickery, Walter N. *Pushkin: Death of a Poet*. Bloomington: Indiana University Press, 1969. Offers no newly discovered materials on Pushkin's death, but a saner approach than others prevailing in the 1960s.

Serial Publications

The following are serial publications containing many valuable articles on Pushkin's life and work:

Literaturnoe Nasledstvo [Literary Heritage]. 16–18 (Moscow, 1934) and 58 (Moscow, 1952).

Pushkin. Issledovaniya i materialy [Pushkin: Research and Materials]. Moscow-Leningrad, 1956–, vols. I–XIII.

Pushkin: Vremennik pushkinskoy komissii [Pushkin: Chronicle of the Pushkin Commission]. Moscow-Leningrad, 1936–1941. 6 vols.

Pushkin i ego sovremenniki [Pushkin and His Contemporaries]. Saint Petersburg-Leningrad, 1905–1927. 39 issues.

Vremennik pushkinskoy komissii [Chronicle of the Pushkin Commission]. Moscow-Leningrad, 1962–. 22 vols.

Index

The Author

Walter N. Vickery is Professor of Russian Literature at the University of North Carolina at Chapel Hill. He was born in England in 1921. He received a B.A. from Oxford in 1948 and a Ph.D. in Slavic languages and literatures from Harvard in 1958. His research on Pushkin and Lermontov has involved spending over two years in the former Soviet Union, mostly with the support of the IREX-organized ACLS-Soviet Academy of Sciences exchange. He has published two books on Pushkin. His next book will study Lermontov's poetry and prose works, with an extensive biographical introduction.

During World War II Prof. Vickery served in the British Royal Navy. Among other accomplishments, he has climbed Colorado's fifty-four "fourteeners."

The Editor

Charles A. Moser, professor of Slavic at the George Washington University, chaired the Department of Slavic Languages from 1969 to 1974 and again from 1980 to 1989. He is a literary historian with a primary specialization in nineteenth-century Russian literature and a secondary interest in Bulgarian literature and Bulgarian political history of the twentieth century. He is the author of *Antinihilism in the Russian Novel of the 1860s* (1964); *Pisemsky: A Provincial Realist* (1969); *Ivan Turgenev* (1972); *A History of Bulgarian Literature 1865–1944* (1972); *Dimitrov of Bulgaria* (1979); *Denis Fonvizin* (Twayne, 1979); and *Esthetics as Nightmare: Russian Literary Theory 1855–1870* (1989). He is also general editor of *The Russian Short Story: A Critical History* (Twayne, 1986) and *The Cambridge History of Russian Literature* (1989).